THE
KNOCKOUT

Sport's Most
Decisive Moment

First published in 2024 by Aurum,
an imprint of The Quarto Group.
One Triptych Place
London, SE1 9SH
United Kingdom
T (0)20 7700 6700
www.Quarto.com

A catalogue record for this book is available from the British Library.

ISBN 978-0-7112-9485-1
Ebook ISBN 978-0-7112-9487-5
Audiobook ISBN 978-0-7112-9615-2

10 9 8 7 6 5 4 3 2 1

Typeset in Baskerville MT Std by Typo•glyphix, Burton-on-Trent, DE14 3HE

Publisher: Richard Green
Editor: Katerina Menhennet
Art Director: Paileen Currie
Production Controller: Rohana Yusof

Printed in the UK

ANDY CLARKE

THE
KNOCKOUT

Sport's Most
Decisive Moment

Aurum

Contents

Foreword

Damian Hughes

One of my favourite pieces of boxing footage are the images of a callow, sixteen-year-old Mike Tyson training in a boxing ring, by responding to a random series of number sequences shouted by a short, stout man who, according to Tyson, didn't possess 'a happy muscle in his face'.

Cus D'Amato, one of the sport's greatest ever coaches, and the man who plotted the development of Floyd Patterson from a troubled thirteen-year-old to an Olympic gold medallist and on to world heavyweight champion before almost repeating the trick with José Torres (he won Olympic silver) at light-heavyweight, was engaged in his last dance. He was employing his intoxicating combination of tough, intelligent coaching and a deep interest in what he described as 'the workings of the inner man' to shape Tyson into the sport's youngest ever heavyweight champion.

In the grainy images, Tyson, as with Torres and Patterson before him, is discovering that D'Amato was no mere trainer. He would later recount that D'Amato spent two hours a day working with him in the gym but much of the waking portion of the remaining twenty-two teaching him about the psychology of the sport. This footage shows us the intersection where the two disciplines overlap.

Everyone knows 'one-two' is the instruction for a fighter to throw a 'jab and straight right' combination. D'Amato was teaching Tyson a new numbering system that would make his commands incomprehensible to an opponent before Tyson's execution of them would soon render the opponent incomprehensible himself.

In this wonderful book, Andy Clarke has done a magnificent, D'Amato-like job of providing us with our own sequence to follow. Fortunately, it is a simpler one to understand than the one Tyson would come to master, but its effect makes it equally as compelling as those images captured within the Catskill boxing gym. It requires us to remember our ABC.

Child psychologists have a classic sequencing template for analyzing and explaining problem behaviour in children, which is known as ABC. This stands for antecedent, behaviour and consequence. The antecedent is the event that prompts the behaviour. The behaviour creates a consequence.

A common classroom example: a student is distracting other children instead of completing their assigned work. The teacher asks the child to finish the task (antecedent). The child reacts by throwing a tantrum (behaviour). The teacher responds by sending the student to the headteacher's office (consequence). That's the ABC sequence. Armed with this insight, after several repeat episodes the teacher concludes that the child's behaviour is a ploy to avoid class assignments.

The ABC sequence is a perfect way of understanding the key themes of this book and indeed boxing's most thrilling moment: the perfectly executed knockout. Andy Clarke's access to the action, his keen eye for detail and his compelling way with words gives us a ringside seat to those practitioners, who explain the build-up, the moment and the aftermath – the ABC – of both delivering and receiving the concussive blow.

If I may, I can offer my own insight into this sequence, gleaned from my adolescence spent in a boxing gym in inner-city

Manchester. Or, as the *Daily Telegraph* once charmingly put it, 'an unrelenting place', in which 'only the foolhardy would park a car . . . unless they enjoyed returning to find their vehicle propped up on small piles of bricks, its wheels expertly removed by a team who works quicker than Michael Schumacher's pit crew.'

The newspaper had ventured to the city to meet my father, Brian Hughes, once referred to as 'the Cus D'Amato of British Boxing' by Tyson Fury. In his gym, world-class standards were expected. Many of his protégés went on to achieve success in the Olympic and world championship boxing ring through 'listening to his wisdom, presented with a mix of gruffness and enthusiasm delivered in the kind of accent and phraseology that seems to have stepped straight from the pages of an Alan Bennett script', as the *Telegraph* described his style of instruction.

He knew the ABC sequence inside out, back to front and upside down. It was an important part of his coaching armoury.

I once travelled with him to San Remo in Italy to support him as he guided Runcorn's Robin Reid to the summit of a world title. Reid was facing the redoubtable champion Vincenzo Nardiello in his hometown of Milan.

Whilst the action was enthralling enough, I watched my dad watching the proceedings with a silent intensity that fascinated me.

I'd read about the state of flow – defined by the wonderfully named psychologist Mihaly Csikszentmihalyi (pronounced six-cent-mihaly) as the place where mind and body work in harmony to produce their optimum performance – and I watched him completely in sync with the action, anticipating events seconds before they happened. His game plan, prepared after hour upon endless hour in front of video footage and then repeated in the dusty old gym, had taken its physical form and he watched for any slight insights where he could adapt.

As the bell to signal the end of the sixth round rang, he stepped between the ropes and became the boxing equivalent of a one-man

Formula One pit crew, busily apply fluids, respite, direction and advice in this minute-long intervention. In total, he uttered a mere five words.

'Sit down when you punch.'

'Sit down when you punch.' The plan had been for Reid to box at range, constantly moving and presenting an ever-shifting mirage. 'Sitting down' signalled a change of plan. It meant stillness as opposed to speed. It indicated that Reid was to move from A to B: the antecedent had been spotted, the behaviour must now change.

My dad had observed that Vincenzo Nardiello's mouth had begun to fall open, desperately gulping down oxygen to his burning lungs; his hands, usually carried high, had begun to resemble lead weights. In short: his resistance was falling fast.

Reid understood the context behind these five succinct words. He nodded his understanding, stood up, adjusted his shorts, punched his gloves together to indicate his readiness to continue and stepped back into the centre of the ring's canvas for the seventh round of the WBC super-middleweight title fight, the most prestigious of the alphabet titles which confusingly litter the sport.

Two minutes and fifty-nine seconds later, he seamlessly moved between his own coaching alphabet, from B to C: Reid had executed the signalled change in behaviour and landed a series of concussive blows, which led him to the consequence, a much-heralded victory for Reid and for my dad, who had become the first Manchester man in fifty years to train a world boxing champion.

In this book, Andy Clarke has done a masterful job of inviting you to witness the ripple effects of a knockout from every perspective: how it feels to administer the concussive blow, as well as the impact – literally, physically, psychologically and spiritually – on the recipient. The retelling of these experiences are as compelling as watching the great fighters engage in the art of war. If you'll forgive the pun, it is a knockout.

Preface

I've been writing this book now for seven months and over the last few weeks, as my deadline has loomed ever larger, I have inevitably been turning my thoughts towards what it is that I have learned during the process. It's a strange exercise, attempting to boil something that has been so all-consuming down into easily digestible morsels for consumption. I have an obsessive personality and I knew I would obsess about the writing of this book, to the extent that at no point have I tried to fight that impulse, choosing to embrace it instead, to surrender to it. I didn't know what I would discover and entered the enterprise with an open mind. I never attempted to lead anyone I spoke to in a particular direction, my credo being that there could be no bad answers, my approach being that I would be as brief and clear in my questioning as I could and listen to what I was told. I suspected it would not be simple, I didn't want it to be, and I was not disappointed.

CHAPTER ONE

A Unique Moment in Sport

> I love the knockout, the big finish. I love how conclusive it is. It settles the argument once and for all.
>
> *Carl Froch*

Saturday, 31 May 2014, Wembley Stadium

The eyes of the sporting world are focused on a roped-off square of canvas sitting in the middle of the Wembley pitch, glowing like an ember in a vast, oval fireplace. If you're up at the back it's hard to make out exactly what's happening under those glaring lights as two fighters tread the boards, circling and manoeuvring, feinting and exchanging. The fight is in the eighth round and the contest is yet to burst into flame. At ringside some have Carl Froch ahead, others favour George Groves, plenty are thinking it's too close to call, and whilst it hasn't been the war we saw in Manchester the previous November, it's tense and absorbing. There's a lot at stake and you can feel it. Both men are aware of the other's ability to wreak havoc, leaving both wary of making too bold a move; at this level of the sport one mistake and it can all be over, in the blink of an eye, and there's plenty of time left yet.

Midway through the eighth and Groves is having a good round, starting off with some quick, snappy jabs, thrown from his familiar wide crouching stance. The Londoner has a ring posture and body language that seems to beckon his opponent in: lead hand low, head slightly forward, 'Here I am, look, what are you waiting for?' But it's a siren song. Locked, loaded and ready to fire is that right hand and Froch knows it, he felt it in Manchester, it nearly finished him in the first round. The Cobra, to give Froch his ring moniker, is taller in his stance, stiffer. There can be a slightly robotic look about him, but he's a highly effective fighting machine, he's proved it time and time again, and he tends to get stronger as the rounds go by; either that, or it just appears that way because his relentless pressure makes his opponent incrementally weaker. Either way, the effect is the same.

But there are signs that this encounter isn't going according to that script. Saint George continues to slip and slide and pick his punches well and Froch is cutting a frustrated figure; he's losing the round and hasn't really landed anything clean. But early in the final minute he catches up with his man, sets his feet square and sinks in some solid blows to the body, feeling ribs on his knuckles through the 10oz gloves. Froch rolls forward and goes to the body again, walking through the return fire, and pushing Groves towards the ropes. He throws a feint, suggesting he's about to spear in a jab, and Groves, back to those ropes now, covers it with his right hand, but the punch doesn't come. Froch steps in and this time he does let his left hand go, aiming a hook to the head which is blocked by that right glove. But it's a decoy. As soon as the punch touches that right gauntlet, like cutting the rope on a catapult, his own right hand comes sailing through. At exactly the same time, Groves attempts a left hook but the Cobra's straight punch has less distance to travel and is always destined to land first, and land first it does, exploding on an exposed jaw, and the Saint immediately falls, like he's been switched off at the mains. His head and right shoulder buffet the ropes on their way down and he ends up on his back, right leg bent underneath him. Referee Charlie Fitch swoops in on the stricken fighter, takes a second to look deep into his eyes and then waves the fight over. The suddenness of it is shocking. It almost doesn't seem right, or fair, that something that until so recently was so full of potential and possibility can just end like that, without warning, without consultation. But that's boxing and that's the knockout, and you won't find anything like it anywhere else in the world of sport. It is truly unique.

Boxing has fascinated writers for millennia. The earliest surviving description of a knockout was written by Homer, in the twenty-third book of the *Iliad*, his epic poem about the Trojan War. Late on in the piece, the Greeks held a number of sporting events as part of a funeral for Patroclus, one of their fallen warriors, and amongst them was boxing. A gentleman called Epeius was first to throw his hat into the ring, followed by Euryalus:

> When the two men were dressed they stepped into the middle of the ring; they both put up their mighty hands, and they fell to. Fist met fist; there was a terrible grinding of jaws; and the sweat began to pour from all their limbs. Presently Euryalus took his eye off his man, and the excellent Epeius, leaping at the chance, gave him a punch on the jaw which knocked him out. His legs were cut from under him and he was lifted by the blow like a fish leaping up from the weed-covered sand and falling back into the dark water, when the North Wind sends ripples up the beach. His chivalrous opponent gave him a hand and set him on his legs. His followers gathered round and supported him across the ring on trailing feet, spitting clots of blood, with his head lolling on one side. He was still senseless when they put him down in his own corner.

I love how evocative the description is – 'like a fish leaping up from the weed-covered sand and falling back into the dark water' is wonderful – but what strikes me most is how it stands the test of time. It stands that test because what is being described, the dynamic at play, is the same now as it was then (1184 BCE being a plausible date for the fall of Troy, the setting of the *Iliad*). Two pugilists, both of whom know the risks and possible consequences of agreeing to face each other, square off and a momentary lapse by Euryalus is instantly and ruthlessly punished by Epeius. It's what happened at Wembley 3,197 years later.

Thankfully George Groves wasn't as badly hurt as Euryalus. I cut off my description above at the very point of the knockout but something that remains largely forgotten about that episode is that a few seconds after being flat on his back and seemingly dead to the world, George, showing superhuman powers of recovery, got back to his feet. He didn't need Froch to 'set him on his legs' as Epeius had sportingly done for Euryalus and nor did he need his corner to support him 'across the ring on trailing feet'. He regained his feet by himself and remained on them until he got back to his dressing room deep in the bowels of Wembley Stadium, after conducting himself admirably during the post-fight interviews. That is a key element in what made Froch vs Groves so special and why I've chosen to start the book with it. Knockouts don't get any better than Froch vs Groves. It had everything. A great rivalry, an incredible stage, and the signature shocking finish that only a knockout can bring. But crucially, thanks to the fact that Groves wasn't in the same state as Euryalus, it could be enjoyed by spectators free of any guilt. Further to that, that colossal right hand turned out to be the last punch Carl Froch ever threw in a professional ring, providing a fairytale ending, the like of which I don't think can ever be beaten. For George Groves it was devastating but it wasn't the end of his story. Four months later, he was back in the ring, boxing at Wembley Arena, in the shadow of the stadium, and he went on to win his world title just over three years after the Froch defeat. Groves's triumph was a long time coming and the result of skill, perseverance and a refusal to allow defeat, no matter how spectacular, to define him.

Comparing Froch vs Groves to Epeius vs Euryalus is a useful exercise because it demonstrates that boxing is as old as sport gets and that fundamentally it hasn't changed. The knockout has existed since well before the relatively modern concept that is sport emerged, because as long as humans have had hands to throw, they've been throwing them. Neil Scott is consultant maxillofacial / head and neck surgeon at Royal Glamorgan Hospital and head office medical adviser to the British Boxing Board of Control and knows as much as a person probably can know about what happens to a human being when they get punched in the head and knocked out. I had a long conversation with him about exactly that, after which he sent me a paper written by Anders Hanell and Elham Rostami, published in *Frontiers of Neurology* in October 2020, entitled 'How Can a Punch Knock You Out?' The beginning of it caught my eye:

> The proportions of the human hand differ from other primates, which tend to have longer fingers. The most likely cause for this is evolutionary pressure aimed at improved manual dexterity to allow better tool use. However, the shape of the human hand also allows it to form a fist which can be used to deliver forceful punches. This was likely very common in prehistoric times, and it has been suggested that the ability to forcefully dominate others also contributed to the evolution of the human hand.

They go on to say, 'Even though the earliest use of punching was likely violent conflict solving, there are mentions of organized competitions in early historical records, such as the *Iliad* by Homer.'

The knockout started life as the ultimate means of conflict resolution, then over time became the ultimate expression of sporting victory and defeat and has remained so ever since. There is no other moment in sport that can rival it for its utter finality. Other sports can of course provide moments of great drama, but a last-second goal or a basket on the buzzer to win the game require whoever scores them to be within striking distance, to be close enough to their opponent's score for that final act to be decisive. A knockout doesn't. A fighter can be ten rounds down on the scorecards and change everything with one punch. There is no response to a knockout either, no opportunity to come back, it renders the clock irrelevant. The knockout is instantaneous and it is that quality which, in the opinion of Steve Bunce, a journalist and author who has spent his entire working life at ringside, makes it sport's most decisive moment.

'In all sports there's a finish line, or a whistle or a klaxon, or some other kind of time limit. In boxing, we also have a time limit, we have the bell, but we also have the knockout. And what distinguishes our knockout from any other contact sport that have their own finishes is that our knockouts, when they come, are instantaneous. When you're knocked out, properly knocked out, it's over, the fight's over. Sure, they have it in taekwondo but they have it connected to points and they don't knock each other out. Sure, in MMA [mixed martial arts], they can catch each other on the chin and knock people out, but if you combine a bit of artistry and a bit of skill, that's what makes boxing knockouts, in my opinion, the greatest finish in all of sport.'

The closest thing to a knockout I've seen in a non-combat sport is the Golden Goal that FIFA introduced to football in the late 1990s, early 2000s. Essentially the Golden Goal was sudden death. Once a match went into extra time then whoever scored first in that thirty-minute period won instantaneously, whereas previously the two teams would play for the extra half-hour and if at the end of it they were still deadlocked, a penalty shoot-out would ensue. The idea was that it would create incredible drama, that teams would go hell for leather from the beginning of extra time, desperate to score that goal, to land that finishing blow. But it didn't work. Coaches, and players, weren't willing to roll the dice in that way, because the more a team went on the attack, the more vulnerable it made them and, more often than not, extra time was a cautious affair, with teams instead preferring to take their chances from the penalty spot. Spectators didn't engage with it either. They found the sudden finality of the Golden Goal too brutal, preferring a dynamic where if a team went behind then they were still afforded time to come back. It just seemed fairer that way. I remember watching the final of Euro 2000, which France won by a Golden Goal when David Trezeguet rifled the ball into the top corner twelve minutes into extra time. It's a brutal scene. The Frenchman lashes the ball in and sprints off, pulling his shirt off in celebration whilst the France bench invade the pitch and the French fans explode with joy in the stands. Meanwhile the Italian players go limp, like all the air has been sucked out of them. Some manage to stay on their feet, others slide to the turf, watched by supporters who are numb with shock, unable to understand how a situation can be so full of hope one second and so utterly bereft of it the next. The Golden Goal was a failure, lasting for just two World Cups and two European Championships. Why? Because athletes and fans alike couldn't reconcile themselves with the suddenness of it, it was too shocking for them, it was too much.

What does it feel like to win in that fashion? What does it feel like to lose in that way? How does a person commit to that sporting life? I've always wanted to know, and that's why I'm writing this book.

My own fascination with boxing started with the knockout. My first boxing memory is from 1986, when I was eight years old, and watching a British welterweight called Darren Dyer knocking out an Australian fighter called Darren Obah on his way to winning a gold medal at the 1986 Edinburgh Commonwealth Games. I haven't been able to find any footage of the fight but I distinctly remember the opponent was Australian and that Dyer flattened him. It's possible that the scene wasn't as dramatic as I remember it – the human memory can tend over time to reframe events as best suits a person – but my recollection has always been one of a conclusive and sudden finish, a knockout, and it had an effect on me. I liked it and, even at that age, I knew what it represented. One man had knocked the other man to the ground and that meant that he'd won. I didn't need to read the rules and regulations to understand that. I didn't debate the morality of it with myself, I didn't shrink from the violence of it, I revelled in it. Almost forty years later it still has the same hold on me.

It's not the only constituent of boxing that satisfies me; I appreciate a fine exhibition of pugilistic skill followed by a points decision very much but, as renowned US boxing writer Thomas Hauser said to me, 'If you take the knockout out of boxing then you no longer have boxing.' I agree with that sentiment but it's more than that, it strikes a deeper, more resonant chord than that within all of us. Thomas summed it up nicely when he added: 'There's something very basic and primal about it both for the participants and for the people that are watching.'

That sentiment was echoed by Frank Warren, somebody else who's been around boxing for a long time and, like Hauser, has seen all there is to see from ringside and who is still as engaged by the spectacle now as he ever was. I spoke to him at a gym in Bermondsey where he was stood watching his young heavyweight Daniel Dubois train ten days out from his fight in Poland against unified world heavyweight champion Oleksandr Usyk. It was August and boiling hot. I was sweating profusely whilst Frank stood there suited and booted, impervious to the heat. I mentioned how he seemed to be the only person in the place without a bead of perspiration on him, at which he smiled and pointed up to the ceiling above him. He was standing under the air-conditioning vent, being blasted by lovely cold air. Frank Warren is a man who for decades upon entering a room has swiftly identified the most advantageous position to be in and this was no exception. He was happy to talk about the knockout; he was after all fervently hoping Dubois would knock out Usyk.

'It's a funny thing. Watching a person getting knocked out is a pretty callous and cold thing to think about but in boxing it's the most exciting part of a fight, you know, when a guy goes in, especially when they're a big puncher, and does the business, it brings out our primeval side. If you look at Tyson, the early days of Mike Tyson, when he bulldozed through the division, knocking people over, it was so exciting, so it's the ultimate in sport. And it can happen in so many different fashions; a guy can be miles behind on points and suddenly he pulls it out of the bag. It's just so dramatic.'

Basic, primal, callous, cold, exciting, dramatic: an interesting set of adjectives. As a collection it suggests that the subject is taboo, one that, against their better judgement, people find themselves drawn to. The knockout provokes conflict within people, a conflict that will have to be confronted at some point; it is an emotional event and demands an emotional reaction. For the spectator, like the fighter, there is nowhere to run and nowhere to hide. The knockout comes at a cost for every single person involved in it and to witness it is to be involved in it, to be complicit in it, whether an individual cares to admit that or not.

As a subject, I don't believe the knockout has been explored in the depth its merits deserve. Part of the reason for that could be that people have been afraid to ask, assuming that the knockout would prove to be too dark a subject and one best left alone, but people have been willing to talk, eager even, to share what they know of something that the vast majority of the population will never experience. Carl Froch, Tony Bellew, David Haye, Ricky Hatton, Amir Khan, Matt Macklin, Jamie Moore, Teddy Atlas, Kenny Bayless, Joe Gallagher, Billy Graham, Frank Warren and Eddie Hearn have all been on the inside of the knockout and they, along with numerous others, will provide testimony and insight into sport's most decisive moment.

CHAPTER TWO

What Is the Knockout?

> No hope. And that's not something you want to be part of
> the human experience or the human psyche, but in real
> life, sometimes it can be, and a knockout brings it to you
> fast, it brings it to you very quick.
>
> *Teddy Atlas*

I've seen a lot of knockouts from ringside and I can honestly say
that I've never become immune or anaesthetized to the pure
adrenaline of it. I don't think I ever will. Whether it's the shock
of that bolt of pure lightning that comes with the single-punch
knockout or the surge you feel rising like a storm around you when
you can see that one fighter is on the brink and the end is nigh, it
reaches right into your soul. It's what you come for, it's what you
want, it's human instinct to marvel at it. That rush, that surge, is like
a blinding flash but it doesn't last long and when it fades and your
eyes readjust to the light the scene that greets you never looks that
euphoric; to me it seems more like a grim juxtaposition of relief and
despair more often than not. The victor felt that high, that quickening, no question, but they're already in withdrawal and when they

look at their fallen opponent, it doesn't appear to be joy they feel. I don't think it's necessarily sympathy either, I don't really know what it is, maybe just relief that it's not them? At least that's how they look. Strangely empty. It can be a melancholy or slightly hysterical scene but triumphant it's often not and I've never once felt an ounce of envy at knowing I'll never experience what the winner is experiencing. But you don't spend much time looking at the winner because your eyes are immediately drawn to the fallen fighter. You want them to be OK, a split second after riding that rush you got from watching them go down. You want them to get up to applause from the crowd and backslaps all round. Sometimes that's what happens and they appear to be in good spirits but when you've seen a few you realize that's a mirage, that's the disorientation talking, that they don't really understand what's happened, not yet, but that when they do the disappointment will be crushing. Other times you can see they know exactly what has just happened and the hopeless despair of it has already got a hold of them, like they're having the worst kind of out-of-body experience. And other times they're being wheeled out on a stretcher, unable to think anything at all.

The reaction of the crowd, I reckon, is similar to mine but I can't be sure about that, one difference being that I have to control what I'm feeling whereas most people watching don't. But I don't have to control it all that much, just enough so that I don't swear or use any inappropriate vocabulary (I remember getting gently picked up by my producer for describing a left hook as 'murderous' once and I understood why). I find it hard to describe the effect the knockout has on me, to be honest, what it is to me. Is my life better or worse for watching people getting knocked out more than most people would think is healthy? I don't think there's any way of quantifying that. But it's a very serious thing, an entity of its own, and that's why I've given it the definite article in the title of this chapter. Originally I went for 'What Is a Knockout?' but realized I needed to change it to 'What is the Knockout?'

I'm not squeamish about it though. I don't watch through my fingers and I've never once found myself questioning my appetite for the sport after seeing a particularly vicious and damaging knockout. I know people that have had that experience, that crisis of faith if you like, and I understand it, I'm just not one of them.

But a person doesn't need to have seen as many knockouts as I have to be familiar with the concept of the knockout; it is a dynamic that everyone understands. But what specifically is meant in the context of this book by the term knockout?

I'll start by explaining the letter of the law in UK boxing when it comes to what can and cannot strictly be described as a knockout. The record books, such as Boxrec.com, the bible of boxing statistics, use the initials KO (knockout) and TKO (technical knockout) to describe how a fight has been won or lost, when it's finished inside the distance due to one opponent rendering the other physically incapable of continuing. A KO is a finish to a fight where one participant is knocked down by a legal punch and isn't able to get back to their feet before the referee reaches the count of ten. Sometimes the fighter appears to have no prospect of getting back up, whilst on other occasions the referee counts to ten during which time the fallen fighter is struggling bravely to get back to their feet only to find themselves unable to accomplish that task in the allotted time. One of the most famous examples of the latter scenario occurred on 11 February 1990 at the Tokyo Dome in Tokyo, Japan, where 42–1 outsider James 'Buster' Douglas tangled with the undefeated, 37–0, unified world champion and unstoppable force that was Michael Gerard Tyson. In the tenth round, Douglas, producing the performance of his life, hits Tyson with an uppercut followed by a swift left, right, left, which sends Tyson pitching onto his back. Referee Octavio Meyran starts to count, down on his haunches, calling the numbers out slowly, loudly and deliberately just inches away from the fighter, whilst also counting off with his fingers. Tyson rolls onto his side and then onto his knees, scrambling around on the canvas for his mouthpiece. He doesn't know where he is, the body is just about working but the signals from the brain are weak. Meyran reaches ten, at which point Tyson somehow gets back upright, but it's too late, the referee waves his arms and embraces the boxer. It's over. The unthinkable has happened. Mike Tyson has been knocked down and counted out in one of the biggest sporting upsets ever, and the record books record it as a KO, a knockout, one of the most famous of all time.

A TKO can come in a number of ways. If a fighter regains their feet before the count of ten but the referee isn't satisfied that they're in any fit state to continue and waves the fight over, that event constitutes a technical knockout. If the referee stops a fight with a fighter still on their feet because they're taking too much punishment then that's a technical knockout. Equally, if the corner stops the fight by throwing the towel in or making it known to the referee in some other way that they wish to stop it because their fighter's taking too much damage, that's a technical knockout. But also, if a fighter gets knocked down and the referee makes the rapid evaluation that they're not going to be able to continue and either doesn't count at all or starts the count but then swiftly suspends it then, in the UK, that is also a technical knockout. Also, if the corner throws the towel in whilst the referee is counting, that can serve to cancel the count and constitute a technical knockout rather than a knockout. What this means is that in the UK ring some clean, pure knockouts, where a fighter is caught by a terrific punch and knocked unconscious, don't get officially recorded as knockouts. Froch vs Groves was a technical knockout, not a knockout, because referee Charlie Fitch looked at Groves, decided he was unconscious and stopped the count. Oleksandr Usyk vs Tony Bellew was also recorded as a technical knockout because referee Terry O'Connor waved it off before he reached ten. But O'Connor did count Amir Khan out against Breidis Prescott, even though there wasn't much prospect of Khan being in any fit state to continue, so therefore a knockout was recorded. Those three examples all occurred in British rings, but in Las Vegas in 2009 Kenny Bayless correctly didn't feel the need to count to ten when he was crouched over a prostrate Ricky Hatton at the end of his fight against Manny Pacquiao. Bayless didn't count at all, he just took a good look at Hatton and signalled that it was over. But under the rules in Nevada that was recorded as a knockout.

Boxing is not a sport governed by a single over-arching body, which leads to inconsistency in a number of areas, and official record-keeping, definitions and annotations are subject to that inconsistency. The rules, therefore, regarding what defines a knock-out and a technical knockout vary according to whose jurisdiction a fight falls under; in the United Kingdom it is the British Boxing Board of Control whilst in the United States of America it will be the athletic commission of whichever state hosts the fight. These kinds of differences can be a point of frustration, but a general awareness of them is what is required here, no more than that, because I'm going to clearly define what constitutes a knockout in these pages. Our working definition is as follows:

A knockout occurs when a person has had the ability and possibly also the desire to continue, to effectively defend themselves, knocked out of them by their opponent. They may be unconscious or they may, like Mike Tyson, be forlornly attempting to get up and continue, even rising on the count of ten, but whatever the circumstances, the observer feels able to view the physical scene and conclude that the contest is over.

One of the very first people I spoke to in my research was Teddy Atlas. It was a stroke of good fortune because it just so happened that I'd booked him in for an appearance on Macklin's Take, the podcast I host with former European middleweight champion Matt Macklin, on another subject. Teddy had already been very generous with his time so I was pushing my luck a touch when I asked for a few more minutes at the end to talk to him about the knockout.

His willingness to engage with the subject would prove to be a taste of things to come. Atlas is a character who exudes boxing. If you closed your eyes and slowly, gently, ran your hands over his face, traced the contours and contusions, it would be like reading a boxing life story in Braille. That's the kind of face he possesses. He's very well known to fight fans the world over as a man of passion and opinion, integrity and experience.

Born in Staten Island, New York, he was a decent amateur fighter, training under the legendary Cus D'Amato, but it was as a trainer that Atlas made his name, working with D'Amato at his famous Catskill gym and assisting in the development of a young Mike Tyson. The relationship with Tyson ended after Atlas put a gun to the teenager's head in protest at the way he'd behaved towards a young female relative of his. I don't know Teddy, our conversation via Zoom was the first time I'd ever spoken to him, but from what I'd read about the kind of person he is, that story spoke volumes about him. When it had come to any point of principle during his life, it did appear that he had always been one of those individuals who had done what he felt had needed to be done without hesitation or regret. He's operated at the top of the sport for a long time, both as a trainer and a TV commentator. His company is stimulating. He engages fully with the subject in hand and with the person he's sharing a conversation with and there is no choice but to reciprocate. I started by asking him what emotions the word 'knockout' stirred in him.

'The end. Over. No hope. And we should always have hope. But with the knockout there is no hope, for that moment at least. There's no coming back. There's no putting the lights back on. To me that's as down as it can get. In the totem pole of human emotions, in the human journey, there always has to be a flickering of light. But knockout . . . it suggests that there's only darkness. And as human beings, people strive to be better, strive for accomplishment, to get up in the morning and go forward. They're optimistic, to be able to accomplish something in front of them that day. But when you hear knockout, it's like, "That ain't happening right now. That's not in play. That's off the board. That's not a possibility any more. Right now, you're knocked out." No hope. And that's not something you want to be part of the human experience or the human psyche, but in real life, sometimes it can be, and a knockout brings it to you fast, it brings it to you very quick.'

This is the knockout. It's a full stop. Swift, decisive, unmistakeable. A traumatic physical event that can have a huge effect on a person mentally, a shattering blow from which not everybody can recover.

But the knockout comes in different forms and it is important to differentiate between them. There are lots of different ways for a fighter to knock out another fighter, and whilst it would be possible to pare them down and catalogue them all, that depth of categorization isn't necessary. Experience has taught me that there are just two main types of knockout, from which all knockouts derive.

Type one is the single-punch knockout. That one punch that lands and turns the lights out. It can, and often is, preceded by other punches, the purpose of which are often to disguise the telling blow, or are followed up by further blows but that one shot is identifiable as being the one that extinguished all hope. Boxers describe it as a punch they don't see, with the fact they don't see it being the reason it's so decisive. If a trained, professional fighter sees a punch coming then they will try and avoid it altogether, block it, or dissipate its force somehow, but if they find themselves unable to do any of those things then at the very least they can brace for impact and survive it. If a boxer doesn't see it, cannot brace for it and it's a solid, accurate, clean punch, then that combatant is going down and that can be true for anyone. This is a key point and worth emphasizing as it's something everyone agrees on, every single boxer, trainer, referee, promoter and observer I've spoken to. That community includes Dr Neil Scott. He was very clear that based 'on physiology, anyone can be knocked out, it just depends on how difficult that process is going to be'. He's aware of course that there are plenty of professional boxers who've never been knocked out but in his estimation that's simply because 'they haven't been exposed to the level of force or that exact "everything lining up" moment, Swiss cheese effect [all the holes needing to be in a row] that would lead to that knockout for them.'

I caught up with Dr Scott via Zoom one Thursday afternoon. He was at work, at the Royal Glamorgan Hospital, sitting in his green scrubs in what looked like a claustrophobic break room. He'd just finished an all-day clinic but his energy levels were impressively high.

Neil's been medical adviser to the British Boxing Board of Control since August 2017, having started as a board medical officer working at ringside in 2012. He's been to myriad boxing shows, so has seen a lot, although his appearances at ringside have become less frequent since he became medical adviser. It's a demanding role and one that colleagues generally don't understand his desire to perform, alongside his duties as a consultant maxillo-facial / head and neck surgeon, as physicians don't tend to approve of boxing. Recruiting doctors who are willing to lend their time and expertise to boxing, Neil told me, is not easy.

We'd met a few times, mainly at Anthony Joshua fights, and when I'd asked if he would be willing to share his expertise he had been very obliging, mainly because, as he said before we started our conversation, 'It's a very difficult thing you've chosen to write about.' That piqued my interest immediately as it suggested there could be aspects to the knockout that could not be explained by medical science, a notion I found intriguing. I started with the obvious, most simple question: What happens when a human being gets knocked unconscious in the boxing ring?

'It varies from person to person. But essentially what happens physiologically within the head is that you've got an impact and you've then got a shift or movement of the brain within the skull, which is a container essentially, with the brain sitting in it, in a bit of fluid. The jolting force [of the impact] totally disrupts the nerves and the nerve signals within the head, and the response to that is that the system momentarily almost shuts down. It's like a protective kind of mechanism, resulting in a temporary loss of consciousness. But also, when someone gets a blow to the head or the neck, that can alter blood flow within the brain, and if that force is significant enough there can be a potential change in the volume of blood flow and the oxygenation that's reaching the brain and that also can trigger that blackout or protective mechanism.'

A type-one knockout involves 'getting caught with a shot that you aren't fully prepared for' and because you're not prepared for it 'you haven't got that brace system set up', meaning that the 'transmission of force' from the initial impact, the punch, causes even greater movement of the brain within the skull, and the greater the movement the less chance the recipient has of staying awake.

The readiness is all. Teddy Atlas explains why in a less technical but equally effective way:

'A guy comes up and hits you with a club on the head pretty bad. But you survive it, you know you're messed up but you survive it, you saw it coming and you survive it. Not everybody will but some people with that kind of endurance, mental and physical endurance, and constitution can survive it. But now, you walk in, take that same person with that same ability to endure and he walks into a dark room and from behind the door the guy hits him over the head, maybe not in quite the same way, maybe not even as hard but hard enough, but hits him over the head. He's knocked out. That same guy that had got hit that same blow but had endured that blow when he saw it, can't endure it this time when he don't see it because again, there's no ability to ward it off, to steel yourself, to ready yourself to use the abilities that are there.'

An important thing to add with reference to type-one knockouts is that they often occur early in a fight, before fatigue has become a significant factor. Froch vs Groves was an unusual type-one knockout because it came in the eighth round, but the previous seven rounds had been cagey, both men still had plenty of gas in the tank, so although it happened later than is typical, it still constituted a type-one knockout.

In the case of type-two knockouts, fatigue is a major factor because these are the knockouts that come deep into a fight, the kind of fight fans salivate over and describe as 'wars', in which the pace is intense and the two combatants punch holes in each other for round after round, battles in which it is possible to see their resistance levels lowering and therefore their ability to survive punches diminishing. Towards the end of the fight one of the boxers lands a good, clean punch on their opponent and even though the opponent sees it coming, their brace system isn't as effective as it was in earlier rounds and they are no longer capable of surviving it. In such an instance, mental and physical exhaustion, dehydration and the cumulative effect of a hard fight leaves fighters, as Teddy describes it, 'disoriented to the point they can't obviously defend themselves in a proper way any more'.

Concussion is also almost certainly going to be a factor in a type-two knockout. People outside boxing are sometimes shocked to discover that boxers continue – and are allowed to do so – when concussed. Anthony Joshua's trainer Rob McCracken was asked by a newspaper reporter after his fighter's defeat to Andy Ruiz in Madison Square Garden to explain why Joshua performed in such uncharacteristic fashion after the Mexican knocked him down for the first time. McCracken, who's been in boxing his whole life, and who is now performance director of GB Boxing, and so one of the more responsible people you will meet when it comes to fighter welfare, answered honestly and correctly when he said that from that point onwards Joshua was dealing with concussion and that if a fighter has never had to deal with that feeling in the ring before then it can be very hard to handle. It was an answer that he was vilified for, with the newspaper that ran the article suggesting that Joshua could have died as a result of a reckless, callous corner not stopping the fight. But fighting on having sustained a concussion is something that boxers have always done. A type-two knockout, therefore, results from a combination of factors. Fatigue is obvious, it's apparent when someone is physically exhausted. Concussion isn't always so apparent, at least not to the untrained eye; it's more insidious than exhaustion, more of an ambush than a clear and present danger, and once the seeds of it are sown then that fighter most likely has an insurmountable problem. Neil Scott's trained eyes can identify it almost immediately.

'There's exhaustion, yes, but I think at that stage [i.e. deep in a fight] you have to talk about concussion in that mix, because that is going to influence how that person is going to respond and it's going to influence what happens next because if they've had an extremely tough fight, are exhausted, their brace mechanisms aren't there, then probably to a certain degree, although they might not have been showing a lot of outward signs of concussion, they are concussed. In the past, to highlight concussion, I've slowed contests right down when rewatching them with people, and said, "There, that's a subtle sign." Nobody's going to pick that up. The referee's not going to pick that up in real time, the corner won't, media at ringside, it just won't register because it's subtle, but from that point on the boxer then is really up against it.'

There is no better example of the type-two knockout than the conclusion to the British light-middleweight title fight between Jamie Moore and Matthew Macklin from September 2006. It's a fight that's gone down in British boxing folklore and is the perfect illustration of two fighters pushing themselves to the brink, of being willing to do whatever it took to get the win, regardless of the consequences.

Of all the fighters featured in this book, Macklin is the one I know best. He had a terrific career, winning British and European titles, and challenging for world titles on three occasions. He was always prepared to take up the challenge, any time, any place, and so was Jamie Moore, who also had a career to be extremely proud of, becoming British, Commonwealth and European champion. Between them these two men achieved an awful lot, but it's the fight they had for the British title that they're remembered for.

When they met, Jamie was twenty-seven and the reigning, defending British light-middleweight champion (11st weight limit). His record stood at 24–3 (twenty-four wins and three losses), boxing out of Salford under the guidance of trainer Oliver Harrison. Matt, twenty-four, from Birmingham but based in Manchester where he was training under Billy Graham, had notched seventeen wins and one defeat since turning pro at eighteen, to much fanfare, after boxing for England and winning a senior national amateur title. Matt's unusual in that he didn't have to box as a career, he had other options, but chose to turn his back on them, walking out on a law degree one year in to pursue his dream of becoming a world champion.

The fight should never really have happened. Jamie wanted to move on from British level and was seeking a tilt at the European title when his manager, Steve Wood, asked him if he wanted to defend his British title one more time because Brian Peters, Matt's manager, had called and declared that Jamie would need to either vacate his belt or fight Macklin for it, with the clear and impertinent inference being that Jamie would choose to vacate. Moore took the bait. As he said himself, 'It was my stubbornness that made it happen. My ego got the better of me.' There was no business sense in doing it, he didn't stand to gain anything from beating Macklin, but if he lost it would be a long way to fall. Jamie had a young son, Mikey, and his partner Colleen sat at ringside on the night of the fight five months pregnant with their daughter Olivia. He couldn't afford to lose. Macklin didn't have the same weight of responsibility on his shoulders but he didn't need it to light his own fire: he was young, hungry and burning with ambition.

Finding a venue proved difficult and Moore vs Macklin ended up at the George Carnall Leisure Centre in Urmston, a tight, compact venue that on the night was boiling hot as Manchester found itself in the middle of an unseasonal autumn heatwave.

I sat down with Jamie and Matt to look back on the fight for a podcast in New York in the summer of 2019 and it was fascinating to listen to them share their recollections. Matt admits he was over-confident going into the fight. He felt he was 'too big, too strong and hit too hard' and that he 'was gonna go through Jamie'. Moore, for his part, very much recognized the physical threat Macklin posed. He and Harrison knew he couldn't afford to go toe to toe with Macklin but also knew there was no point trying to run either. It was a conundrum and they came up with a bold and demanding plan. Oliver believed Matt fought in bursts, that he liked to step in, let his hands go, throw rapid combinations, and then step out and look to recover for a spell before going again. The trainer told his fighter that he had to 'sit right in front of him and make him miss', and then 'in them little pockets you've got to jump on him'.

'That's gonna be some fuckin' fight,' was Moore's response to Harrison's proposal, and they proved to be prophetic words. Macklin started very quickly, too quickly, and found himself in trouble.

'I remember coming back at the end of the third round, sat back on the stool and it was almost like a blur, I was that tired, and I remember thinking, vividly, "How the fuck am I gonna get through this?"'

He dug in, knowing that if he was feeling the pace then his opponent had to be too. Looking back, they both agreed that it was the defence of Moore that proved the difference; he'd worked hard at his defensive moves in the gym, drilling them day in and day out until they became second nature, whereas Macklin's defence was pretty much non-existent.

'My defence was basically my nose, I was just blocking shots with my jaw and my nose, the shots I took were unbelievable.'

The resistance levels of both boxers were dropping round by round. It was clear watching it that the fight was not going to go the distance, that it was a case of who could stand the heat the longest, who could find that one telling punch in the fog of exhaustion and concussion that engulfed them both. Jamie distinctly remembers hearing his trainer's voice cut through that fog, delivering the simple advice that can be so crucial in the heat of any battle, but especially one so hideous.

'I remember going back to the corner at the end of the ninth and Oliver said, "He's finished, I promise you, he's finished. Forget hooks and uppercuts, basic one-two straight down the pipe, one-two straight down the middle."'

As the tenth round starts Macklin stands with his mouth open, gulping in the air, his swollen features drenched in sweat. He's on autopilot, dog-tired and operating on instinct, whilst Moore, although also exhausted, has a slightly more alert air about him and is still able to think. Forty-five seconds into the round, Macklin goes down on one knee, collapsing from fatigue more than from any punch. He gets back up, still wanting to fight on, still believing he can win, somehow. Moore is biding his time, tucking up, protecting himself from the marauding attacks and waiting for his opportunity to let that loose left hand go in precisely the manner Oliver Harrison had prescribed, and midway through the round he does exactly that. Macklin falls forward, looking to grab hold of his opponent, but Moore disentangles himself, moves his feet back slightly, lets that one-two flow and catches Macklin with a well-timed left. It's not the biggest punch he's ever thrown but the technique is perfect and for Matt it was just one too many.

'He'd hit me with much better shots but at that stage the tank had been empty for a while. The needle had broken on red but it was a good, accurate shot when I had completely nothing left and it got the job done.'

This chimes exactly with what Dr Neil Scott told us about the effect of concussion on a fighter. Neil is confident that were he to watch the fight back slowly, he'd be able to 'pinpoint that initial change from which point on there was a concussion and that's led to what's happened later on'. So those 'much better shots' Matt mentions, those are the ones that really did the damage. He was exhausted and concussed, the combination of which made him, in boxing parlance, 'ready to go'.

The left hand lands and Macklin pitches forward, landing face first on the canvas, his body unable to do anything to break his fall, that last tiny scintilla of strength having been finally wiped out. Referee Victor Loughlin waved the fight over immediately, there was no need to count.

It's a fight that gets replayed regularly, a modern classic that both fighters get reminded of all the time and with good reason. It was incredible to watch, scarcely believable that two humans could endure such an inferno for as long as they did, steadfastly ignoring the pain and refusing to betray any sign to the other of the purgatory they were experiencing.

But although boxers may seem invulnerable, in reality they are not. They are made of flesh and bone, not steel, and as adept as they are at concealing damage, they are not always able to do so. Their legs buckle, their knees dip, their balance deserts them and it is very much worth examining these physical manifestations because they often precede a type-two knockout. Neil Scott has described what happens physiologically when a fighter gets hit hard but what does the fighter experience? It is a fascinating subject.

What happens to a boxer when they get hurt?

When any boxer talks about getting hurt or 'buzzed', as they often describe it, what they're referring to is a disturbance to their equilibrium, either mental or physical, or both.

This is how Carl Froch describes the feeling: 'If I ever said "I've been hurt" it's not hurt as in "Oh, my eye's stinging or my nose is sore or my eardrum's perforated or my rib's really sore." "Hurt" for me in the boxing ring is either getting really badly winded with a body shot, or with a head shot, where you get punched in the chin, your legs feel a bit uneven, like they're not under you, and the space around your head feels numb, almost like you've had too much to drink and you feel like you can't keep your balance. That's being hurt, that's getting hurt in the boxing ring, not getting your nose bleeding or getting a stinger on your eye.'

Barry McGuigan painted a vivid picture of it in his autobiography. The 'he' he's referring to below is Juan Laporte, a very good Puerto Rican fighter McGuigan beat on points in February 1985, four months before he won his world title at Loftus Road stadium.

> This is the honest truth: When he hit me with that right, I was transported back to when I was a child and used to go to Mrs Keenan's toy shop down the road. For a split second I thought I was in the toy shop again. I had the sense to grab La Porte, to try and allow my head to clear. It was a bit like when you've been walking along in the rain and get into your car: the windscreen steams up and you put on the fan to clear and it takes a bit of time before you can properly see out again.

Strange things happen to fighters when they get hit and almost everyone has a story like McGuigan's. When asked if anything like that has happened to them, their brain and mind seemingly playing a trick on them like that, boxers tend to take on a conspiratorial air, nod, lean in and whisper their answer, like they don't want to be overheard, afraid they might get their membership of the Pugilistic Brotherhood revoked if it comes to the light that they've been discussing private business with an outsider. I've heard stories about fighters who, after a hard fight, have returned to the changing room, showered and then, having sat back down on the bench, have started to put their kit back on, asking when they were due in the ring. Billy Graham, trainer to Matt Macklin and Ricky Hatton and a former professional fighter himself, told me how he was knocked down in one of his fights but doesn't remember it and only knew it had happened when a friend told him afterwards. He remembers the rest of the fight and he boxed well after the knock-down, his explanation being that the knockdown didn't affect his confidence because he didn't even know it had happened. He also told me about a fellow fighter who, having been dropped, found himself sat on his sofa in his front room at home, or at least that was where he thought he was. When Froch got canvassed by George Groves's right hand in the first round of their first fight he then doesn't remember anything until the second half of the contest and only recalled that he'd been knocked down when he was halfway through his post-fight interview. When Carl won his first world title in 2008, in front of his adoring Nottingham fans, on points over twelve rounds against Jean Pascal, he recalls being hit hard by the Haitian-Canadian in the eighth round and then the next thing he remembers is being back in the changing room after the fight. He has no recollection of that defining moment when the MC announced him as 'the new WBC super-middleweight champion of the world . . . Carl "The Cobra" Froch,' no remembrance what-soever of that moment he'd been working his whole life for.

Simon Brown was a Jamaican fighter operating in the 1980s and 90s, a two-weight world champion, a terrific competitor, a winner, but he's also remembered for what he did during one of his defeats. In 1995 he took on Vincent Pettway for the IBF light-middleweight title. In the sixth round he walks onto a left hand he doesn't see coming and instantly is knocked unconscious. His hands still up, he drops backwards, legs split wide and straight, his back hitting the canvas hard. As he lies there, out cold, with the referee counting him out, he starts to throw his jab from his prone position. Hands still up and in position, he pushes that lead left hand out but his eyes are closed and he's still unconscious.

Things like this don't just happen on fight night either, they happen in the gym too, with regularity. The following was told to me by former IBF middleweight champion Darren Barker:

'There was one in Repton when I was sparring with an African guy, he'd just come through the doors, apparently he was in the Commonwealth Games. I got hit with a jab, I thought "wow" and next thing I know I was sat in the ring, I was sat down and I had no recollection of what had happened. Tony Burns was saying, "You alright?" I carried on training but it was the first time I'd ever been concussed. But I carried on as normal, then got on the scales, as I was fighting Timothy Bradley two weeks or a week later, and Tony Burns walked up to me and went, "When you fighting next?" "I dunno, Tone." He goes, "Where do you live?" I went, "I dunno, Tone." I remember thinking, "I'm here, I know what's going on, my body's working, I'm on the scales." I'd carried on training but he's asking me these questions and I cannot answer them, for the life of me I cannot answer them, the answers weren't there.'

How does a person keep on fighting when they're in that state, when they're 'out on their feet' as it's described in boxing? The answer, Dr Scott told me, is muscle memory, training and instinct. Boxers in that condition are concussed and so the 'signals coming out of the head aren't appropriate and aren't working'. Essentially, the body isn't responding to instructions from the brain, but instead is doing what instinct dictates in that situation, which is to attempt to continue fighting. In a civilian, in a person with average physical strength and a different mentality, that instinct wouldn't be there, but in the case of a boxer, especially those who operate at a high level, that raw instinct would have been there naturally from the beginning and then refined and reinforced over thousands of hours in the gym, along with muscle memory.

I give Dr Scott a case study involving the reverse situation, so rather than a scenario where the brain's not working but the body continues to function, it's one where the brain seems fine but the body won't work.

Anthony Crolla is a former WBA lightweight champion. From New Moston in Manchester, he is one of the most approachable athletes you could ever meet. He had his ups and downs, including having his world title shot delayed when he suffered a fractured skull chasing burglars out of his neighbour's house just before Christmas one year, but through that mixture of skill, perseverance and self-belief that all champions have to have, Anthony got there in the end. His win against Darleys Perez to claim that WBA belt was one of the most popular results in a British ring in recent years. That victory came in 2015 and in 2019, after he'd lost the belt to Jorge Linares, 'Million Dollar' Crolla had the chance to win it back. The only problem was that he had to fight the supersonic Vasiliy Lomachenko. From Ukraine, Lomachenko won Olympic gold in both 2008 and 2012, losing just one of his 397 amateur fights. As a professional he challenged for a world title in his second fight, won one in his third and by the time he faced Anthony was a three-weight world champion, having won eleven world title fights in a row. It was a tall order that awaited the affable Mancunian in Los Angeles.

I'd been wanting to ask Anthony about the fight, and its conclusion, for a while, I just hadn't quite found the right moment, but when I bumped into him during a fight week in London in early August 2023 I made my move. I sidled up to him in suitably sheepish fashion at a hotel in Liverpool Street where we were both waiting for the arrival of Anthony Joshua for his press conference ahead of his fight against Robert Helenius and asked him if we could talk about Lomachenko, and specifically his state of mind when he found himself lying face first on the canvas unable to move with a minute remaining in round four.

'I didn't realize until after it, just how bad it looked. In the dressing room my phone obviously was going mad, people concerned, wanting me to let them know I was OK, and then you look a little bit on social media, which probably wasn't the best idea, and people are saying, "That was brutal," and this and that. And the team's in there, most of the lads from the gym are in there. Eddie Hearn's in there, and I feel absolutely fine and I say, "I don't really understand all of this. I mean it's really nice of people and everything but it's not like it was a really bad knockout." And the room just went a bit like quiet.' Antony starts laughing at this point.

'And I could see people thinking, "Ah, awkward, who's gonna tell him?" And to be fair Eddie went, "It was pretty bad, you know, Croll." And I went, "What?" and he said, "Yeah, it was pretty bad." But I still thought he was on the wind-up so I got my phone and watched it and thought, "Oh."' By now he's laughing pretty hard.

'But it was mad because I could remember everything really clearly, how he set me up, the shot he hit me with. And I remembered being on the floor, face first, and I remember thinking I must look stupid, but I couldn't move, it was like I'd been tasered. And I'm talking to the referee and I was telling him I was fine and I genuinely was, I just couldn't move for a little while. It was like, well, I've never actually been tasered, but I can only imagine it's something like that. I was trying my hardest just to roll over but I'd face-planted and couldn't. I remember thinking, "I look like a right silly fucker here and there's nothing I can do about it." But yeah, listen, I can laugh now and it wasn't long before friends were sending me GIFs of me on a luggage conveyor belt, I think later that night mates sent me pictures of me on a conveyor belt, face down, like a suitcase. But that was the feeling; my senses were all there, I just couldn't really move. I could remember it so clearly. And it didn't hurt one bit. Lomachenko came over after and said he'd broken his hand and I told him he'd broken my heart and pride!'

The only feeling most people will have had that will be in any way equivalent to the one described above will have been experienced in a dream, one of those dreams in which it proves desperately difficult to achieve a relatively simple physical task, such as navigate an obstacle to make good an escape or something of that nature. But this happened to Crolla in real life. Or did it, though? According to Neil Scott, all may not have been as it seemed to Anthony.

'He may well have been knocked out and then the impact [of face planting] has woken him up, but he's immediately exhibiting signs of a concussion, because he's disorientated, he's trying to start movement, trying to get his balance and get his legs to move but they just won't because the nervous system at that stage is still in shock from the impact and there aren't appropriate signals firing from his brain and down his spinal cord to get his limbs moving. He may look back and think that he was trying to get his legs up but I suspect that actually in that moment, if we'd had the benefit of looking at what was actually going on in his brain, I suspect that wasn't even going on, but with hindsight he feels like he was trying to get up.'

According to Neil, Anthony's memory of being clear-headed and wanting to get up has, at least to some degree, been inserted after the event somehow, the reason being that getting up is what he has trained himself to do, what he would expect himself to try and do in that situation.

Talking to boxers about these out-of-body experiences is a bewitching world to step into and there is no better raconteur in whose company to finish this trip than Muhammad Ali. The Greatest described the condition of being hurt, of being in that state of not knowing where you are and whether you're capable of continuing, as being 'outside the Near Room'. Famed boxing writer George Plimpton related how Ali described the Near Room to him in his classic book *Shadow Box*:

A place to which, when he got in trouble in the ring, he imagined the door swung half open and inside he could see neon, orange and green lights blinking, and bats blowing trumpets and alligators playing trombones, and where he could see snakes screaming. Weird masks and actors' clothes hung on the wall, and if he stepped across the sill and reached for them, he knew that he was committing himself to his own destruction.

The Near Room calls to hurt fighters, woos them, but it must be resisted. Appealing though it might appear to be in that strange twilight of semi-consciousness, a fighter has to resist the temptation to enter that room, to go under, until, as Barry McGuigan described it, the windscreen clears and 'you can properly see out again', at which point the Near Room will recede into the distance.

But it's not just the responsibility of the hurt fighter to ward off the temptation of the Near Room, it's also the job of others to recognize when a fighter is hurt and dangerously vulnerable.

A referee has to know when a fighter has been knocked out so they can ensure the fight doesn't continue and they also have to be able to spot when a fighter is exhibiting that level of vulnerability which looks like resulting in them getting knocked out and so stop the fight before it happens. The first part might seem straightforward, as it would be easy to assume that it's obvious when a person has been knocked out and lost consciousness. In the case of an average person, not trained in absorbing and recovering from punches, that would be true because, having been knocked unconscious, it would take some time and a considerable degree of assistance for that person to come round and regain their feet. But referees aren't dealing with average people, they're dealing with highly trained athletes, who, having been knocked unconscious, are then somehow able to recover within the count of ten and convince the referee of their fitness to continue fighting. Referees have to know a knockout, however brief, when they see one.

Charlie Fitch, the referee for Froch vs Groves II at Wembley Stadium, gave me an instructive breakdown of how he makes his own instant diagnosis when he's in the ring, holding fighters' lives in his hands:

'You kind of put all knockdowns in one of two camps; one where there's a parachute fall and one where there's not a parachute fall; the difference being, a parachute knockdown is where the fighter braces himself because he's aware he's going down, and the non-parachute is when he's out, he doesn't know he's going down. The way Groves went down was a non-parachute knockdown. He didn't try to brace himself, he just completely went down. And the evidence of that was the way his left leg was bent back, it was clear to me, "He's knocked out." But even though I was pretty sure he was knocked out at that point, I didn't wave it over. I took the time to look at him, to look in his eyes and see, "Is this guy truly unconscious?" So I do remember, I looked over into his eyes, and although his eyes were open, nobody was home. It was clear to me, "OK, he is knocked out." So at that point I waved it over and did not continue with the count for him. And at that point, to George Groves's credit, he woke up, which really shows how hard he trained for that fight, that he was able to do that. I think he probably wasn't even aware that he was trying to get up, he was out, but it was just like his instinct, desire, determination and willpower had him try to get up. I don't think he could get up though, as he starts to stand, he falls and I have to catch him or he would have just gone down, so I don't think he would have beaten the ten-count had he been given the ten-count.'

Referees also need to be able to see the knockout coming and save a fighter from that fate. No referee can be expected to predict a type-one knockout and, even if they could, they wouldn't have any grounds to stop the fight. If a referee stopped a contest because they strongly suspected a perfectly fresh and unharmed participant was about to get hit with a wonder punch there'd be uproar. But type-two knockouts are different; those a referee might be expected to see coming. But that doesn't mean that making the decision to prevent them is easy. If the contest has become one-sided and all that awaits one fighter is a prolonged beating, probably ending in a knockout, then it's a straightforward decision to stop the fight. But if it's an even fight, one in which both participants are exhausted, very possibly concussed, one where either could be about to win with one more solid blow or combination – and, further to that, one where there's a major title, a big reward, on the line – then in that instance the decision is a lot more difficult. In that situation, though, it's not just the referee who has a big responsibility – the trainer does also. All trainers want their fighters to win but, as much as they want that, they don't want them to get badly hurt. The conflict for the trainer comes with the acknowledgement that if a fighter is going to win a hard fight – and the bigger the fight, the higher the level, often the harder it will be – then most likely they're going to get hurt. A trainer, therefore, can't just pull their boxer out at the first sign of danger or distress, they have to take calculated risks with another human's health, based on what they know about their physiology and strength of will. A trainer has to know when they have a fighter who has reached their limit and they also have to know when they have a fighter who has no limit, who would risk death if allowed to, and save them from their own bravery. It's difficult and it often brings trainers and referees into conflict.

Type-two knockouts drain the physical, mental and emotional energy of all those involved in an entirely different way to type-one knockouts. They are borderline barbaric. It's their nature, they cannot be anything else, and Billy Graham, Matt Macklin's trainer, was happy to explain to me why that is.

Graham's an interesting character. Pure Manchester and pure boxing, he was a pro fighter himself, notching twelve wins against two defeats, mainly at middleweight in the mid-1970s, but it was as a trainer that he became best known, working out of the famous Phoenix Camp, where he trained numerous champions, with his most famous charge being Ricky Hatton. The duo enjoyed an incredible ride together as Hatton's success established Manchester as Britain's boxing capital in the early 2000s and Graham's gym as the hub of that thriving scene. They conquered the world and the bond between trainer and fighter seemed unbreakable, but over time it deteriorated. Hatton suffered his first defeat, in his forty-fourth fight, against Floyd Mayweather in Las Vegas in 2007 and not long after that, he and Graham split. It was acrimonious and it left a scar on them both.

Billy, in his late sixties now, withdrew from the boxing scene in about 2010 and has largely steered clear of it since then, so it was by no means guaranteed that I'd be able to tempt him into talking to me, but after a bit of negotiation I found myself invited to his house on a Thursday evening in summer. He lives about ten miles outside Manchester, in a little town in the Tame Valley, where the Pennines start, in a cottage next to a stream. It's very peaceful, about as far from the madness of professional boxing as it's possible to be.

Billy agreed with everyone else that the one-punch knockout is something nobody can do anything about. He's wondered at times whether there's a sweet spot and has always reckoned it to be located around the ear, one of the areas identified by Neil Scott as potentially being more vulnerable than others. But the type-two knockout is what really gets his juices flowing:

'I always looked for the knockout, to finish it inside the distance. You might be looking for a certain shot that you think you might be able to knock him out with but just in case you don't knock him out, you've got to drain that man, you've got to torture him really because you've got to make him work harder than he wants to. And then any time he wants to rest, you pop things in, so you're constantly draining him, torturing him, because you can't always count on the fact that you're gonna knock him out with one shot, so you've got to be physically draining him, so you can take him into a position where you can stop him, because he's exhausted and you've broken his will. The easiest way to break someone's will is to make them exhausted because when you're exhausted you've got less courage. You can still be brave as fuck, but when you're fucked, you're fucked. That shot you could have taken a few rounds ago, you can't take it any more. It's all about breaking his will and then you can stop him and when it comes to breaking his will, the best way is exhaustion. Then you can take more chances because he can't hit as hard any more.'

Torture. Breaking the will. That's what a type-two knockout is about. Type one is spectacular, shocking, an adrenaline shot, whereas type two is slow by comparison, gruelling and, at least in theory, much more preventable, which makes it more problematic for those involved. A characteristic of the type two is that it demands answers to difficult questions, it is confrontational, and there is no avoiding its inquisition.

One question it demands be answered is: when is enough, enough? It is possibly the most excruciating question in boxing. Billy Graham could have stopped the fight between Jamie Moore and Matt Macklin at the end of that ninth round and saved Macklin from getting knocked out but, just as a fighter needs to be prepared to do whatever it takes to win, as a trainer, 'You have to get your fighter to do unnatural things to win because you want them to fucking win and they want to fucking win. You can't be squeamish.'

It is a trainer's job, though, to know when a fighter under their care is spent, when they have no more to give and are either unable or unwilling to continue. This is critical because some boxers, the bravest ones, may be unable to continue and they may know it, but they'll never be unwilling. They'll keep walking into the gunfire until they are cut down. That is the exit they will willingly choose. Death before dishonour. I found it genuinely shocking that a person would choose that route, to the extent that it took me a few years to accept it, but once I had accepted it, it begged another devilish question, whispered in my ear by the Lucifer-like figure that is the type-two knockout. Could it be classified as surrender? To make that decision to go out swinging, 'on your shield', to use boxing parlance? Were these knockouts, that come as a result of torture and exhaustion and concussion and unnatural things, were they actually a form of submission?

One person who adheres to that theory is Teddy Atlas. His hypothesis is that outside of that perfect type-one punch, every other knockout involves a level of submission. There is, he claims, 'a reason why certain fighters never got knocked out'. And it is this.

'The will to refuse to be knocked out. Some people will say that's crazy. No. There's a history that will show you certain fighters never got knocked out. They got dropped, they got hurt, but they never got knocked out. They got hit hard. And they had long enough careers to get hit by soft-hitting, medium-hitting and really, really hard-hitting guys. But they never got knocked out and the biggest part of it is that they refused to oblige the knockout. I know it sounds foreign to people, but they refused to be a co-conspirator in their own knockout, in their own demise, if you will. They refused to go along with it. They got hurt, they got hit, they saw the flashes that we see, they saw the darkness that we see. But then they insisted that they get back to light. And that insistence is what kept them from being knocked out, to get back to the light.'

They refused to be beckoned into Muhammad Ali's Near Room.

But others succumbed. Their will to continue had been broken and at that point they made the decision, whether consciously or subconsciously, to 'oblige the knockout'. The Atlas Theory is an unforgiving theory but not without merit and therefore, as a line of inquiry, worth pursuing.

The person I found most in agreement with Teddy Atlas was former WBO cruiserweight champion Johnny Nelson.

'The one-punch knockout you don't see coming, there's nothing anybody can do about that, it can happen to anybody. But the one where you get beaten into submission, it's hard for a fighter to accept that's what's happened, because he knows it has, he knows he has accepted that, and although people might say, "Wow, what an amazing fight," he knows he's submitted and he regrets it because there's a side to him that thinks, "If only I'd just stuck it out, if only I'd just believed in myself more because I was doing a lot better than I thought." Often you'll see a fighter give it one last hurrah because they're thinking that if they catch their opponent with something then they might win and if they don't then they're done and it's over.'

Billy Graham largely agreed with it, reiterating his own belief that the type two is all about breaking the will and that 'the higher you go up, the better the fighter is, the harder it is'. But he qualified that, saying that when that stage of a fight is reached, the trainer needs to be able to identify almost to the second the point at which the will gets broken and pull the fighter out, because the trainer knows that their fighter won't quit and that the fight will therefore end with them getting knocked out.

Jamie Moore agreed with it to an extent, saying that often when a fighter gets stopped it's a decision they've taken, a choice they've made to submit. This is true and there are numerous ways a fighter can go about it. They can refuse to get off their stool and force their trainer to stop the fight; they can look sorry for themselves, stop throwing back and force the referee to stop it; they can go down to a knee and stay there; or deliberately rise to attempt to beat the count fractionally too late. I saw Daniel Dubois submit in Poland against Oleksandr Usyk when he challenged the Ukrainian for his unified world heavyweight titles in front of 40,000 at Wroclaw's Tarczyński stadium. In the ninth round, well behind on the score-cards and exhausted, having been put down at the end of the previous round, he got hit with a jab and went down to a knee. I was about twenty feet away and this time I knew he wasn't going to continue. He stayed down as the count rose higher and then, a split second too late, he got back to his feet, just to show that he could, but knowing that when he did so the referee would wave it over. That was the exit he chose and I understood it because he couldn't win the fight at that point and had nothing left.

But Moore was clear that that wasn't what Macklin had done in their fight, that there had been no submission on his part, even in circumstances where plenty of other fighters would have engineered the stoppage of the fight via one of the methods prescribed above.

Macklin considered the Atlas Theory. 'I know what Teddy's saying,' he said. 'With a lot of stoppages, not all, but a lot, you have broke the other fighter and when the fight gets stopped maybe he's glad it got stopped. They didn't quit, but they weren't complaining either.' But the 'they' he refers to? 'They' are not him. The idea that he could have been a co-conspirator in his own knockout, that, even on a subconscious level, he gave up, was not something he could accept:

'Anyone who gets caught with a good shot late on in a fight, they can get knocked out. Any man who gets caught early in a fight with a shot he doesn't see can get knocked out. And that's boxing.'

But that's not just boxing.

Anyone can find themselves in a position where they get blind-sided by something they didn't anticipate happening. Equally, anyone can find themselves in a situation where they've given every ounce of energy and effort to a certain cause, only to discover that it wasn't quite enough.

Those experiences aren't unique to the squared circle; people everywhere experience them, every day.

That's life.

CHAPTER THREE

A Strange Kind of Glory

> You feel like a god. You feel very powerful. You feel . . . oh,
> man . . . it's an indescribable feeling. Especially when you
> see that body and the effect that it has after you land that
> punch. The aftermath of it, it intensifies your feeling. You
> feel like a god and a powerful one at that.
>
> *Deontay Wilder*

What does it feel like to win by knockout?

Fighters will be sharing their experiences, emotional and physical, of landing that knockout blow, but first it's worth examining both winning and losing in more general terms, as it's my belief that attitudes towards them and towards an athlete's required reaction to either result have changed significantly over the last thirty years, a period that constitutes my own viewing lifetime.

I grew up watching sport in the 1980s and 90s and the binary nature of victory and defeat appeared to be just that, with the celebrating of wins and mourning of defeats appearing to be a straightforward psychological process. The scenes at the end of finals were easy to interpret: winners danced and losers slumped.

It was simple, with everyone behaving in the manner that observers expected them to.

But then around 2000 something changed. It was exactly at that point that I started working in sports broadcasting, so I will concede that it is possible that the greater proximity I had to professional sport from then on allowed me to see things that had always been there but previously had eluded me. Nonetheless I am convinced that there was a shift in mentality that affected winning more than it did losing. The agony of coming up short stayed as it was but winning seemed to become a much less joyful affair. The driving force behind it, I believe, was how much bigger sport had become. There was more coverage, more scrutiny, more money, and it all combined to create the attitude that true winners didn't celebrate. True winners expected to win so victory did not constitute the hitting of any kind of jackpot, but instead the forecasted yield on an investment. If teams or individuals celebrated in too spontaneous and extensive a manner then that betrayed a lack of confidence, a lack of ambition, because it indicated that those involved were surprised by their success and didn't believe it would necessarily be repeated. I understood how this shift in mentality had occurred, as professional sport is in many ways the ultimate groupthink environment in which any method or mode of behaviour that seems to facilitate or even coincidentally accompany a successful outcome will often be instantly adopted across the board – but I never agreed that it had to be that way. I found it baffling and somewhat depressing and what it did was create a generation of athletes who didn't enjoy their successes as much as they should have, whilst feeling their losses as deeply as their kind always have. Athletes from that era admit now that they wish they'd celebrated more, stayed in the moment longer and allowed themselves to be at least satisfied with their efforts, if only for a brief period, before refocusing on the next challenge. When the England women's football team won the European Championships in 2022, they celebrated with abandon, they lived that experience for all it was worth, and it was fascinating to see how that totally authentic reaction was received because everyone loved it, the joy was infectious. Nobody was suggesting that the Lionesses over-celebrated and numerous competitors from the aforementioned era expressed envy at how those players were able to behave with that freedom in victory, a freedom that they either hadn't allowed themselves or hadn't felt like they were allowed, or a combination of the two, and they regretted it.

This subject became something I pondered more and more as my career progressed. I vividly remember covering the parade in London after the 2008 Beijing Olympics, which was held to celebrate what had been a very successful Games for Team GB. Numerous floats were deployed to transport medallists around central London and my brief was to interview as many as I could. A conversation I had with one Olympian specifically stands out. Victoria Pendleton had won gold in the sprint as part of a very successful cycling team and therefore was part of the proceedings but didn't seem at ease with being paraded. I conducted my interview, recorded for radio, but when I'd finished asked her if I could pose one more question, not for broadcast. She looked slightly unsure but consented.

My question was very simple: What did it feel like to win? She looked pensive for a moment and then told me it was relief. Relief that after four years of hard work she'd achieved what she'd expected of herself and what others had expected of her. Relief that it hadn't all been for nothing. Relief that she'd avoided the despair and crushing disappointment that would have come with not winning. Relief that it hadn't somehow all gone wrong, as it always can in elite-level sport where the margins are so impossibly fine. I found her answer very relatable. I hadn't asked her the question because I had expected or wanted a certain answer, I'd asked it because I didn't know what the answer would be, but the one that she gave me made sense. Winning an Olympic gold medal might not seem like a relatable experience, it is something very few people get to do, but when you strip that experience back it is the realization of a dream, of a long-held ambition, and that is something anyone can relate to, whether there's a gold medal at the end of that rainbow or not.

Victoria's response instantly made me recall the fate of another athlete at that same Olympics: Lolo Jones. Jones, like Pendleton, had arrived in China expecting and expected to win. Her event was the 100m hurdles, a precarious pursuit, and as she stood on the start line in the final, she was a strong favourite. She'd won the US trials as well as the world indoor championships earlier in the year and in her semi-final had almost broken the Olympic record. She had a great story and the NBC coverage of her final was all about her. At twenty-six she was at the peak of her powers and the rest of the field barely got a mention. When the gun went Jones got away slowly in lane four but by halfway she was on the charge, bursting to the front and streaking away from the rest of the field, hurtling headlong towards the podium and a gold medal. But then the unthinkable happened. She hit the penultimate hurdle with her lead foot and lost all momentum. Jones managed to stay on her feet somehow but in the blink of an eye went from first place to seventh. As soon as she crossed the line she sank to her knees and beat the track in frustration. All that work undone by a rare and fractional error made at precisely the worst time. She managed to give an interview, very soon after the event, during which she showed remarkable poise, but the story goes that she was later to be found crying in a hallway, repeatedly asking herself, 'Why, why, why?'

Jones's fate is a cautionary tale, a sporting *memento mori*, the like of which all athletes are aware. Like the knockout, these tales are brutal and, like the knockout, nobody is immune. Athletes know that what happened to Jones can happen to any of them, and that knowledge makes winning, and how a person reacts to it, complicated.

Olympic sport is brutal. Windows of opportunity are brief, with no guarantee of second chances. In my estimation, both victory and defeat in an Olympic context bear comparison with the knockout, hence the examination of it. But even Olympians do not experience the pure, unadulterated jeopardy that the knockout can deliver.

So, to return to the chapter's original question; what does it feel like to win by knockout, to seal victory in that most decisive fashion?

One man who knows is Carl Froch, the three-time world super-middleweight champion whose final punch as a professional saw him win by knockout in front of 80,000 people at Wembley Stadium.

Froch is not the kind of man you meet every day. I enjoy his company immensely but his personality defies description in many ways and I'd been wondering how exactly I was going to approach the task for this book. But, as luck would have it, when we met to sit down to talk about the knockout, before we started recording, he painted a Rembrandt-like self-portrait.

I met him at the Park Lane Hilton in central London. We'd been trying to organize a rendezvous for a while and, although he'd been very willing, it had proved tricky. But when he was invited to London for a poker tournament the timing was perfect. I strolled into the lobby of the Hilton late afternoon to be greeted by the man himself and quickly found myself immersed in a scene that, if you spend enough time with Carl, you get used to. He shook my hand and immediately showed me the ring he'd been given at his induction into the International Boxing Hall of Fame in Upstate New York a few weeks previously. It's a huge honour to get invited into the Hall of Fame and one that he thoroughly deserved after the career he'd had. The ring was a big, American-style band. It was good, he said, for poker because it attracted, or rather distracted, people's attention. He had a beer in his hand, which was a bit surprising for him, and he explained it, telling me that there'd been a mistake with his booking which had meant his room hadn't been ready when he arrived and so the hotel staff had furnished him with a beer to appease him. He was on very good form. One of the hotel staff then appeared beside us and told Carl very politely that drinking alcohol was not permitted in the lobby, so either he would have to repair to the bar to finish his beverage or relinquish it if he wished to remain where he was. As soon as I heard that I knew this poor, unsuspecting fellow had a battle on his hands. I could see the connections being made in Froch's brain and knew what was coming next. I wasn't yet recording but the exchange went something like this from Carl's side:

'OK. But your colleague gave me this beer because there's been a mistake with my booking and my room's not ready, so he gave it to me by way of an apology. So why would he give me a beer to drink in the lobby if you're not allowed to drink alcohol in the lobby?'

There was no logical rebuttal to this and Froch knew it. The gentleman reiterated the hotel policy of no alcohol in the lobby but Carl was never going to have any truck with that level of illogicality. So our friend submitted and made his exit, which really was the only option available to him. There was nothing about Carl's behaviour that he could take any exception to; he was unfailingly reasonable. There was, of course, another factor in play, which I'd imagine made the situation a touch more daunting than normal for the Hilton employee, namely that Froch is unmistakeably what he looks like: a tough, tough man. He achieves this without any effort or posturing on his part, without any marking out of his territory; there's no need for any of that, the boundaries are obvious, and that's true for all fighters.

We started chatting again and were about to get started when another hotel employee, a more senior person this time, emerged. I was willing him to posit a better argument than the 'no alcohol in the lobby' angle, I genuinely was, because I knew how far that would get him, but, like his colleague, that was all he had to offer and his fate therefore was sealed.

'OK, your colleague has already said that to me. But what I'm saying is that I was given this beer by another of your colleagues. So why did he give me the beer to drink in the lobby if I'm not allowed to drink it in the lobby? It makes no sense. Either he doesn't know the rule or you don't. Which one is it?'

Reasonable and rational with a touch of provocation, it was both painful and funny to watch. After what seemed like an eternity Carl suddenly tired of the situation. Ever the athlete, what he wanted was a contest, a verbal spar, some entertainment, but, upon realizing that his adversary wasn't equipped to provide serious opposition, he told him to take the beer 'if it makes you happy' because he had work to do. He sat down next to me and started laughing. 'I know it's silly,' he said, 'but I just love the awkwardness.'

That is Carl 'The Cobra' Froch in a nutshell. There's an old boxing adage that states that if you want to succeed in the ring then you have to 'get comfortable with being uncomfortable'. I've never met anyone more comfortable with being uncomfortable – and making other people uncomfortable – inside and outside the ring than Froch.

The benefit of that exchange for me was that it served to loosen him up, like a session on the pads before entering the ring. There was no need to start slowly so I began by asking him how it felt when he landed his right hand on George Groves on the evening of 31 May 2014 at Wembley Stadium?

'As soon as it hit him I remember feeling it go down my shoulder and thinking, "Fucking hell, I caught him sweet, right on the chin." I saw him drop and I thought, "Fucking hell, that's a great shot, probably the best shot I've ever landed." Because I threw the check hook my body was coiled to my right side so everything then exploded like a golf swing or a tennis shot or a big fucking right hand from the Cobra. And I remember when it landed thinking,

"Fucking hell, if he gets up from that I'm in for the big finish here and it'll look great." I wasn't thinking, "Stay down," I was just thinking, "Keep cool." I'd been there a few times and when I saw the ref wave it off I just thought, "Game over." I wasn't thinking too much, I didn't get too emotional, I was that much in the zone, it was just seek and destroy.'

TV coverage of the fight doesn't show Carl's immediate reaction as the cameras focus on George, but fourteen seconds after the punch lands, after the referee has waved the fight over, they home in on him, standing in the blue corner, his corner. His promoter Eddie Hearn is already in the ring and you can see Carl's girlfriend, now his wife, Rachael, standing in the front row, huge smile on her face, as her man kisses his right glove and raises it, in an understated manner, before brother Lee barrels through the ropes and hoists him up into the air. The huge adrenaline surge that comes with a knockout has swept ringside, leaving people giddy, but not the man at the centre of it all. What was he feeling at that point?

'It's a mixture of emotions and I don't think until you wake up the next day you understand actually what you've done. You wake up the next day and you still think you need to go on a run, you think to yourself, "Have I done it?" Two weeks after sometimes you wake up and you think, "Have I had the fight? Yeah, I've had the fight. Of course I did." Because your mind's in a mad space. But once it was stopped I just thought, "Yeah, I've done it," like I'd done it thirty-odd times before.'

I point out that this wasn't like the 'thirty-odd times before', that this was different due to the scale of the occasion and that that must have struck him, surely?

'No. Not anything major, no, that's not going through my head. Nothing like that.'

There were no raucous celebrations. He went back to the post-fight party briefly and then back to the flat he'd rented for the week with his brother and one of his friends. But he couldn't sleep so at about 5am he decided he wanted to get back to Nottingham, got on the motorway and headed home.

'I got home and then it was like, that's it, mate, it's all done and dusted, finished. It was a bit of a comedown but obviously I've been smiling about that fight for years and milking it. But it meant so much to me to get that win in my last fight. Maybe if I'd lost, maybe I'd have fought again, to try and satisfy myself and do something different, but it's like, that was it, I did what I did and it was so conclusive, there was no argument. The first fight was controversial in a lot of people's eyes and it had to be settled, it had to be done.'

His reaction is matter of fact, low key, but not blasé. It is a reaction that is not coloured or influenced by his opponent either. He and George Groves had developed an intense rivalry but once it was resolved that animosity no longer served any useful purpose. Wembley wasn't the adrenaline spike for Carl that it was for almost everyone else who was there, it wasn't that mind-blowing natural high that one might assume it would have been. At first glance that might seem disappointing but on reflection what it did give him was something better, a memory that he can enjoy for the rest of his life. Remembering things that happen to you in the boxing ring, good or bad, is not guaranteed; he doesn't remember the moment he first became world champion, but he does remember Wembley.

But I still wanted to know what it was that created the reaction, or lack thereof, that he described? It wasn't that surge that footballers tell us floods the system upon scoring a goal in front of tens of thousands, it wasn't that, but *why* wasn't it that? I wondered whether it was something that had changed over time? Whether back in his early days, when he was a kid boxing as an amateur, winning was a joy and it was the prospect of winning and the joyfulness that came with it that motivated him, but that as he grew older and boxing became his profession things changed?

With that in mind, I veered away from Wembley and raised a subject he's always been very open about, much more so than a lot of boxers. Nerves, and fear. What was he afraid of? What didn't he want to happen?

'I'm not so much nervous about getting knocked out or getting hurt, I'm nervous about under-performing, about not winning. I've got to win, I've got to win the fight, I've trained all this time, I don't want to let anyone down, I want to get a step closer to that world title. It was the fear of not achieving or the fear of letting myself down, because I did that a couple of times in the amateurs. It's that feeling of going back to your room crying, thinking, "Fuck me, I've missed out on the Olympics and I've got fly back to England now with the team and tell everyone I've lost."'

It was almost exactly what Victoria Pendleton had described. The joy of winning can largely be the relief of not losing or, to put it another way, the euphoria that athletes feel is fuelled largely by relief. It's a very relatable reaction, although one that can present as negative. But in the context of a sport like boxing, and in the context of the knockout, it is not, I would argue, a negative reaction. The stakes are unbearably high in boxing. There is no avoiding defeat by playing for a draw, no match next week in which to make amends; and if a fighter gets knocked out there's possibly no further career. It's no wonder an individual feels such palpable relief in victory.

'Losing in boxing's horrible, it's not like losing in tennis. It's a personal thing, but you're also letting people down. Like my mum. I didn't want to tell my mum that I'd lost, or my coach. "What did you get beat for? You boxed for England and you got fucking beat?" My brothers and my mates. In boxing a loss is so bad. It's so detrimental. In tennis if you lose you play again next week, or if it's a team sport it's different. In golf, Tiger Woods won 15 per cent of his matches and he was the best. But in boxing it's that air of invincibility, that unbeaten record, protecting that zero.'

In boxing, if you have the mentality for it, the best way to ensure you don't lose is to go for the knockout.

'When I was boxing I wanted to stop everyone, I never wanted to go the distance. I always wanted to finish it. You've got to get into range, to put yourself in danger to get the stoppage. It's risk versus reward.'

Froch was happy to take that risk and he never got knocked out. But he accepts that it could have happened. He accepts that a type-one knockout, like the one he unleashed on George Groves, could have happened. What he doesn't accept, however, is that he could ever have been the victim of a type-two knockout. That kind of scenario, where a fighter gets ground down and put to sleep late on in a gruelling fight, was not something that could ever happen to Carl Froch.

It was exactly that kind of knockout that he inflicted on Jermain Taylor in April 2009 and it provoked quite different emotions to those he experienced at Wembley.

Carl won his first world title in 2008 when he claimed the vacant WBC super-middleweight title in Nottingham against Jean Pascal. His first defence was a very tough one, taking him to the USA in spring 2009 to defend his belt against former undisputed world middleweight champion Jermain Taylor. From Little Rock, Arkansas, Taylor had dethroned Bernard Hopkins at middleweight (11st 6lb) but after losing twice to Kelly Pavlik had decided he needed to make the move all the way up to super-middleweight (12st). He was mandatory challenger for Carl's title, which meant Carl had to fight Taylor or give up his belt. Team Taylor produced the money to host the fight in the USA and were very confident. In their eyes Froch was an unknown fighter, who'd got a little lucky winning a vacant title, and although he looked like he had some toughness to him, they didn't believe he would cause Taylor many problems. Preparations for the fight weren't ideal for Froch: he had some injuries and then during fight week found himself the victim of some old-fashioned chicanery perpetrated by his American hosts. On the night of the fight, which was held at Foxwoods Casino in Connecticut, nobody came to collect Team Froch to take them to the arena. When they did eventually arrive they were shown into a tiny, freezing-cold dressing room. They were then hauled out of said dressing room five minutes after starting their warm-up and shoved in an elevator that took them up to a holding area where they were made to stand for twenty minutes whilst the home fans showered them with beer and insults. The champion was like a fish out of water and when the bell went things didn't get much better, with Carl getting knocked down in the third round. Everything was going perfectly according to the home team's script, or so it seemed. But Froch was made of much sterner stuff than they thought. He was far from finished; he was just warming to his task.

'After round one, two and three when you've got caught with a couple of tough shots your body and brain kind of adapts and numbs to it and you just get used to getting belted round the head and the effects aren't there. But that depends how solid your chin is.'

Froch's chin was solid. Solid enough to allow him to get back to his feet and to keep going, even though he doesn't remember any of the fight between the knockdown and the final round. He was operating on that autopilot Neil Scott referred to, relying on that instinct and muscle memory, and it was serving him well because he wasn't just hanging in there, he was working his way back into the fight. He can't remember exactly how he did it that specific night but he's been there enough times to be able to explain how it feels, bit by bit torturing his opponent, drowning him.

'When you get up close you can feel them getting weaker. You hit them with shots that you can feel landing flush, clumping them, and you just think, "I'm getting him," slowly but surely, round after round, I'm getting to him, he's crumbling. And even though I'm tiring and getting more and more towards being exhausted, I'm not gonna let that bother me because he's in a worse place than me.

Whatever I'm feeling, he's feeling worse, and I'm not gonna be the one to quit, to submit, I'm not getting out of that red-hot sauna before you, I'm gonna stay in here until I fucking faint, you can get out first. Do you know what I mean? I'm not gonna stop pedalling up that hill. I can't lose, I can't quit. Never.'

Heading into the twelfth and final round he was four points down on two cards and four points up on the other. He needed a knockout. It wasn't an easy fight to score, with Showtime analyst Al Bernstein, a very respected observer, stating at the start of that last round that he had Taylor two points up on his own, unofficial scorecard but that it could easily be a draw or Froch by a point. The instructions from the corner were to 'put it on' Taylor. They didn't want Carl to be overly gung-ho and search too desperately for the knockout but they knew that in all likelihood he needed to win the round and probably win it big courtesy of a knockdown. Three minutes is a long time, and trainer Rob McCracken knew better than anyone what Carl Froch with the scent of blood in his nostrils could be capable of doing in that time against a tiring opponent.

What unfolded was one of the greatest rounds ever produced by a British fighter. Not much happens in the opening minute but just into the second minute Froch stuns Taylor with a solid right hand and you can see immediately that he's in trouble. From that point on Jermain Taylor has nowhere to run and nowhere to hide and with forty-three seconds remaining he goes down in the corner. There's a faraway look in his eyes as he picks up referee Mike Ortega's count and rises at nine, as if he knows what's coming next but has resolved to meet his fate anyway. There are just twenty-six seconds left for him to survive when boxing resumes but it's far too long. Froch comes stalking out of the neutral corner and rains in punch after punch before a right hand causes Taylor's gloves to drop and his body to lose its rigidity, at which point the referee stops the fight with fourteen seconds left on the clock. Amazing drama. Very different to Wembley and, by the evidence of Froch's reaction, a better feeling than Wembley, certainly a more euphoric feeling. He celebrates in the ring, clenching his gloves and bellowing to himself. This was his kind of knockout, that knockout that you can feel rising like a storm, that the fighter and the arena knows is imminent, as does the opponent if they're still able to think straight. A Colosseum-style duel and execution. Blood on the sand.

'I just used to love the stoppage. I'd see them stumble back, the crowd makes a noise, you feel and hear the noise, the adrenaline kicks in and you think, "Fuck me, I've nearly got him here." Left hook, right hook, left hook, you miss, he grabs, get off, fucking boom, boom, boom, the ref's in the corner of your eye, and I'm thinking to myself, "The ref's gonna jump in." And then I'd have another fucking go and then another go. The referee's stood there and watching and the crowd's going mental, and you're thinking, "I've only got to hit him with a proper, sweet shot," and I want nothing more when I'm catching him with shots than that stoppage, I won't stop throwing punches. I threw eighteen unanswered punches in the final round against Jermain Taylor, I counted them all. And when it was over I was like, "Fucking hell, I've done it." That was probably the best one. You know when it's over – I mean, I can't remember technically what happened, what punches I threw, I can't remember any of that, I can't remember it, but I can remember the stoppage, the towel coming in as the ref jumped in as his arms are down and I'm thinking the ref's definitely going to jump in and I'm going to make sure I hit him with two or three he doesn't need, I'm prepared to kill him.'

Sitting in the Hilton lobby, Froch is a lot more animated talking about this than he was talking about Wembley. His voice is still low, it's still a private conversation, nothing is being done for show here, but he's moving his hands as he speaks, digging the shots in, a glint in his eye. He remembers it so clearly, he tells me, because the adrenaline surge caused by the anticipation of the stoppage woke him from the autopilot he'd been on since round three. It brought him back into the ring, or maybe more accurately to a position somewhere above the ring, from where he could look down on himself and watch the carnage.

'It's like an out-of-body experience, a big stoppage or a big finish.'

The big finish was what got his juices flowing and this is what he means by a big finish, not a one-punch knockout. It's how he'd have preferred to finish things at Wembley if he could have, and if that's how it had ended at Wembley I believe we'd have seen a different reaction from him. The Groves knockout was clinical and so he reacted accordingly but it wasn't the kind of contest he wanted and so couldn't provide the conclusion he craved. The Taylor fight, however, was everything he wanted from a fight and the knockout satisfied him in a way that a type-one knockout never could, regardless of the stage, audience or career context. Wembley was too abrupt, a single, sudden act, whereas Connecticut was a process, a hypnotic countdown in which he was able to be present and live the part he played.

Sunday, 29 May 2016, Goodison Park, Liverpool

In the bowels of his beloved Goodison Park Tony Bellew waits.

He hears master of ceremonies Michael Buffer call his name. It's nearly time to go. There's a video playing on the big screen, showing the moments that have brought his career to this point, a brief snapshot of a lifetime grinding and dreaming and telling anyone who'd listen that this day would come. He'd always believed, even when nobody else did, especially when nobody else did.

'I remember fighting in a novice final in a sports centre versus Mohamed Youssef. I go into this final, a little bit apprehensive, and I knocked him cold in six seconds, absolutely flattened him. And I ran, jumped on his corner, with the corner team underneath while he was fast asleep on the floor, and I was screaming at the whole sports centre, "I'm the best fighter you lot will ever see. Don't ever forget my name." A fucking amateur boxer with a headguard on, a vest on, fucking screaming.'

The sequence begins with the setbacks, the defeats in world title fights. 'Twice vanquished' looms on the screen in large letters, as it shows him knocked to the ground by Adonis Stevenson, who stopped him when the two met in Canada for Stevenson's WBC light-heavyweight title. It cuts to the announcement of tonight's fight and Bellew standing in the middle of the Everton pitch, suited and booted: 'I'm gonna put a ring in the middle of that park and I'm gonna fight, and I'm gonna fight to a finish. Everything happens for a reason and it's got me to the place I'm at now.' His words echo around the stands. 'Destiny brought him here,' the screen tells the audience, and then the images segue into a highlight reel. 'Can Bellew realize his dreams?'

The man himself answers, a disembodied voice riding the air currents around ringside: 'It's a lot easier to say enough's enough when they're all against you, it's impossible when they're all with you, there's nothing that's gonna stop me on that night.'

But that night is now this night and still he waits. His opponent for the vacant WBC cruiserweight title, Ilunga Makabu, has long since made his way to the ring and paces the canvas whilst the sound from the screen dissipates into the night air. The crowd fills the void, and then surfing over the top of them comes the voice of Russell Crowe, the Gladiator himself, Maximus Decimus Meridius: 'Are you not entertained? Are you not entertained? Is this not why you are here?'

Finally Bellew appears, at the top of the tunnel steps, hood up, flanked by security. He knows why people are here; he's always known.

'They're not turning up to see someone win on points. They're turning up to see someone get rendered unconscious and that's what you sign up to. And I love doing that to people, I'm not going to lie, and I miss it like a fucking hole in the heart, I miss it bad.'

As he reaches the pitch, the sirens start to wail and the Everton Football Club theme tune of 'Z-Cars' fills the air. It's a jaunty yet menacing tune, the drums and flutes lending it a piratical vibe, a cheerful call to arms, and now he's walking to that ring of fire. There's no going back. It's now or never.

'I had a massive injury going into that fight; the only reason I never postponed that fight is because I couldn't have got Goodison Park again. That was my one chance, I would never have gone ahead with that fight if it wasn't at Goodison. I had a detached floating rib. I remember being in a hyperbaric chamber for two weeks before it for three hours at a time.'

That was the last obstacle on a long road that he'd first set foot on years beforehand. He started boxing as a ten-year-old, a boy wanting to impress his dad. It was tough. He wasn't as talented as other kids in the gym but he stuck at it, winning national championships and boxing for England. Maybe there was something in those bold claims after all. When he became a professional he turned up the volume. Plenty of people reached for the mute button when he appeared, but he didn't care. He wasn't bothered if people loved him or loathed him as long as they couldn't ignore him. He won Commonwealth and British light-heavyweight titles and then fought Nathan Cleverly for the Welshman's WBO title, in front of a home Liverpool crowd, but this time it didn't go his way, a points decision favouring the champion. A rebuild followed and in late 2013 he was in world title contention again, this time travelling to Canada to take on Adonis Stevenson for the Haitian-Canadian's WBC title, the green and gold belt he coveted more than any other. It didn't end well, with the referee calling a halt in the sixth after he'd been knocked down and hurt. He had very little chance of winning that night; making the twelve and half stone limit of light-heavyweight had become almost impossible, and he knew it as he walked to the ring

'I knew I had one good round in me, I was that drained. But I still had the willingness and the belief to walk to that ring, knowing how fucked I was. It's just what you do, it's the way you are. Not everyone's wired the same and I don't take anything away from any other fighter because there are fighters far better than me who've gone to a knee and said, "I've had enough here." And I give them credit because they put their own health first and their own family first and I don't knock that. It's just that I'm stupid. Whether it's because I'm pig-headed or too brave for me own good or whether it's probably me upbringing and wanting to impress me dad all the time, it could go as far back as that, I don't know. But I've never quit anything in me life. Ever.'

But walking to the ring at Goodison Park on this night, things are different. He's up at cruiserweight now, giving himself a blissful extra 25lb of weight to play with. He's undefeated at his new weight, having beaten Cleverly, an adversary he genuinely despised, in a rematch and having become European champion too. Incredibly, Hollywood had even come calling, with Tony cast by Sylvester Stallone as 'Pretty' Ricky Conlan in his *Rocky* franchise revival *Creed*. The film had come out earlier in the year and it depicted Conlan defending his title at Goodison Park. Life imitating art.

As he gets closer to the ring you can see him mouth the word 'unbelievable' to himself, before raising a glove to the crowd. But there's still a way to go. That Green Mile (the ring walk) a fighter has to tread, as Carl Froch once described it, can seem to stretch too far sometimes. It affords plenty of time for those who walk it to think about what they're walking into, about how much is at stake. A fight can be won and lost on that walk.

'I remember going to the ring that night just thinking, "I can't lose here. I can't afford to lose." If I lose I'd have been the biggest fraud ever and I'd have never come out of me house and I'd have never gone back to Goodison Park and I've been going to Goodison since I was ten. And I was five seconds away from losing at Goodison Park by fucking knockout, in the first round. It's madness.'

Finally he's at the steps and up he goes, pausing on the apron to salute the crowd and beat his chest. He dips through the ropes and canters into the ring. Waiting for him patiently is Makabu, a 19–1 Congolese mayhem machine with a 90 per cent knockout ratio. He's five years Tony's junior and a slight favourite with the bookmakers. Michael Buffer makes the introductions and at long last everybody is ready to rumble. Bellew kneels in his corner, offers up a final prayer, kisses the corner post and takes some last instructions from trainer Dave Coldwell.

After a cagey opening couple of minutes Bellew backs his man up to the ropes and lets his hands go. It's a good beginning but then in the last ten seconds before the bell he walks onto a straight left hand and down he goes. He manages to effect a backward roll as he's dumped onto the canvas and, contrary to his personal recollection, is on his feet before the timekeeper has reached the count of two. Bellew's acrobatics make it look like a flash knockdown but it was a solid punch, solid enough to break his nose. The bell goes and he heads back to his corner. 'You got greedy,' Dave Coldwell tells him. But Coldwell's fighter isn't fazed, because getting knocked down by Ilunga Makabu in the first round of a world title fight at Goodison Park wasn't a new experience for Bellew. It had happened to him dozens of times.

'For months I'd have the same dream. I'd get knocked out. When I went down I'd seen the knockdown, it'd happened in me dream. That exact knockdown happened in them dreams and that was the fight over. He did me different sometimes but that exact knockdown, I'd had in the dream. And I was done, the referee waved it off. As soon as that fight got announced, every night I'd have a dream about the fight. And I'd never win.'

He boxes a more circumspect second round. 'Don't think about entertaining the crowd, think about winning the fight,' counsels Coldwell. In the next three minutes the trainer watches his fighter do both.

After about fifty seconds of round three, the Bomber lands a left hook on Makabu, feels it register and goes for him. He's taking chances and walks onto a couple of punches. 'He's got to be careful,' warns commentator Nick Halling, but Bellew doesn't care about what's coming back. He knows. Fighters always know. He backs Makabu up to the ropes and throws with spite, every punch loaded with venom. His eyes are cold, he's in the zone. His opponent is trying to bob and weave, to stay out of the way, but then a left hook lands and Makabu goes limp, gloves dropping, heading lolling to the side, upright but enmeshed in the ropes, unconscious on his feet, like a dead fly in a spider's web. A couple more land before referee Victor Loughlin can get in and stop the action as the beaten fighter flops onto his back, parallel to the ropes, almost under them, knocked out.

Goodison Park explodes. Tony Bellew sinks to his knees, gloves at his hips, and screams into the night air.

What was the feeling, I ask him, as we sit outside Caffè Nero in Stratford station, east London. Tony's one of those people who looks at you when he talks to you, more than most people do. He's an uncomplicated character, one who values honesty and loyalty above all other things, something that anyone who finds themselves in his circle quickly learns about him. There can be a depth and intensity to him too, born, I imagine, of a life dedicated to something that so few people could ever understand.

'Relief. Relief. Relief that I'm not a bullshitter. I'd been telling people for the last ten, fifteen years that I was gonna win a world title at Goodison Park and I think everyone put me in that bracket that I was a bullshitter. "He's full of shit. He chats shit. He just talks and that's it." And the moment that punch landed I know I'm not a bullshitter, that I've done everything that I've set out to do and I think that's where it took me. It took me to the point of no return. I'd done everything in boxing that I said I'd do; I'd been British and European champ and the one belt I wanted, the WBC, that's what gave me it.'

Back at Goodison Park Dave Coldwell gets to him first and wraps him up in a hug. The ring is flooded with people and Tony is mobbed. Eddie Hearn, his promoter, looks over at the still-prostrate figure of Makabu and tries to calm his man down.

'I rendered him unconscious. He was in real trouble. Eddie celebrates everyone's victories, especially their defining ones, and Eddie was like, "Tone, he's in a really bad way, please stop [celebrating]," and I was like, "I do not care." All the emotion . . . people don't understand . . . my whole life had built to this moment, it's just something I can't explain.'

It's one of the most visceral reactions I've seen to anything, not just a sporting triumph. In other sports you'll sometimes see athletes, at the point of victory, perform a choreographed routine, a pre-planned signature with which to underwrite their achievement. But some things there can be no preparing for, some things just catapult a person into obliviousness.

'I had no idea what to do. I just kneeled down and cried. Cried with relief at the fact that everything I'd been saying all these years had come true. It was just the greatest relief of my life. It just validated everything I'd been saying, that I was gonna be a world champion. It was the ultimate goal, I'd reached the ultimate goal. At that stage of my life it was the only thing left I was chasing. I was always chasing becoming world champion.'

He goes to the corner post and beats it with his gloves, screws up his face and roars to the crowd, before reaching down and pulling his son up into the ring with him. His wife Rachael, who very rarely attended his fights, joins them and they fall into a hug. It's at this point that he goes over to Makabu, who by now is awake and on his stool, kneels in front of him and embraces him. All of this, from the final punch to the embrace, and the emotional carnage in between, takes place over barely two and a half minutes. The entire passage, from him emerging from the tunnel to consoling Makabu, takes less than twenty minutes. He makes his way over to Sky interviewer Andy Scott and, surveying the whole scene, tells him.

'Last time I seen that, I was in a Hollywood movie. Now it's real. It's real. I've lived the dream tonight, nothing was gonna stop me.'

Friday, 29 September 2006, George Carnall Centre, Manchester

Jamie Moore has just knocked out Matthew Macklin midway through the tenth round of their fight for Moore's British light-middleweight title. Like Tony Bellew, he'd finished it with a very well-executed left hand. It was over, and, like Bellew, he didn't really know what to do. Initially he did, but then it got confusing, worrying, as knockouts often do. Moments like these are not easy to recall but Moore does his best:

'From what I can remember, the feeling of it was, the instant feeling is like one of, "Yes, fucking get in, I've had a breakthrough." And then I walked to the corner and turned around and he wasn't moving at all. And then me stomach sank, because then obviously, I was, I was happy I'd won but it was more a feeling of concern, rather than euphoria that I'd won. It was a strange feeling.'

His celebrations were short-lived. Jamie turns away with his glove in the air, an instinctive celebratory act, 'a split-second window' as he describes it, but even as he's doing that, he's looking at Macklin and that original feeling of relief and jubilation quickly morphs into something else, in a way that it didn't for Tony Bellew. They're two different people but the situations were also different. Bellew vs Makabu was a high-octane car crash, whereas Moore vs Macklin was a longer, grimmer journey, that took them both to the brink. Jamie knew they'd both pushed themselves to the absolute limit and beyond.

'This sport is beautiful and brutal in equal measure because you want to inflict pain on your opponent because that's the only way you're gonna win. But when you do it to that extent, then for me, from my experience, that scares you, because you think "fuck", and everyone wants to win but nobody wants to go to that extent. So, you know, you're trying to find that middle ground. But when you push it to that sort of end of it, it's a scary feeling.'

This sums up the unique demand that life in the professional ring places on boxers. That 'middle ground' he speaks of? It can't really be found, not deliberately, not as the result of a course being plotted and followed. Every now and again it can be chanced upon and the perfect outcome produced, as it was at Wembley with Froch and Groves. But there's no road map, nobody has any control over it, the wheel spins and it stops where it stops. Boxers know that and so they do the only thing they can do, which is commit fully to the task in hand. Nobody can play boxing, the sport does not afford that luxury; it is a verb in its own right, and if a person chooses to box then the higher they go, the harder they have to go. No middle ground. Here are two takes on this from opposite sides of the ropes:

'Fighters might say they don't want to hurt their opponent but let me tell you, when you're in there, you fucking do, you absolutely fucking do. You want to knock them out, you want to keep hitting them until they drop, so they'll stop fucking hitting you and you can get yourself out of that hellhole. That's exactly what you want to do. Yeah, a few seconds later, when you've done it, when it's over, you might start to think about if they're OK, but whilst you're in there you just want to finish it, to knock them the fuck out, that's the reality.'

'When you go into a ring, if you're going to compete at the top level then you might not come out and you don't think about it. I didn't. I certainly didn't think about it in the sense that I wasn't in the changing rooms thinking I might not come out of this alive, but it is what it is. I didn't think like that. I just blanked it out. Because you have to have that tunnel vision. And you understand that it could happen, but you don't think about it because if you do think about it, you won't commit yourself the same way.'

The first quote is from Billy Graham, Matt Macklin's trainer, the second from Jamie Moore, but both could come from any number of fighters. This is what a boxer has to be prepared to do. They have to be aware of what could happen to them. Denial is dangerous, but at a certain point, maybe early in camp, maybe during fight week, or even on the night itself when they're having that one last conversation with the man in the mirror, they have to decide that the worst won't happen. How different individuals bear that cross is a personal thing and not everybody approaches it the same way, but Moore vs Macklin, the way it finished and the conflicting emotional demands that finish placed on Jamie Moore illustrate very well the contradictory nature of life in the ring.

Thankfully, that choking fear that rose in Jamie's throat upon seeing the state of his opponent released its grip, eventually. After focusing on Macklin, the cameras leave him, still on the floor, and go back to Jamie, who is being embraced by his team. He's exhausted, but quickly he, promoter Frank Maloney and manager Steve Wood all start to bring the celebrations of the crowd down. It's still just seconds since the finish and that adrenaline surge in a tight, intimate venue is in full flow. His supporters respond and all of a sudden it's a different scene. Matt's down for a long time, being attended to by the doctors, and all the while Jamie waits. His team get him sat down in the corner for a spell, on the other side of the ring, but when Matt looks like he's starting to respond, Jamie goes over, kneels down over him, and they manage a handshake. Matt's put on a stretcher and taken away from the ring into a waiting ambulance. The interim period between him pitching face first into the ring floor and the gurney moving down the aisle is about seven and a half minutes. MC Mike Goodall announces that Matt regained consciousness before leaving the ring, before asking the crowd for a standing ovation and announcing Jamie as the winner and still the British light-middleweight champion. His belt is given back to him and for the first time since the fight finished he's able to soak up some of the warmth in the arena . . . but he can't fully relax, not yet.

'Everyone in the family and friends we'd arranged to go back to a house afterwards to celebrate in anticipation of winning. And then I just rung my wife and I said, "Listen, I've got to go to the hospital to make sure he's alright," so I drove straight to Salford Hospital, I just went straight there because I needed to make sure he was alright. I couldn't relax. And I got there. And he was just lying in the hospital bed. So I walked in and we both started laughing. I was like, "What the fuck have we just done?" So by the time we got to that stage and we knew he was okay, I was relaxed then.'

Four knockouts, all of them different and all provoking different reactions. I've watched hundreds of knockouts over the course of writing this book; most I'd seen before, some I hadn't, and during that period fresh ones have been inflicted. I was ringside at Wembley Arena for the rematch between Joe 'The Juggernaut' Joyce and Zhilei 'Big Bang' Zhang, over forty stones of heavyweight sharing twenty square feet of canvas. Zhang had won the first fight, closing Joyce's eye with a metronomic, straight left hand and causing the fight to be stopped in the middle rounds. It was a huge blow for Joyce, who up until that point in his career had traded off the idea that he couldn't be hurt, telling the assembled press in the week leading up to the first meeting with Zhang that 'everybody has a plan until they punch me in the face and nothing happens', a line that would come back to haunt him. It was hard to see how the second fight could go the distance and it didn't. Zhang started to find his feared Chinese power in the second round and every time he hit Joyce it seemed to hurt him. Then in the third he threw a left, not all that bothered whether it landed clean or not, coiled for a right hook, and ripped it through, catching Joyce perfectly and down he went. You could tell from the way he dropped, heavily onto his front, that the fight was over. Incredibly, like George Groves, Joe Joyce did make it back to his feet by the count of ten, but he wasn't steady and referee Steve Gray waved it over. It was savage, but knockouts always are at heavyweight. There's so much human body to fall that they often tend to hang in the air for a split second before gravity takes over and the inevitable descent to earth begins; like watching an old block of flats get detonated. Zhang was jubilant. He's been boxing for a long time but finally had a win that could seal him a fight for the biggest prize of all, the heavyweight championship of the world. His reaction was unambiguous, he looked extremely happy, joyful.

Relief, euphoria, concern (bordering on guilt), joy. Reactions to winning by knockout are varied and complex, born of an experience unrivalled in its intensity in any other sporting arena or walk of life bar the emergency services or armed forces, but nonetheless reactions that remain eminently familiar and relatable to the average person on the street. But to win by knockout you have to accept that you could lose by the same method and therefore life in pursuit of the knockout requires a very particular mentality. In some combatants it can evolve and develop over a period of time, whilst in others that mindset is present from day one. Fighters who possess that all-consuming obsession with finding that devastating punch are rare but they exist. For some fighters, it isn't just about winning, it's about *how* they win. They crave that moment of dominance and resolution that the knockout brings, it's what they train for and what they aim for, every time they pull on a glove. It's an obsession, an addiction. One such fighter is David Haye.

Haye had thirty-two professional fights; twenty-nine of them (twenty-six wins and three defeats) ended inside the distance. He unified the cruiserweight division (14st 4lb) and then moved up to heavyweight where he won the WBA title in Germany against a seven-foot Russian who outweighed him by 99lb. David Haye knocked people out; it was what he did, what he had always done. I arranged to speak to him during the Anthony Joshua vs Robert Helenius fight week. The weigh-in, conducted the day before the fight, was far too busy so in the end I had little choice but to take my chances on fight night itself, which was not an ideal scenario, as I knew from experience that any number of things could scupper me. But I had the luck I needed and at about half past seven, well before Joshua and Helenius were due to take to the ring, we stepped out the back of the TV studio at London's O2 arena and found somewhere just quiet enough to talk. Haye was looking typically cool; casually but immaculately dressed, sunglasses in place. He asked me who else had spoken to me on the subject and, satisfied with my answer, nodded for me to start recording.

I will now reproduce the conversation we had, almost in full, as it happened, with the occasional interjection for the sake of context. This is not something I had planned to do but this was one of those occasions when the interviewee so comprehensively covered the subject at hand as to render interpretation or explanation obsolete.

Do you remember the first time you knocked someone out?
'Yeah, I was probably four or five years old. I was at school and I had a feather, and a kid took it off me. I told him to give it back, he didn't, so I then hit him, punched him and knocked him out. I hit him in the chin, his head hit the concrete. I got in trouble obviously. That was the first time I remember knocking someone out. I didn't really mean to do it, I just hit him out of anger, but it was obviously right on the button and I was a really powerful kid and kids aren't used to getting punched in the face.'

Did you enjoy it? The feeling of it?
'Yeah, I love it. It's a way to completely eradicate the situation, you know. It's got me out of many, many scrapes, being able to render someone unconscious very quickly, and I could do it with an open hand, slap people on the jaw, and that would probably be my ideal choice, so you save the knuckles, punching with an open hand, you can knock someone out, hit them hard enough and they just go to

sleep. So I realized that as well, and technically knocking someone out is easy.'

So you were a knockout artist from the beginning when you started boxing?
'Yeah. Because I'd knocked so many people out I just automatically assumed when I went to the gym when I was ten that I'd be able to knock everybody out and it didn't quite work out that way. It's all about timing and when the other person knows you're trying to knock them out, they can move away, they can counter you. So it took me a little while to realize that just because I can punch hard it doesn't mean I'm gonna land.'

How long was it before you realized that looking for the knockout would put you in more danger yourself?
'My instinct was always just to swing, a bit more Nigel Benn than Naseem Hamed. My first idol was Nigel Benn so all-out assaults was something I loved to do and when you're a kid, other kids aren't used to that type of intensity in combat, but when you go up in levels they are. They know how to negate it, tuck up, pace themselves, and I didn't know how to pace myself so that was always something I struggled with, but nine times out of ten I could get away with it because my intensity of trying to knock them out was far superior to their ability to survive, so I was able to get the knockout if I committed to that.

'It's about committing but not only in the fight, also committing in training. If you commit every punch in training to be a knockout punch . . . all my punches in training when I first started boxing were as hard as I could do it. A lot of coaches tried to get you to punch with technique, gently and gradually increase the power, whereas I was like a baseball pitcher, trying to throw the ball as hard as I could before I had any aim, so when my aim became good I'd already been throwing at a hundred per cent from the start, so I was able to have that natural, athletic, explosive punch power.'

What does it feel like to win by knockout, in that moment?
'It's a beautiful feeling. It ends the conflict. We love the battle but to end the conflict in one fell swoop, the buzz . . . you can't compete with that, particularly in a hard battle where there's been beef, where there's been thousands of people travelling, particularly if you're the underdog and you need to prove that you can knock this person out and you then do it, I've never found any additional high that can come close to that.'

So was it a pure high of winning or relief at not losing?
'It's a mixture of all of it. It's definitely a nice relief. But it's the fact that I told myself I could do it and put myself in a position . . . For instance, before I fought Derek Chisora I told myself I'd knock him out in five rounds and there was nothing to suggest I could do that. He'd just gone twelve rounds with Vitali Klitschko and was granite-chinned apparently, but I said I'd knock him out in five rounds and if I don't knock him out in five rounds I'd consider it a loss, that's the pressure I put myself under in front of the public because I wanted that pressure . . . you know, if people tell you that you can't do something then you tend to do it, so I told the universe I was gonna knock him out in five rounds and that's exactly what I did. If you don't intend to knock someone out then it's very difficult to do it.'

What was your attitude to your opponent? Some fighters have spoken about guilt at knocking someone out?
'I've never felt guilty about knocking somebody out before. Even when I fought Audley Harrison, and Audley's a good friend of mine, and even when I knocked him out [I didn't feel guilty]. You've got to go into a beast mode. I kind of go into another zone where it's just victory and everything else is secondary. Other people's feelings, I couldn't give a shit, you're just here to win and when I'd won that was it.

'But once that initial euphoria's worn off then you're kind of back in the room and you think, "OK, there's a guy here motionless on the ground, I hope he's actually OK." You can see his family around him screaming. I knocked out a guy called Peter Haymer when I was like sixteen years old. Tough fight but I knocked him out in the third round, and he was "asleep" asleep and that was a relief because it was a real tough fight. I won the first round, he won the second round and I needed a big third round to win the fight and I knocked him spark out and I remember his coach, his mum, his girlfriend, everyone rushed the ring, he was in a bad way. But he woke up and had a professional career afterwards.

'I think that equalizer gives you the confidence that no matter how beat up you are, no matter how the situation is, even when I fought Tony Bellew on one leg, there was no time where I didn't think I was gonna win, I still thought I was gonna win because I know if I catch you, you're gonna go. So I keep swinging, because I know I can still win, even on one leg I know I can still win and when the towel came in I was like, "What the hell did you stop the fight for?" In my mind I'm on the floor but I'm thinking, "Great, I'm not hurt, but he thinks I'm hurt, so I'm gonna hit him with a big uppercut." So I get back up, I make the count, I'm ready to throw a big uppercut and the towel comes in and I'm like, "Fuck, that could have been it. That could have been me turning the fight around as he rushes in to finish me." So I always know, if I'm still on my feet, that I can render you unconscious if you give me the opportunity.'

(Haye ruptured his Achilles tendon during his 2017 fight against Tony Bellew, after which, as he says, he was essentially boxing on one leg, with the fight ending in the eleventh round when Haye's trainer, Shane McGuigan, threw the towel in.)

What was your attitude to the possibility that it could happen to you? Everyone tells me that it can happen to anyone, if you get caught with that shot you don't see. Did you accept that?

'I didn't accept it until I got put on my arse for the first time, when I was eighteen against a guy called Jim Twite. He threw a southpaw overhand left, I saw it coming but the next thing you know the ref's counting . . . seven, eight, and I'm thinking, "Why the fuck did he start at seven? Aren't you supposed to start at one?" I'd blacked out and then I watched the tape back and I'd got up and then fallen back down again and I don't remember falling back down again. Another time when I fought a guy called Lolenga Mock, my fourth fight I think it was [it was his seventh and he won by TKO in the fourth round of six scheduled], and he put me over real heavy and we were sitting in the changing room afterwards and the referee's asking me what my name is and where I live and I'm thinking, "Did I win the fight?" And he was like, "Yeah, you won the fight, you knocked him out." "Why don't I remember it?" "You got put down pretty heavy in the second round."

'So I've been fully aware of my frailty and the fact that I can be knocked out, and my understanding and being fully aware of the ability of someone to knock me out has allowed me to devise a style that avoids me taking unnecessary punishment. So when I fought Wladimir Klitschko [a points defeat over twelve rounds in 2011 when they met in a world heavyweight title unification], I'm aware that he's big enough and strong enough and punches hard enough to knock me out if he hits me on the chin, so I couldn't allow him to hit me on the chin and in the fight he hit me on the chin and it was alright, I actually overestimated what I needed to do to make sure my style [stopped me getting hit]. But I knew being lackadaisical and not being bothered about getting hit was a surefire way of getting knocked out. Imagine your opponent's got razor blades on their hands and it's [a game of] don't get cut, that was my mindset.'

So the awareness that getting knocked out is a possibility is a good thing?
'It's a brilliant thing. Chris Eubank Junior didn't have that when he went in against Liam Smith. He didn't believe there was a version

of reality where he could get knocked out because it had never happened before in sparring or training, so now it should alert him to "OK, I can't be getting hit, I've got to adapt, I've got to roll my head, take my head out, I don't want to get put down again." So being a realist in the fight game is so important.'

(Eubank was stopped by Liam Smith in January 2023, having talked a lot in the build-up about how he'd never been put down either on fight night or in the gym. Smith knocked him down in the third round and although Eubank managed to get up and was allowed to continue, his coordination had completely deserted him, and when Smith started landing on him again the referee stopped the fight. Eubank had come up with a great line with regard to the mentality of top-level boxing a few years previously when he'd said that in the ring 'it was you or me, and it's not going to be me, not in front of all these people'. Eubank went straight into a rematch with Smith eight months later and managed to win by stoppage himself, which was hugely impressive after what happened to him in the first fight.)

'I used to prepare for it [getting knocked down]. I used to do roly-polies around the ring and do spinning around and around and then have to try and hold my form to do the pads to replicate that feeling you get when you get put down or hurt. So I used to prepare knowing that there's a chance. Before I fought Jean-Marc Mormeck [in a world cruiserweight title unification in 2007] I did roly-polies around the ring and then the pads because I knew there was a chance with his style that he was going to clip me and he did in the fourth and put me down real heavy, and when I was on the floor I was thinking, "Thank fuck I've practised this because the room's spinning and I'm used to this." So I got back up, got to the end of the round and three rounds later I knocked him out.'

But that acceptance never translated into any kind of fearfulness or hesitation? Because it does with some people.

'No, no, no. If you hesitate you get chinned. You have to commit to it and my style is slipping and countering, drawing him in to hit him with a counter. I've got good reflexes so I could slip their punches and counter them, to get them fearful of letting their hands go and then when they're fearful of letting their hands go then I'd start to lead off. So I devised my style so I used my superior speed to my advantage.'

Pro boxing is one level of commitment, but being a knockout fighter, committing to the knockout, is another level of jeopardy, like an Assassin's Creed. Do you know a fellow Assassin when you see one?
'I can tell straightaway. You can see how much a fighter is committing to the shot, how much he's rotating through. Yeah, I can tell straightaway if he's got that X-factor. I can see if someone's got mean intentions in their punches. Some fighters have learnt to try and keep it long and keep you on the end of their jab, but my jab was there just to load up for my right hand, my jab was there to knock your head out so I could hit you with a right hand.'

Did you always know that minerals-wise you always had it? That when it got hard in there you wouldn't quit?
'I used to watch *Rocky* and that's what Rocky did. Rocky just kept coming. I used to watch Rocky Balboa.'

In the eyes of fighters, Rocky is like real life.
'Yeah, yeah, yeah. For me it was. I never gave up, I just kept coming.'

Is there any way to replace that feeling of boxing, of winning by knockout?
'There's no way to replace it. A big, strong lad getting stretched out, it's a beautiful thing.'

Did that edge ever blunt? Did you ever get civilized?
'I definitely got more civilized as I got older, for sure, but when you're in there, in the heat of the battle, you're not civilized. The

civilized side of it changes your training and your way of life, living in a big mansion, private jets and all that shit, versus living in a shit-hole flat, grinding away. But when that bell rings, all of that doesn't matter. Are you willing to die when that bell rings? Who is willing to drown the longest? And that's always there and will always be there; you don't think of anything other than the fight. Sensibly in that first Bellew fight I should have thought, "OK, my Achilles tendon's ruptured, let's pull out with the injury and get a rematch." But I'm like, "No, this is how I live and die, I have to find a way to win this fight." At no stage did I consider pulling out.

Were you prepared to die in pursuit of victory?
'That's the winning mentality. All the fighters who've made it have been willing to die. Some say they wouldn't but how do you know when you're about to die? You don't know. It's not a decision. You just keep going. And some fighters have fought until they've died, or been put in a coma, or paralyzed. It happens. That person didn't know that next round that was what was going to happen, no one gets that heads-up, but you're all aware that if it gets tough, that is the potential repercussion. Every fighter who goes beyond that, who's come back from defeat, a knockdown, or kept coming back, they're all willing to die in there, to put themselves in the firing line.'

Commitment. Realism. Acceptance. A holy trinity of qualities that a fighter needs, that a person needs, if they're to succeed.

Haye describes life in pursuit of the knockout, sport's most decisive victory, perfectly and it is a strange kind of glory indeed.

But I'll conclude this chapter with Deontay Wilder.

When I was mapping out an ideal landscape for this book, a conversation with Wilder formed part of it. I made an approach early on but didn't hear anything back, which neither discouraged nor disappointed me as he's someone who receives a lot of interview requests. I remained hopeful as I suspected at some point I would find myself within striking distance of the Bronze Bomber, and so it proved. Just before Christmas I found myself in Riyadh working on the Day of Reckoning, a bumper card that featured, amongst numerous heavyweight showdowns, Deontay Wilder vs Joseph Parker. On the Monday he and all the other fighters had to engage in a day of interviews and although he wasn't on my list of duties I asked if he'd be amenable to a couple of questions about the knockout; although in heavy demand and pushed for time, he obliged. Wilder is the pre-eminent heavy-weight knockout artist of recent times, and possibly of all time. His stats support that description but bare statistics, impressive as they are, do not do him justice. Six foot seven, sinewy and slim, Wilder possesses an elasticity that allows him to punch from seemingly any position with mind-blowing power, to knock an opponent out at any second and from any angle. He has a greater familiarity with that lightning-bolt surge that comes with the knockout than any person alive.

'You feel like a god. You feel very powerful. You feel . . . oh man . . . it's an indescribable feeling. Especially when you see that body and the effect that it has after you land that punch. The after-math of it, it intensifies your feeling. You feel like a god and a powerful one at that.'

But he also knows what it's like to be on the receiving end. In the second fight of his trilogy with Tyson Fury he found himself stopped in seven rounds and subjected to the kind of beating that he would never have believed possible, and then in their third fight Fury knocked him out in the eleventh round of what will probably always be the best fight I've ever commentated on. The bravery and mental fortitude that Wilder showed on that Las Vegas night, in walking, without hesitation or fear, straight back into the fire that had burnt him so badly and swinging until his last breath was inspiring. He was still willing to roll the dice, to play that high-stakes game, even though he knew it was a game he could lose.

'You have to understand that the business consists of that. That it's a hurt business, that anything can happen, so you have to have that mindset that what you do to others can be done to you and you have to accept that fate, you know what I mean? Because nothing is promised. So whatever happens you have to able to deal with it because when it does happen to you, you're going to have to deal with it alone anyway.'

How do you deal with suffering a knockout? That is the next subject for discussion.

CHAPTER FOUR

An Inconvenient Truth

> When I hit the canvas, my mouthpiece came out and as the ref was counting, I was trying to stumble to my feet and grab the mouthpiece at the same time. I was operating on pure instinct. I was totally out of it. The ref hugged me after he counted to 10. I walked back to my corner totally dazed. I was chewing on my mouthpiece but I didn't even know what it was.
>
> 'What happened?' I asked my corner.
>
> 'The ref counted you out, Champ.'
>
> *Mike Tyson talking in his autobiography,* The Undisputed Truth, *about getting knocked out by Buster Douglas in Tokyo in 1990*

The inconvenient truth is simply this: For someone to win by knockout, someone has to get knocked out. You cannot have one without the other and the effects can be devastating.

The first person I asked about losing by knockout was Scott Welch. It was late May in Bournemouth and we were a couple of days away from a fight at Bournemouth Football Club involving local hero Chris Billam-Smith and WBO cruiserweight champion Lawrence Okolie. Scott's son, Tommy, was featuring on the card that weekend. The Brighton Rock, as Welch was known during his fighting days, had been a formidable operator during the 1990s, winning British and Commonwealth titles before going on to star opposite Brad Pitt in *Snatch*, sharing a ring with him whilst playing Horace 'Good Night' Anderson, a bareknuckle fighter. He'd been knocked out by James Oyebola on a Lennox Lewis undercard in Atlantic City in 1994 only to then exact his revenge in a rematch. We were staying in the same hotel, an old-fashioned place up on the cliff overlooking the sea, and were being treated to perfect weather. That was the backdrop against which I raised the spectre of the knockout as we sat in a sunlit lobby, a cooling breeze filtering through the front doors. I brought the conversation around to the current heavyweight scene and what was a hot topic, whether Anthony Joshua was still capable of making that commitment to the knockout, or whether that instinct to gamble ultimate defeat in search of the ultimate victory had left him. I wasn't expecting Scott to speak to Joshua's situation specifically, that's something fellow practitioners rarely do, but what he did do was answer the question within the framework of his own experience and tell me what he knew to be true after a lifetime in the sport.

'In this game we know that to get the best out of yourself you have to accept the worst that can ever happen to you and in boxing that's death, right. It's a very dangerous game, especially the heavyweight division, one wrong shot and you're knocked out, what it does to you we don't know, all through history it's done different things to different people.'

There is no standard response to the public, sporting execution that is getting knocked unconscious in front of a crowd of people. What did it do to him?

'It's not a very nice place, it's a terrible, terrible place. To come back from it I had to refind myself, reinvent myself. If I could have found a rock to hide under I would have done and I probably would never have been seen again. But we couldn't, we had to come back, and rebuild and put it back together again, find the reasons we got beat. I was winning the fight and I dropped my hands for a split second, next thing I know . . . But you have to find yourself, there's not many people who do come back, you come back either better or you don't come back, or you come back broken and you never get there again.'

Getting knocked out is a physical event and the physical damage it can visit upon a boxer can be extremely serious, but it's a different kind of damage that fighters fear, the damage to their ego and identity, and those wounds can take a lot longer to heal, if they indeed they ever do.

'Getting knocked out is just the worst thing. I felt embarrassed, I felt I was an idiot, I mean every single thought went through my head. I can't go see people, and no matter how you try and tell people it's OK, you're fine, when it actually happens to you . . . We watch boxing every day, what do we want to see? We want to see knockouts. I've got seventeen knockouts on my record out of twenty-two wins, fantastic. What did I do in the gym? Knocked as many people out as I could. Did I think about it? No. But when it happened to me my whole world collapsed. For three months I was just walking around in tears, just coming out of my eyes, running down my face.'

For a proud warrior like Scott Welch, the embarrassment, the humiliation, of being knocked out was a fate worse than death. Revenge was paramount. He had to exact it and he did so, at the Brighton Metropole Hotel, seventeen months later, to win his British and Commonwealth titles. That helped him, as he described it, 'get over it easier.' For his own recovery he had to send somebody else into that same dark place, a one-in, one-out system, breathtaking in its ruthlessness.

'It's a disgustingly terrible thing but it's a wonderful feeling when you do it and unfortunately people pay a lot of money to watch people do it. What do I want to see still now, after all these years in the game? Do I want to see boxing and winning on points? No. Do I like a tough fight? Yeah, I like a tough fight, I like to see knock-downs. The beautiful, brutal game of boxing, that's what it is isn't it? It's a beautiful, brutal game.'

His career ended with a reversal on points over twelve rounds. Nobody wants to end on a loss but Scott could handle the manner of it because, to fighters, whilst a points defeat is a loss, it isn't a defeat, and that distinction is very important. A knockout is a defeat and 'to deal with a knockout at the end of your career, and to go through life after your last fight was a knockout is very, very difficult to deal with'.

The story of Ricky Hatton's rise from the humble streets of Hattersley to the shimmering lights of Las Vegas is extraordinary. He ended his career with a haul of trophies that would make even the most seasoned engraver wince, but it wasn't the titles he won as much as the journey to those wins that made his pugilistic odyssey so unique. Tens of thousands of his supporters descended on Las Vegas to walk in a Hatton Wonderland, all drinking the same intoxicating brew, never fearful of the inevitable hangover that follows defeat.

In December 2007, 43–0, two-weight world champion Hatton met a 38–0, five-weight champion in Floyd Mayweather. The fight was at welterweight, 10st 7lb, a division above Ricky's strongest of 10st. He felt invincible, in the way that all undefeated fighters do. But there was nothing gung-ho about his confidence, no whistling past the graveyard, he was too intelligent a fighter for that. He'd been knocked out as an amateur so he had that acceptance of what could happen in the ring, but he never allowed that realism to dampen or dilute his resolution that when the bell went he would find a way to win. He'd been with trainer Billy Graham his entire pro career and it was that attitude, just as much as his boxing ability, that convinced Graham he had someone special on his hands. 'If ever anyone was born to be a pro fighter it was Ricky Hatton,' Graham told me. He went on to describe how before their British title fight against Jon Thaxton in 2000, the pair of them had been out walking in the afternoon, killing time, and Billy, nervous about Thaxton's power, had been running through all the things Ricky had to look out for:

'And then he turned around to me and said, "I'm not scared of getting a good hiding, you know." And he's the only fighter that's ever said that to me, before or since. And that's the attitude he had.'

For Billy, that's the attitude a fighter must have and it was a huge part of what had taken them so far, from sitting on the back steps of his Salford gym talking about conquering the world, to head-lining the MGM Grand.

But on 8 December, in front of a packed house, a huge TV audience and mainstream global attention, the unthinkable happened. Ricky Hatton got knocked out. Going into the tenth round he was well down on the cards and needed a knockout himself. Mayweather knew it and was ready to exploit his opponent's increasingly desperate attacks with his trademark surgical skill. He hit Hatton with a left hook that sent him bouncing off the corner post to the canvas and then when an unsteady Hitman was allowed to resume after beating the count, Mayweather clipped him with another left and Hatton again collapsed to the floor, with referee Joe Cortez immediately waving the fight off as the towel came sailing in from Graham. It was over. He wasn't invincible after all.

'When I got beat by Mayweather, I think it left a dent in me because I thought I was gonna beat him and then when I didn't . . . it's not just the after-effects physically, when you've been knocked out. You know, for someone who's beaten this guy and beaten that guy and won four world titles in two weight divisions and with record numbers of fans coming to watch him, and then to get knocked out; it was the after-effects mentally that ruined me, it was the mental side that I struggled with. You're bullying everybody and bashing everyone and then the next minute you're knocked out and that's very hard sometimes to get your head round.'

I spoke to Ricky whilst he was on his way to a speaking engagement in Lincoln, where he was appearing alongside Frank Bruno, Nigel Benn and Joe Calzaghe. He's always in huge demand for events like that, and always will be. He can make a room laugh but he can also make a room cry, and that's where his magnetism really lies, in his humanity, his relatability. When he was fighting people loved him because he was, as he always said, just a kid from a council estate, and if you went out in Manchester of an evening and you bumped into him then you could have a beer with him and walk away with your own personal Hatton memory, he would give you that. But he's become even more relatable in retirement because of what he's been through since boxing finished for him. It's been very tough and although getting knocked out isn't responsible for all of it, it was certainly a catalyst.

'When I got beat by Mayweather, I cancelled all my functions, all my appearances, I was walking down my hometown in Hyde down the street and I thought people were laughing at me. They weren't, they were proud as punch of me, but in my mind because I'd told everyone I was gonna win and not only did I not win but I got knocked out . . . So I cancelled all my functions and I actually found it hard walking down the street of my own town, which I know is crazy but that's what ended up in my head. For several weeks I just couldn't leave the house, it was the embarrassment. And people would say that there's no embarrassment in getting beaten by Floyd Mayweather, which there isn't, but some people can cope with a knockout well and move on and get past it, and get back in the gym, which I did eventually, but it took a lot to get my head around the fact and to rebuild again. You know, some people can just shrug it off and say they'll come back stronger. And I didn't feel that way at first. I didn't think I'd come back stronger. I didn't want to see anyone. It was bad.'

He needed to somehow erase the defeat. Unlike Scott Welch, a rematch with his original nemesis was never on the cards, but there was another fight out there that, should he win it, would put him back on top. If he could beat Manny Pacquiao, who at that time was contesting the crown of best pound-for-pound fighter in the world with Mayweather, then he could exorcise the demons of December 2007. So it was that in May 2009 he was back in Las Vegas and back at the MGM Grand Garden Arena looking to do exactly that.

In theory it made sense, however in practice, as insiders would later reveal, it was a doomed enterprise. But there was optimism regarding his chances. Ricky had had two fights in 2008 post-Mayweather: a huge homecoming at his beloved Manchester City and then a good eleventh-round stoppage win in Nevada against Paulie Malignaggi. And, further to that, against Pacquiao he would be back down in the 10st light-welterweight division, his strongest. But behind the scenes his world was falling apart. He'd split with Billy Graham and his relationship with his parents was also strained, so the two pillars that had formed the architecture of his boxing life had all but dissolved. To replace Graham he'd chosen Floyd Mayweather Sr, the father of his ultimate foe, which, in retrospect, seems insane. It could be argued that if anyone knew Ricky's weaknesses and how to improve them then it would be a Mayweather, but what was indisputable was that the Hattons and the Mayweathers were very different people. Training camp had not gone well. Ricky tells a story about how, two weeks out from the fight, after a poor gym session, he sat on the ring apron, buried his head in a towel and sobbed, because he knew that he had no chance of hitting the peak he needed to come fight night.

'I probably should have been pulled out but, I mean, everyone's flights are booked, everyone's hotels are booked, everyone's tickets are booked, so you know, you go with it, don't you?'

This is a key point about huge fights and the boxing business. The repercussions of a no-show are so big it just isn't an option. He was more vulnerable than he'd ever been, both mentally and physically, and up against a superb fighter at the peak of his powers. Walking to the ring for any fight, there is no room for doubt, no room for apprehension, but that night, that was all Hatton had.

'Against Mayweather I was walking to the ring thinking, "I can beat him, I can beat him." Going into that fight there was no doubt in my mind but for the Pacquiao fight I felt like I was going to my own funeral. It's scary to admit that but it's true.'

The packed arena had that feral feel to it. People knew something was coming, they could smell it; the nerves, the adrenaline, the expectation, the blood lust that the biggest fights create. There's an overhead shot of the ring before the bell sounds which shows Hatton standing in the middle with Mayweather Sr, waiting for Pacquiao to join him to receive final instructions from referee Kenny Bayless. Ricky looks like he's all alone, whilst Pacquiao until the last possible moment has a throng of people around him, protecting him, shielding him, believing in him. Bayless issues his final instructions and the fighters go back to their corners. You can hear the Hatton fans in the background. Larry Merchant, on commentary for HBO, captures the moment perfectly, saying, 'They are warrior kings with armies of fans who follow them to the battle. Now they will be alone in the battle.' Nobody felt more alone at that moment than Hatton.

The bell sounds and Hatton tries to bring the fight to his opponent but gets knocked down twice in the final minute of the first round and, although he looks clear-eyed as he takes a knee before rising to beat the count each time, the writing is on the wall. Nobody is closer to the action than referee Kenny Bayless. He can feel it, that quickening, that heightening of the senses: 'I had never had an adrenaline rush in a fight, never, but I did in that fight, because the crowd was so loud and excited after those first two knockdowns. I could feel my heart racing as if I'd just a run a four-hundred metres and I'm standing in the corner and I can feel my heart beating and I'm thinking, "Heart, calm down, because the bell's getting ready to ring and I have to go back out there."'

Mayweather Sr talks to Ricky in the corner, telling him he needs to move his head, to feint, but his fighter is miles away.

In the second round Hatton continues to try and land that one shot that could turn things around. Bravery is all he has at this point but it's boxing suicide. In the dying seconds of the round Pacquiao pummels him with a ramrod left hand and Hatton drops, straight onto his back, head bouncing off the canvas, gloves flying back over his head and cannoning off the ring floor before settling neatly at his side whilst his legs stretch straight out in front of him; an act of spontaneous violence creating a scene of almost perfect, serene symmetry. The overhead camera zooms in and we can see that his eyes are open. Kenny Bayless can see that too as he crouches over him and takes up the count, but after a few seconds he gives up on it, waves his arms, takes the gumshield out and urgently ushers in the medics. The American coverage flicks to Pacquiao celebrating but then goes back in on Hatton. A cameraman has managed to get in the melee in the ring and we're treated to a close-up as Hatton is rolled onto his side, his glazed eyes still open as the latex-gloved hands of one of the medical staff supports his head. It's too much. The pictures switch to the parents, Ray and Carol Hatton, and Jennifer Dooley, his fiancée, her face strewn with tears, blind with anxiety. She's peering into the ring, where thankfully Ricky has come round and is now sitting up. That's what happened, but what does he remember?

'I was knocked out cold and then after a couple of minutes you come round. And there's people around you, "Hiya, Rick, how are you doing? Are you alright?" Your team and your corner are there. It just takes time to get your head back together. You wake up and then you realize you're in the ring and then you realize you've been in a fight and you go back to the changing rooms after and then you talk to your coach and ask so what was it? What was the punch that caught me? "It was the left hand over the top. He got you down twice in the first round, but in the second round, it looked like you'd got through the worst of it but then he hit you with a few seconds to go." And then you say, "Yeah, yeah, I remember now, that's right," and it just takes you a while to absorb it again.'

The one saving grace was that it was a quick, type-one knockout, rather than the type-two stoppage he'd suffered against Mayweather.

'I had to go to the hospital after for a brain scan which every boxer has to do and they take your blood pressure and your heart rate and all that and because the fight was over that quickly, there's nothing wrong with me blood pressure and there's nothing wrong with me heart rate and you wouldn't know I'd even been in a fight. Because it was over that quick there weren't that many after-effects, you know, physically. After the Mayweather fight because it was ten rounds and it was a gruelling fight, my body was in a much worse state. [With Pacquiao] It was over that quick, there wasn't much physical damage.'

But whilst it wasn't as bad physically, mentally it was much worse.

'With the Mayweather fight, even though the fight was pulling away from me down the straight, I did give him a fair good run for his money but against Pacquiao, when you get destroyed in two rounds, that was embarrassing. With the Mayweather fight I was devastated but at least I could look in the mirror and go, "You give him a fair go, Rick," but getting knocked in two rounds, that was an embarrassment and ultimately after that fight, I knew I had to retire. I've been knocked out in two rounds, that's it now, my career's over, I'm never going to fight again. Something you've done from ten years of age. I've got destroyed in two rounds so I need to retire now because I know I haven't got it any more. That was very hard to cope with.'

The aftermath was horrific. He suffered terribly with depression, he was suicidal and attempted to kill himself 'several times'. The wins, the former glories, were no consolation, just a painful reminder of what he used to be. He'd had some incredible highs but now was experiencing an unimaginable low, living his life in the darkest of shadows:

'People would say, "What's he got to be depressed about? Yeah he got beat by Mayweather, yeah, he got beat by Pacquiao, but look, he's got a nice house, he's got a nice car, he's got this, he's got that, what does he need to be worried about?" But they don't realize, you know, the state it leaves you in. When you're a fighter and a winner, you have to have that belief in yourself and that attitude that no one can beat you, that you're the best, and if you don't have that attitude, you're not going to go very far in boxing, so when you do get beat and you have to retire it hits you harder. If you're a proud, proud man, a proud boxing champion, you know; I mean, it doesn't matter what you put in the bank and how big your house is, it fucks you up a bit.'

Ego and pride, the things that got him – that get any athlete – to the top now bite the hand that used to feed them. He can feel his identity being stripped away and that loss cuts deeper than any reversal in any sporting arena. It's crippling.

If the story ended there then this would be a bleak tale indeed. But Ricky Hatton managed to find a way through those long nights, sat on his sofa with a knife at his wrist. He wanted to submit, but in life, just as in the ring, something inside him wouldn't allow him to do it. He had to refind himself though, as Scott Welch described it, and although he wasn't going to box Pacquiao again, just as he wasn't going to square off with Mayweather again, he decided he had to return to the ring, to the Manchester Arena, the scene of his greatest triumph, and show people, most of all himself, that no matter how low you sink, it's always possible to return to the surface.

Such was Hatton's fame, to many it would have looked like a typical boxing comeback; a former champion, well past their best, returning to chase that rush one last time, or in need of one last big cheque having seen the money run out. But it wasn't that. It wasn't born of any delusions of future grandeur either. It wasn't about beginning a new career, it was about finding a different end to the original one because that ending harboured a level of regret that it wasn't possible for a proud champion to live with. It was about closure.

'You don't want to end your career on a second-round knockout, do you? But also, due to my knockout defeat and a few personal problems, I went off the rails and my life went to shit. So it wasn't just getting beat in the two rounds in the fashion I did, I wanted to go out on a better note than that, but also because of what had happened in my personal life I felt like I'd let my fans down, people down and family down, because mentally I was a very, very poorly guy. The comeback was because I wanted to end it on a good note, not just two rounds. And I wanted people to say, "Well, listen, we all have problems, Ricky's no different and look how he bounced back." And even though I ended up getting beat I think that's what I proved. I wanted to get a little bit of respect back for myself. And even though I lost, I was able to move on with my life better and I think people looked at it and thought, "OK, wow, well done, fair play." You know, I mean, so even though I lost it was probably one of the best fights of my career.'

I was in attendance on 24 November 2012, to hear 'Blue Moon', Hatton's legendary ring-walk anthem, echo around ringside and it was quite a moment. Right up until the first bell went, it was like the old days: the arena was packed, Michael Buffer was the MC and on commentary was Ian Darke. You could tell from the beginning that the old timing wasn't there, though, and that his trademark body attacks had lost their snap. But it didn't matter, he was still in there, in fighting shape and trying for all he was worth, against an opponent in Ukrainian Vyacheslav Senchenko who just seven months previously had been world champion. That Hatton had managed to get himself back to a place where, mentally and physically, he was able to compete at that level again was extraordinary. And compete he did. It was close on the cards, but at the end of the ninth round he got sunk by a body shot and couldn't beat the count, hearing the referee toll 'ten' whilst on a knee, totally aware of what was happening. In the record books it went down as a knockout but it was nothing like Mayweather or Pacquiao. In years gone by, when winning at any cost was all that mattered, he'd have beaten that count, but as Ian Darke said, during what turned out to be Hatton's final round, this had been 'an exercise in redemption' for Ricky and when viewed in that light the exercise had been a success. He could finally put the nightmare of 2 May 2009 behind him and move on with his life, and in doing so inspire countless other people to do the same, to take arms against their own sea of troubles and, by opposing, end them. Ricky Hatton's story hasn't, to my knowledge, often been described as Shakespearean, but it was without doubt an epic tale, one that explored the human condition in agonizing detail but that, thankfully, stopped short of tragedy due to the resilience of its lead character.

Tony Bellew got knocked out in the final fight of his career, after which he closed the book. He'd always seemed at peace with it but I wasn't entirely sure how keen he'd be to discuss it as, although I'd heard him speak on it, I hadn't heard him do so in any great detail. Added to that, some typical London travel chaos had scuppered our original plans to sit down at the plush hotel he was staying at ahead of a fight we were both covering, which was why we'd had to seek refuge at a train station café after a long journey on the London underground. The whole thing ended up being a lot more public than I'd planned, which wasn't ideal as Bellew's fame meant that he had a steady stream of people approaching him for photos. I wouldn't have blamed him had he run out of patience and requested we do it another time. Thankfully he didn't, which was entirely consistent with the type of person he is.

We'd already discussed the Makabu win so it was time to move on to 10 November 2018 and his fight for the undisputed world cruiserweight crown versus Oleksandr Usyk.

After beating Ilunga Makabu to realize his lifelong dream of becoming a world champion, Bellew defended once and then moved up to heavyweight to fight David Haye, in what seemed like a mission impossible. But he pulled it off and then repeated the trick in a rematch. Tangling with the Hayemaker had been extremely taxing mentally and physically, so when he stopped Haye for a second time, in May 2018, he'd decided enough was enough. But then, in late July, Oleksandr Usyk, a London 2012 gold-medallist, had won the World Boxing Super Series with a string of formidable performances to become undisputed cruiserweight champion of the world. When interviewed in the Moscow ring after his victory against Russian Murat Gassiev, adorned with all four major championship belts, including the WBC strap that Tony had vacated when he set his sights on Haye, the undefeated Ukrainian ring wizard called Bellew's name. As far as Usyk was concerned, he had to beat Bellew to be the true champion and was happy to fight him at cruiserweight or heavyweight. Any time, any place.

Bellew was listening. He shouldn't have been, but he was. On honeymoon with Rachael, he'd had to sneak off to watch the fight. As soon as his name passed Usyk's lips he wasted no time in replying, firing off a tweet at one in the morning declaring, 'Usyk I was BORN READY!! Let's get this done!!' Sitting on his sofa back in Rotherham, trainer Dave Coldwell's phone lit up and he knew what was coming: 'When he rang me after Usyk called him out on TV, I knew he was going to do it. And I remember saying to my wife as I'm watching Usyk call him out, "Oh shit, Tony's going to come back." And I didn't want him to but then when we had that conversation, and he said to me, "Coach, what do you think?" I said, "Look, not at cruiserweight. You've been a heavyweight for last two years. For you to go back down to cruiserweight now, my worry is, number one, your energy levels, and number two, that you're not gonna take a shot as well as you did at heavyweight. I'm talking about your resistance. And at thirty-five years old, if you come back down, your resistance goes. That's my worry." And that's what I said to him. And he said to me, "Look, if I pull Usyk up to heavyweight people won't give me the credit. If I'm gonna get in there with him I want all the belts." So I understood. So even though I didn't want it at cruiserweight I understood why it was at cruiser.'

His retirement lasted all of eleven weeks. After an awkward conversation with Rachael, the fight was set for the Manchester Arena.

I worked on the fight and it was one of my favourite build-ups. I remember going to Coldwell's gym in Rotherham on the Friday before fight week to see both trainer and fighter. It was their last ever session in that gym together and there was a melancholy sweetness hanging in the air that is often detectable when people are knowingly doing things together for the final time. They were both adamant this really was the last dance. I wondered if it would be, though, because Tony hadn't managed to retire off the back of a massive win and, although I understood the lure of the fight, I thought he was pushing his luck taking on Usyk because there was a good chance he'd lose. And walking away out of the wreckage of defeat is a difficult thing to do, boxing history is very clear on that.

Fight week was one for the purists. The pair of them were very respectful of each other and although that meant the event probably wouldn't sell as well on pay-per-view as the bile-soaked vendetta Tony had waged with Haye, it was great for the sport to see such a good example set. Bellew was the underdog again, not that he cared.

The fight did not pan out like people thought it would. Bellew, who hadn't scaled the heights Usyk had as an amateur, was fundamentally still a very sound boxer and he used those skills to good effect early on. Through five rounds he was very possibly ahead and, as the halfway stage neared, at ringside people were beginning to wonder if he could pull off the shock yet again. On commentary during the sixth round, though, Carl Froch tells us that his friend looks like he might be starting to feel the pace, that Usyk's making him work hard, something that could tell on him in the second half of the fight. Then, right on the bell at the end of the round, Usyk clips Bellew on the chin with a left hook and you can see his legs buckle slightly. Coldwell guides him back to his stool and knows he's got a problem.

'I knew straightaway, his legs were heavy. Not gone but heavy and when he came back to the corner, I lean into his ear, and I said, "This is very important, this next round." Because he's boxing well and he's winning the fight. And I said, "Take a round off and don't punch until you feel your legs are back. He'll start cranking it up but keep him missing so you don't get caught with anything big. Get through this round for me. Then we'll have another shot." But he gets up from the stool and the last thing he says to me, and you can see it on TV, was that he was fine. So I'm trying to get into his head, because I know, and it doesn't matter about bullshitting anybody else. I know. So I say it again and he tells me again that he's fine, walks out into the middle of the ring and starts fucking swinging.'

Usyk's left hook at the end of the sixth was that moment in a fight that Neil Scott talked about previously, that one punch after which concussion sets in and from which point the boxer is up against it. That left hook hurt Bellew. The damage is in his eyes as Coldwell puts the gumshield back in and sends him out for the seventh round. He's fighting on muscle memory and instinct now and his instinct isn't to stay away and try and recover. Usyk meanwhile is seemingly everywhere, demonic, gap-toothed grin hypnotizing his prey. At this point Coldwell knows the writing is on the wall.

'Round seven for me was a disaster. That round Usyk made Bellew work, made him trigger, made him panic and throw punches at the wrong time, get nailed with shots on the way, wear him out. And that energy level just went down, down, down, down. So when he came back to the corner at the end of round seven that's when I thought then, "We're fucked."

What does Tony remember?

'I remember most of it. I remember everything up to the end of round seven. I remember going back to the corner and Dave Coldwell asking, "Are you tired?" And saying that I was absolutely fucked.'

At the end of round seven, just before he sits on his stool, he looks outside the ring and shakes his head. Who was he shaking his head at and what did he mean by it?

'I don't remember doing it. I just remember being fucked. I remember thinking, "I am absolutely gassed." And I know Dave would have wanted to pull the plug then but he knew that could never happen. I just knew, I was spent, I was absolutely exhausted. And then I don't remember anything of round eight. The next thing I remember after sitting in the corner talking to Dave is me wife coming in the dressing room crying.'

Coldwell did want to pull the plug, it was the rational thing to do, but this is boxing and it has a logic of its own.

He says, 'What happens in round seven completely takes away your hope. So then when you come back to the corner at the end of round seven and you're looking at your man's eyes, you know when a fighter kind of knows he's done and I know my fighter and at that point, because you know that he knows that he's done, that he's gonna roll the dice. And there's been nothing so far in the fight to make you think that rolling the dice is going to pay off because you're in against a man who's not showing any signs of fatigue, who's actually in the ascendancy, and that's a horrible, horrible feeling. And because it's for undisputed, you can't then just turn around and pull him out and say you're saving him for another day because there is no other day. Because that is it. That was always Tony's last fight ever. No matter what. That was always his last fight. He'd come out of retirement for that reason only, to become undisputed. So you've got to give him that chance. So there's no regrets. And there is no regrets for me. He tried his best in that fight and that's why I think he can be at peace with it.'

Coldwell knew what was coming and there was nothing he could do about it. Watching at ringside I couldn't tell the situation was so dire. There'd been a shift, that was easy to identify, but I didn't know how close to the edge the fight was and outside of the two corners, I don't think anyone in the arena did.

The bell goes for the start of the eighth and Bellew's rolling that dice, not swinging blindly, but letting his hands go. Blood's beginning to come from his nose and mouth. At the midway point Usyk starts to pick him off. Every time he lands he can feel his gloves sucking the tensile strength out of his opponent. He's circling him, homing in on him in rapid, ever-decreasing circles. And then he strikes, the jab and left hand finding the target in rapid succession. There doesn't look to be all that much power in them, they travel no distance at all, but it's deep in the fight, Bellew's resistance has gone and he crashes into the ropes behind him, head bouncing off the bottom strand. As soon as he starts to fall Coldwell is on his way into the ring, an official grabs at his leg as he's on his way in, so quick is he off the mark. Bellew somehow pulls himself up onto his knees and the camera looks up at him as he grasps the second rope with his right glove, determined to wrestle himself to his feet as the count echoes around him. But at seven and with Bellew still on his knees referee Terry O'Connor has seen enough and waves the fight over.

Tony doesn't remember it and he doesn't remember any of what comes next as he manages to get back to his feet and then after the announcement give an interview. He's fulsome in his praise of Usyk and is very affectionate towards his opponent, congratulating him and embracing him several times. He's not all there, not in the room, concussion does that to a fighter. The way he is behaving brought to my mind a description former heavy-weight champion of the world Floyd Patterson gave of the feeling of getting knocked out (something that happened to him in spec-tacular fashion, more than once), as he is quoted in W.K. Stratton's *Floyd Patterson* on the occasion of the second consecutive knockout defeat he suffered to Sonny Liston, who at the time was very pos-sibly the most feared fighter in modern boxing history, in Las Vegas, in July 1963:

> It's not a bad feeling when you're knocked out. It's a good feeling actually. It's not painful, just a sharp grogginess. You don't see angels or stars; you're on a pleasant cloud. After Liston hit me in Nevada, I felt, for about four or five seconds, that everybody in the arena was actually in the ring with me, circled around me like a family, and you feel warmth toward all the people in the arena after you're knocked out. You feel lovable to all the people. And you want to reach out and kiss everybody – men and women – and after the Liston fight somebody told me I actually blew a kiss to the crowd from the ring.

That warm, fuzzy feeling, a few drinks down and the happy side of blurry, that's what it sounds like and that's what I thought of when I looked at and listened to Tony up in the ring. For him though, it's gone for good.

'No. It's gone. I can't remember a single fucking second.'

I explain the Atlas Theory to him, the idea that all forms of stoppage defeat, outside of the single-punch, type-one knockout, are a form of submission. I am asking him if, when he walked out for the start of the eighth round, his will had been broken; if, as Dave Coldwell had suggested, he knew he was 'done'; and if, therefore, he'd gone out there to oblige the knockout, to submit to it, albeit in the bravest way possible. 'Were you almost choosing to get knocked out?' was word for word my question, and his answer was both yes and no.

'Of course. If I'm going out then I'm going out on my shield.'

A swift addendum then follows: 'I don't remember it but I'd have been thinking, "I can land one more here, I've got a chance still." Because I knew I could punch. If I wasn't a puncher I don't know if I'd have had that same mentality but I've always been able to punch, since I was twelve, so I think that's what gives me that mindset of even when I'm hurt, down and out, I can still pull it out the bag.'

Down and out but still in with a chance. It's a contradiction in terms, an oxymoron, but being a boxer is an oxymoronic existence, one that demands a person be able to accept that something can happen but then decide that it definitely won't or to tell themselves that they still have a chance when they know it's over.

'If I was [capable] of rational thinking me coach would have said, "That's it, he's had enough," and stopped it there and then, but he knew that could never fucking happen, not a fucking chance. I'm happy how I went out. That would have been the greatest shame to me, if he'd have thrown the towel in and I could have went out for round eight, I'd never have forgiven him.'

Happy to risk it all to be able to walk away with no regrets, or, to put it another way, happy to risk not being able to walk away at all rather than live with the shame of quitting.

'It's embarrassing to say this when I look back but I was willing to die to win. I'd rather have been killed than lose dishonourably.'

Embarrassed to admit that he'd rather die than embarrass himself. But then in the middle of this vortex of contradictions he hits me a jab of stunning clarity.

'I'm not a fantasist, I'm a realist. I knew he was far better than me but if I had a great night and he had an off night I could get the job done. But it didn't work out like that and when I started getting tired I thought I had to start rolling the dice and when I roll the dice I get cleaned out.'

And with that he shrugs, unwraps the flapjack my questions have been keeping him from and takes a bite.

He walked away and never looked back after Oleksandr Usyk brought the curtain down on his career in such brutal fashion. I believe him when he tells me he was then, and always will be, comfortable with his exit. It wasn't what he wanted but he could accept it, I believe, because of the respect he had, and will always have, for the man who sent him into retirement, and also – although I would never expect him to admit it – because he knew that same man, on any given night, would in all probability always have proved too much for him. Usyk, to Bellew, was not who Mayweather had been to Hatton. Bellew's ego could sustain a defeat to Usyk in a way that Ricky Hatton's could not when humbled by Mayweather, a key factor that allowed Tony to walk away and never look back. The absence of any antipathy towards his opponent made defeat less personal and easier to accept. He bore no grudge because, as far as he was concerned, there was no grudge to bear.

'I don't really remember the knockout. In fact, the only thing I can remember is being in the ambulance. I must have kind of come round, maybe I'd come round before that but I don't remember any of it. But I remember being in the ambulance and my girlfriend at the time and my brother was in it, and the paramedic guy, and he was asking me questions: "Do you know where you were tonight? Do you know where you are now?" That type of thing, and he asked if I knew where I'd been boxing and I said, "Yeah, Pairc Na Heireann.' It wasn't Pairc Na Heireann, it was the George Carnall Centre in Salford. Pairc Na Heireann's the GAA [Gaelic games] pitches here in Birmingham so I've no idea why I said that, I was obviously concussed. And it was weird because I didn't think it was Pairc Na Heireann but that's what came out, so when I said it, I felt like I'd said the right thing, but I knew I was in Salford.'

Matt Macklin shakes his head and laughs.

We're in his front room in Solihull on a Saturday night in summer and it's quite a comic scene all round. He's sat on one of the sofas, on a pregnancy pillow, and there's baby paraphernalia scattered all over the room. His daughter, Molleigh, had arrived in February, his fiancée Sarah is upstairs giving her a bath, and so it was amid this scene of domestic bliss that I quizzed him on what it was like to chin or be chinned.

Matt got knocked out in the tenth round by Jamie Moore. Jamie has given his side of it, about how worried he was when he saw Matt motionless on the canvas. Given the type of fight it was, of all the knockouts discussed in detail here, this one was potentially the worst in terms of neurological damage. It was the kind of knockout after which a boxer is often never the same again, after which sometimes they breathe their last.

But that isn't what happened with Macklin. He watched the fight back the next day, as soon as he got out of hospital.

'I just remember thinking, "It's fucking boxing, I've knocked people out myself." Do you know what I mean? I just kept it that simple. You know, Roberto Duran got knocked out, spark out, by Tommy Hearns but he dusted himself down, came back and had many great wins after that. I think you've just got to be a bit mentally tougher than that. That's the conversation I was having in my head. In my head I'm telling myself this: "It's alright dishing it out but you can't take it? Fucking man up." That was my internal dialogue about it.'

It worked for him.

One of the reasons he was able to square the experience away was because of the kind of fight it had been. He'd given everything and if Jamie hadn't knocked him out then he reckoned he'd have collapsed through exhaustion before the end of the fight anyway. In his mind, what would have been harder to take would have been a type-one knockout, where he got taken out early before he was able to give every ounce of himself; that could have made him question his punch resistance, but this didn't. He knew why it had happened: he'd underestimated his opponent and set far too high a pace in unusually gruelling conditions. Lesson learnt. But the idea that the defeat had exposed some kind of serious defect, either mental or physical? Absolutely not.

But he didn't come away from the knockout consequence free. In Matt's case the problem was other people. They couldn't believe it was possible he could walk away from the crash site without a scratch. People began to whisper, almost before he was stretchered away from ringside, and those whispers reached his ears quickly. 'He'll never box again,' the whispers said, and 'even if he does, he'll never be the same again', they murmured. 'He hasn't turned out to be what we thought he would be, what we were told he would be,' they complained. Matt couldn't dismiss it completely because he was well aware that his career hadn't gone the way he'd imagined it would. He would never have expected that five years after turning professional he'd wake up in hospital after getting knocked out in a British title fight, live on TV. It was never supposed to be this way.

'I'm texting and calling [his manager]. I'm desperate to get back in there and get my career moving again and put that behind me. And I remember I was sitting in the flat in Manchester and I burst out crying out of absolute, pure frustration. Because here I am, I'm twenty-five and it hasn't happened. I mean, there were positives from the Moore fight in that people were praising me for the courage I showed, but once you get past all that the reality is, I'm twenty-five, I've been beaten twice, I haven't even won a domestic title and I've been knocked out and spent the night in hospital. And I'm in this because I believe I can go all the way.'

Doubt. For Matt that was the major repercussion of getting knocked out. People were doubting him. The fact that he got knocked out was something he was able to deal with; that mode of defeat, that can be so damaging for others, wasn't the problem, the problem was that he'd been conclusively beaten in a fight he expected to win, at a level he had always expected he would sail past. His career was in danger of becoming a shipwreck. Due to fights falling through and the general vagaries of the boxing business, it wasn't far off a year before he returned to the ring. It was an unhelpfully long time. I asked him if he'd been nervous before his return and he said that he had, but more 'because of all the things I'd heard people had been saying, all the doubts they had about me', more than 'any doubts I had in myself'.

I found that a very interesting idea, that an athlete could be nervous about other people's doubts about them without allowing that to metamorphose into that person directly doubting themselves. I'd never heard anyone say that before. People would generally either profess to be unaware of the doubters or would acknowledge their awareness of them only to dismiss them as irrelevant. But to admit not only to being aware of them but also to empower their doubt in such a way was a novel concept and another example of the level of compartmentalization of which boxers are capable. Compartmentalization is 'a form of psychological defence mechanism in which thoughts and feelings that seem to conflict are kept separated or isolated from each other in the mind'. Conflicting thoughts such as accepting the knockout as a boxing reality yet denying it as a possibility on any given night. Thoughts that, should they be allowed to run into each other, could clash and collide with devastating consequences.

Whatever doubts Macklin had, wherever they originated from and wherever they did or didn't spread to, he got over them, the rest of his career proved that. His straightforward approach of treating the knockout as an occupational hazard worked for him. He knew that whatever happened, he could rely on himself to give every last drop of effort in pursuit of victory, and if that turned out not to be enough, then so be it.

'It's like a jigsaw that has just gone smash, into pieces, and you're trying to put it back together as quick as possible.'

Of all the descriptions I've been given of what it feels like to be at the epicentre of a knockout, this is my favourite one. It's provided by Amir Khan. I caught up with Amir in Riyadh, Saudi Arabia, after the press conference for the Battle of the Baddest, the cross-over promotion featuring the fight between boxing and MMA's universally recognised number one heavyweights Tyson Fury and Francis Ngannou. Amir was one of the many famous guests of honour invited to attend the event and was in demand all week, but he'd promised to spare me some time and was true to his word.

He already knew that I wanted to talk about the knockout, but he didn't know what it was specifically that I would want to explore. Time was of the essence so I opened up by briefly explaining the premise of the book and then asked what he remembered about getting knocked out by Breidis Prescott, in what was his first defeat, back in September 2008. He started to answer in general terms, and ordinarily I would have been happy to warm into the discussion via a broader overview, but on this occasion I gently interrupted, saying that what I wanted to get to was the precise event. He was surprised. 'Oh, you mean the moment, at the moment, in the ring, you mean?' But he wasn't offended, he wasn't even reluctant, he was actually enthusiastic, and I got the distinct impression nobody had ever asked him to revisit that experience before.

'You know what, it happened so quick, you don't even remember anything, honestly. It happened so quick and then . . . it's like a . . . I mean, when I was knocked out the only thing that you see is you on your back looking up at the lights and the lights shining. And you're thinking . . . you're just trying to get your mind together, "What's going on here?" you touch down and you think, "OK, I'm on the canvas." Then you try and focus on the referee to see what number is he on and to get up before he . . . and then you do everything you can to get up and your body up, but it's like you're being pulled down. It's like you're being pulled down and that's what it was. And then when you're stood up, you're trying to get your bearings back but you can't because your whole balance is off, you're moving and you're holding yourself to try to be standing OK, but luckily you try to look for the corner rope as well to try to get some stability as well from that, some help. It's the worst place to be in because your eyes are going one way, your head's going one way and you're trying to do . . . it's like a jigsaw that has just gone smash, into pieces, and you're trying to put it back together as quick as possible. That's what it is, that's what it's like because what happens is, you're hearing so many different voices from different people, you're hearing different voices from outside, voices that you recognize, and the referee as well, counting as well, and you're thinking, "Shit, who am I listening to, what should I do?" and you're in a desperate position, you're thinking, "I have to beat the count," and it's a very tough position to be in, man. When you're the number one and you're meant to win the fight and the pressure's on you, but still you're thinking you need to get up because you're thinking you have to beat all odds, you have to be the winner, this wasn't meant to happen.'

It's a totally spontaneous answer to an unexpected and difficult question. It communicates the confusion and desperation perfectly, as well as colouring in some context with the mention of the expectation that was on him to win the fight, an expectation that would significantly affect the way the fight – all fifty-four seconds of it – played out.

When Khan met Prescott, Amir was 18–0 and the hottest property in British boxing. He'd captured the hearts and minds of the nation when as a cheeky seventeen-year-old he'd won a silver medal at the 2004 Athens Olympics. From that point on he was a star in the making and when he turned professional with promoter Frank Warren he was given the red-carpet treatment. Amir Khan was the poster boy of British boxing and expected to transcend the sport. It hadn't all been plain sailing though. He'd hit the canvas against Willie Limond when winning the Commonwealth title at 12–0 and could be too gung-ho at times, but he was still young, learning his trade, and undoubtedly had that X-factor. But the Prescott fight was not a fight that Warren, an expert matchmaker, wanted. The 19–0, big-punching Colombian was dangerous and in Warren's estimation represented a risk not worth taking at that stage, but he was overruled. As he stood there, watching the two fighters take to the scales the day before the fight, he experienced a strong sense of foreboding.

'At the weigh-in I knew he was going to get beaten. The guy looked so much physically stronger, it was like a man against a boy. He just looked physically bigger. I looked at him and I just didn't fancy it. I felt he'd get beat, I could feel it.

His feeling was right and what Warren witnessed in that Manchester ring the following night was fifty-four seconds of pure, unadulterated savagery. Breidis Prescott ran Amir Khan down and was then allowed to reverse back over him for good measure. That may sound like an indelicate description but that's what happened.

The bell goes on that fateful evening, in front of a full house and a big TV audience, and Prescott, tall and angular with wide, rangy shoulders, comes out throwing bombs, oozing intent. Twenty seconds into the first round the Colombian lands a left hook that sends a vibration through Khan from his jaw down to the soles of his boots. His legs judder, feet tap-dancing on the canvas like somebody has just flicked him into fast-forward. Prescott sees this, steps in, lands another left hand and Khan collapses onto the ring floor. He gets back up quickly but he's completely scrambled, eyes glazed and stumbling backwards as though intoxicated.

'He's all over the place, he's going to have to be stopped, surely,' exclaims Ian Darke on commentary. But when referee Terry O'Connor reaches the count of eight and asks Khan to put up his hands and walk forward, the tasks a referee will always ask a boxer to complete in that situation to demonstrate their ability to box on, the youngster complies and the fight continues. Prescott pounces, hitting his victim with a right and then connecting clean with another pulverizing left hand that deposits Khan onto his back for the second time in forty-two seconds. He lies in his own corner of the ring, a corner that just a few minutes earlier he had arrived in, bright and shiny, feted by the crowd, full of hope and potential. But that has all gone now, evaporated into the night air, and people can only watch as the Olympian struggles desperately to rise again. Straining every sinew, he manages to lift his head from the canvas, but the rest of the body just won't follow, those signals from the brain are too weak and can only travel as far as the neck. That force he describes above as pulling him down is too strong. Somehow, through sheer strength of subconscious will, he manages to sit up, pushing off the canvas with his gloves in an effort to get his feet under him, but he falls back down onto his right side, whilst all the time referee O'Connor continues a completely superfluous count. Eventually, just after he's counted out and therefore knocked out, he does get back to his feet, but it's too late. Ian Darke describes it as 'one of the biggest stunners in British boxing history.' It was utterly shocking, in every way. Teddy Atlas spoke of the knockout extinguishing hope and this knockout, in my estimation, possesses that dark, nihilistic quality more than any other featured in these pages.

Boxing journalist Tris Dixon was ringside: 'It was all over in fifty-four seconds and it could have been over sooner. There was that first knockdown that clearly nobody was going to recover from. Terry O'Connor was the ref and he let Khan back out when he was in all sorts of trouble. And you're thinking, "No, no, no, stop the fight," but you know that Khan is the golden goose, for the promotional company, and there must be a lot of pressure on Terry O'Connor there to give Khan every chance. But also this is a sport where we've seen heroic stuff, where a fighter's been on the verge of being knocked out and they've found a punch from the gods and turned things around. But you could see he wasn't there and it was almost like watching a condemned man walk to the gallows because you know what's awaiting him. And he was bowled over by this huge combination and you just felt it was so unnecessary. It was stunning and one of those weird ones where the fight hadn't even got started. We talk about the knockout and people wanting to see the knockout. I would say the vast majority of people didn't want to see those final punches.'

It's a very good assessment from an experienced observer and encapsulates neatly some of the impossible contradictions that can be in play with the knockout. The money and hope invested in Khan had an influence on the fight not being stopped when it should have been. Then there's the ultimate ghastly irony of a fighter who is surely about to get knocked out being allowed to continue because it's just possible he may be able to find that one punch to turn it around himself, because this is a sport in which that can happen. But everyone can see that that is not going to happen, that they're about to witness a young man get knocked out in front of the whole world, and although that's what those in attendance and watching from their sofas tuned in for, they don't want to see it any longer, because that hideous fate is about to be visited upon the wrong fighter. As Khan said himself, 'This wasn't meant to happen.'

Saturday, 6 September 2008, was a disaster for Amir Khan and one that could easily have spelled the end of his career. His unbeaten record was gone, as very possibly was his self-belief. His ability to rebound from such a defeat was being questioned by those of a more balanced disposition and dismissed by those who revel in tearing down our sporting matinee idols. Khan was in a dark, dark place.

'The respect, the respect outside, the embarrassment. That's it, yeah, that's it, hundred per cent, and that's what hurts you. It's the embarrassment to your family, to your wife or to their friends. They don't understand, they think you just lost a fight, they don't understand how hard it was or who you were fighting, they just know that you lost. So it's quite embarrassing, especially as obviously as a Muslim, the Muslim community is very close knit but people will laugh at you, blatantly, openly, and it happens a lot in our culture, people laugh at you and make a joke of it. It's hard to take. It happened after Prescott. But I had to just deal with it.'

There are echoes of Ricky Hatton and Scott Welch here but whilst Hatton admits that his belief that his own community were ashamed of him was a product of his own tortured imagination, for Khan, the ridicule was real. But it wasn't just the reaction of some within the Muslim community that cut deep; a very specific reaction that emanated from the boxing world also struck right at the very heart of his fighting identity. Amir Khan, as a result of getting knocked out by a renowned big puncher, was labelled as 'chinny'. 'Chinny' is a term applied to a boxer who, it is believed, is weak around the whiskers, who is unable to absorb a punch. It is a deliberately demeaning, insulting and emasculating label, a stigma that, once applied, can be very hard to shed. It's ignorant nonsense. As has been confirmed within these pages, any boxer who gets hit by a clean punch they're not braced for can get knocked out. Educated followers of the sport know this to be true and do not indulge in the kind of lazy labelling that sees fighters categorized in such patronizing fashion. Khan has never accepted the term 'chinny' or the idea that he or any fighter that has scaled the heights he has could do so whilst harbouring an apparent genetic inability to take a punch. What he does accept though is that he has a reckless streak, a fighting style that has seen his chin get hit clean too often, but that acceptance allowed him to turn what many would have seen as a weakness into a strength.

'I knew it was gonna happen one day [losing] and I knew it would happen [via knockout] because I had too much of a heart, I used to put everything in. When I used to fight, I used to throw everything in, I never, ever would leave anything behind, I give it my all or there's no point doing it. Anyone can go [get knocked out] because these guys are trained fighters, they know how to punch and how to hurt someone, so I had to make sure, if I am going to get put down, if I am going to get knocked out, there's needs to be a way of me coming back. How do I come back? So I was always mentally strong that way.'

The days and weeks post-Prescott were painful but Amir survived them because he was prepared for it. For some athletes that willingness to prepare for defeat, to visualize the unthinkable, is too frightening. They're afraid that entertaining that scenario could usher in a negative mindset, which in turn could act as a catalyst to cause the unthinkable to become real, that it could act as a self-fulfilling prophecy. But elite-level performers such as Khan understand that the unthinkable and the impossible are not the same thing, that the unthinkable can, and at some point almost certainly will, happen and that when it does a person's chances of rebounding from it will be significantly higher if they have addressed it in advance. Individuals need to understand the business they're in, to be aware of what can happen and plan accordingly. Amir Khan always understood what could happen when he walked up those steps into the ring.

'You have to understand, every second that person is in front of you, he is a danger, he's dangerous, there's a chance of him hurting you or knocking you out, so you have to get him out of the way. There were times I knocked people out so quickly because I was scared that they might knock me out. It's either you or me and it can't be me because there's too much at stake for me, so I have to make sure that I do it quick.'

But on that night against Breidis Prescott, it *was* him, and that is a night that will come for most fighters. Khan was able to recover from what, at the time, many believed would be, if not a career-ending, then certainly a career-ruining defeat. He wouldn't allow his career to be defined by it; that prospect was met with steadfast refusal.

The journey back from a knockout defeat is an individual one but if the journey up until that point has been grounded in reality then a person stands a good chance of successfully navigating it. If they've been living in a land of make-believe, of denial and delusion, then it will be a lot more difficult. When I speak to young fighters at the start of their professional career I often ask them whether they contemplate defeat, prepare for it even, or whether they dismiss it as something that won't happen to them. If the reply that comes back is the latter then I know they have plenty of learning left to do; if they opt for the former response then I know that they already have a valuable weapon in their arsenal in that willingness to confront their most basic fear. To be fallible is to be human and to be aware of and to admit to that fallibility, to embrace it even, is a sign of strength. Boxers know that. They know they will fall but, as they always say, nobody ever lost a fight because they got knocked down, they lost because they didn't get up.

This was exactly the message that Sylvester Stallone communicated through the eponymous boxing hero he created in Rocky Balboa. I am aware that it could seem strange, childish even, to defer to the endeavours of a fictional character in the context of this discussion but it is appropriate because the character of Balboa and the *Rocky* films as a whole command huge respect amongst fighters because although the fight scenes are far-fetched the themes dealt with within the narrative are not. I would have been very keen to speak to Stallone as part of this examination of the knockout because it is a subject with which he deals extensively with the second and fourth films featuring epic type-two knockouts, whilst *Rocky III* is punctuated by two type-one knockouts.

The following excerpt is from *Rocky Balboa*, the sixth film in the franchise series which came sixteen years after the fifth instalment. An ageing Balboa has lost his way somewhat following the death of his wife, and in a bid to rediscover some purpose has decided to make a comeback. His son Robert, with whom he has a difficult relationship, doesn't like the idea, not for fear of his father getting hurt but due to the shadow that having such a famous figure for a father has cast over his own life. It has fuelled a lingering resentment and that shadow will only get heavier with Rocky's return to the spotlight. The father listens to his son air his grievances before responding with a monologue that speaks to adversity in whatever form it may come, that speaks to the knockout:

> The world ain't all sunshine and rainbows. It's a very mean and nasty place, and I don't care how tough you are . . . it will beat you to your knees and keep you there if you let it. You, me or nobody is gonna hit as hard as life. But it ain't about how hard you hit. It's about how hard you can get hit . . . and keep moving forward. How much you can take and keep moving forward. That's how winning is done!

Scott Welch, Ricky Hatton, Tony Bellew, Matt Macklin and Amir Khan all took the hits that they knew were coming and all found a way to keep moving forward. For some it was more difficult than others, for some it took longer than others, but they all found a way back to the light from the darkness that the knockout brings.

CHAPTER FIVE

Dicing with Death

> Against David Haye, I signed a will, I made my wife come to the solicitors with me a week before the first fight and I signed the will because I knew he was capable of killing me.
>
> *Tony Bellew*

Jimmy Cannon, a New York fight scribe of great repute, once memorably described boxing as the 'red-light district of sports', a description its practitioners would concur with. The fight game is also often described as the wild west of the sporting world; a lawless landscape of guerrilla warfare where there is very rarely any correlation between what a person deserves and what they receive. The ultimate aim for all boxers is to leave the sport having taken more from boxing than boxing has taken from them. It is a straightforward ambition but one that few achieve.

In that quest to be able to quit whilst ahead, fighters are prepared to take huge risks if they deem the reward to be sufficient, risks that athletes in other sports are either not required to take or are prevented from taking by the rules and safety guidelines of their sport.

A career in the ring – and this applies across all levels – very often treads the same basic path. If a combatant is able to stay the course then it is a play of three acts. Act one: As a young man or woman, the fighter engages in the sport purely for the love of it; they box as an amateur and are the literal definition of it. Act two: Love becomes an obsession, an addiction, and they turn professional; motivated by the thirst for glory, they dream of winning titles, earning the respect of their peers; money is not their god but they trust that if they can fulfil their ambitions then the money will follow. Act three: Titles won and respect well and truly earned, they are by now pure prize-fighters, looking to secure their financial future and that of their family by making as much money as they can in the time they have remaining, before their powers wane and they have no choice but to exit the stage.

Acts one and two are the journey – lengthy, full of ups and downs, recollected with fondness and frustration – whereas act three is the destination, briefer and less satisfying. The brevity of act three is inevitable because by the time fighters arrive they have miles on the clock, physically and mentally, but also because as a primary source of motivation money rarely sustains a person of passion for very long and pugilists are passionate people for whom financial gain alone cannot keep the flame burning indefinitely.

Act three is also dangerous. When the clock is ticking fighters can be tempted to take grave risks, to gamble with their health and risk the knockout, to dice with death.

Act one for Amir Khan culminated in an Olympic silver medal. It was over by the time he was seventeen but by then he'd already been boxing for six years. Act two was momentous. He recovered from the trauma of the Breidis Prescott knockout and less than a year later became WBA light-welterweight champion at the very same Manchester Arena where it had all gone so spectacularly wrong. Next stop was the USA. Making it big in America has always been the dream for any boxer but one that very few from the

UK have managed to realize. But King Khan pulled it off. He headlined in Las Vegas, beating rugged Argentinian Marcos Maidana in a twelve-round war, and then became a unified champion, adding the IBF title to his WBA belt. Khan fights were must-see events due to his fan-friendly style and willingness to mix it with anyone. The Boltonian was box office and in boxing that is the ticket to the big time. But then he lost, unexpectedly, to Lamont Peterson in Washington, a fight shrouded in controversy for all sorts of different reasons, and then he lost again, this time by stoppage against Danny Garcia, a defeat that caused doubts about the solidity of his chin to resurface, doubts that had receded following his heroics against Maidana. In the space of a few months Khan's career trajectory had been significantly altered so he did what a lot of fighters do in that situation – he moved up in weight, to the 147lb welterweight division, historically one of the sport's richest and financially one of its most rewarding. Over the next four years, between 2012 and 2016, the now former world champion racked up five good wins against very capable operators but the mega-fight he craved, against the likes of Floyd Mayweather or Manny Pacquiao, although regularly mentioned, never materialized. By early 2016, Amir was twenty-nine and, although that might not seem old for an athlete, he was eleven years and thirty-four fights into his professional career and had racked up some hard ring miles. The clock was ticking.

It was at this point that he accepted a fight that ushered in act three. The boxing world, not one that is regularly caught off guard, was shocked when it was announced in spring 2016 that Amir Khan would be stepping up in weight to meet Saul Canelo Alvarez for the Mexican sensation's WBC middleweight title at a catchweight of 11st 1lb (the middleweight limit is 11st 6lb but as the fight would be over the 11st limit of the division below, the lightmiddleweight division, it was categorized as a middleweight fight). I remember seeing the announcement on social media and being convinced that it couldn't possibly be true. Canelo was 46–1–1, his only defeat having come against Floyd Mayweather, and had been a long-reigning world champion at light-middleweight before winning the WBC middleweight title against the great Puerto Rican Miguel Cotto. The flame-haired Guadalajaran was the sport's next superstar, the real thing, and everybody knew it. He was skilful and tough and – crucially – he was too big for Khan.

Boxing is a sport separated into seventeen different weight divisions, from minimumweight where the limit is 7st 7lb to heavyweight where there is no limit. The narrowest separation between weights is three pounds, whereas the widest is the yawning 25lb chasm that exits between the upper ends of light-heavyweight and cruiserweight. These divisions exist to try and ensure that when two boxers face each other, in terms of size, it is a fair fight. To the uninitiated the eight-pound difference between the limit that Khan had been campaigning at and the limit set for the Canelo fight might not seem like much, but in boxing terms it's vast. The problem for Amir was that although he and Alvarez would both weigh almost exactly the same when they stood on the scales at the weigh-in on the Friday before the fight, come Saturday night when they were stood in the ring, there would be a significant difference between them. In boxing a fighter has a fighting weight, the weight they will be when they walk to the ring, and the weight they will weigh in at the day before the fight, and those two weights will hardly ever be the same, with fighters typically weighing around eight to ten pounds more on fight night than at the weigh-in. They will conduct the majority of their training at their fighting weight and then in the days approaching the fight will lose the weight they need to in order to make the contracted weight at the weigh-in and then once they step off the scales will go about rehydrating and replenishing their recently starved body in order to restore it to their fighting weight. It is a discipline that boxers have been adhering to since weight divisions were introduced and it's problematic for many different reasons. In the instance of Canelo vs Khan, it was problematic for Khan because his natural weight was welterweight, which meant that his normal weigh-in weight was 10st 7lb and that his ring weight would most likely be around the 11st 1lb the fight had been set at. Canelo, meanwhile, was naturally bigger than Khan anyway, having been boxing at 11st since 2010, and was rumoured to add considerably more than the typical 8–10lb to his frame in the period between the weigh-in and his ring walk. All things taken into consideration it was likely that when the first bell went Canelo would be over 12st and Khan around 11st. All perfectly legal, if not exactly fair, but Khan knew this when he accepted the fight, and that the risk he was taking was much greater than normal. But so was the reward. Amir Khan crunched the numbers and decided it was worth the gamble.

'It's like me taking four fights for what I'd get paid for that one fight. If I get paid ten million dollars for that one fight then that's four other hard fights I'd have to have to make that same kind of money. I thought to myself, "If I'm getting paid ten million dollars for that one I'd rather get hit and hurt once," but I was so confident I was gonna win that fight, but at the same time I'd rather do that one instead of doing four hard fights and four hard training camps.'

The above speaks straight to the heart of the matter. This was his mindset going into the fight. He maintained the belief that he could win, or at least insists he still had that belief, but accepted that there was a good chance, a better chance than normal, that he was going to 'get hit and hurt', that he was going to get knocked out. For $10m he's willing to gamble with his life. Why? Because that's the business he's in.

'What drives you is financially making sure your family's good, that you are good, that you never have to work again. We're all prize-fighters, that's what we are, you know what I'm saying, and I had to make sure that I got the bigger purses because I never wanted to work again after boxing. I'll give it my all once and I'll never work again.'

On the night, in front of a packed T-Mobile Arena in Las Vegas on 7 May 2016, Khan boxed very well for five rounds, well enough to be ahead on two of the judges' scorecards, but in the sixth his opponent, who had been getting fractionally closer to landing and detonating with every round that passed, did exactly that. With just over thirty seconds remaining in the round, after further adjusting his sights, Canelo touches his opponent with a measuring stick of a left hand and then pulls the trigger on a perfect right hand. At the same time as the Mexican's right homes in, with sniper-like precision, Khan opens out to throw a left hand, clearing the way. The punch lands and the effect is instant. It's a circuit-breaker, in method and execution very similar to the shot Carl Froch landed on George Groves. A pure type-one knockout. Khan drops onto his back, arms and legs settling either side and out in front with the same impeccable manners that we saw exhibited by the limbs of Ricky Hatton. Like Hatton, Khan stares up at the ceiling with open eyes as referee Kenny Bayless, the same man who stood over the prone Hatton a few years earlier, looks into those vacant eyes and signals the end. At that moment in time nobody can know, least of all him, if his gamble will win out or if he and his family will pay the ultimate price and lose a son, a brother, a husband, a father. In those few seconds, it's all in the balance, the dice yet to stop rolling. Ringside is Gennady Golovkin, who has been invited to the fight so he can be unveiled as Canelo's next opponent. Khan has served his purpose, the red-light district of sports is ready to move on with its trademark callousness, but first Golovkin and everybody else must wait and hope that tonight's sacrificial lamb hasn't literally been slaughtered – a fatality would be bad for business.

Amir Khan survived. He took the ultimate risk and he didn't lose. He lost the fight but it wasn't an 'L' on his record that was at stake, it was his life. By the grace of his god he was able to walk

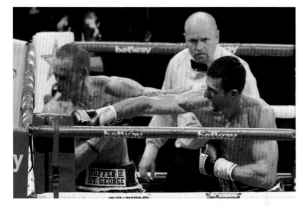

Carl Froch knocks out George Groves during the **IBF & WBA** world super-middleweight title fight at Wembley Stadium, on 31 May 2014.

Jermain Taylor loses by TKO 14 seconds from the end of the twelfth and final round of his WBC super-middleweight title fight with champion Carl Froch at the MGM Foxwoods in Mashantucket on 25 April 2009.

In round three of the Froch vs Taylor fight, it was Carl who was knocked down.

Jamie Moore lands a left hand on Matt Macklin in their epic encounter at George Carnall Leisure Centre, Manchester, on 29 September 2006.

Macklin is assessed by the ring doctor and his cornermen after being knocked out by Moore which ended their epic light-middleweight title fight.

Saul Canelo Alvarez stands over Amir Khan after delivering a knockout punch in the sixth round of their WBC middleweight title fight at T-Mobile Arena, Las Vegas, on 7 May 2016.

Referee Kenny Bayless signals the end of Khan's vain attempt to win the WBC world middleweight championship after Alvarez's devastating knock-out punch.

Amir Khan lies on the canvas after being knocked down by Breidis Prescott in the first round of their WBO Intercontinental lightweight championship fight, at the MEN Arena, Manchester, on 6 September 2008.

Khan's perfect 18–0 record ended after just 54 seconds against 19–0 Prescott.

Tony Bellew knocks out Ilunga Makabu in the third round to win the vacant WBC World Cruiserweight Championship fight at Goodison Park, Liverpool, on 29 May 2016.

Boxing promoter Eddie Hearn, right, checks on Tony Bellew after he was beaten by Oleksandr Usyk to end their WBC, WBA, WBO, IBF and Ring Magazine world cruiserweight championship fight at the Manchester Arena on 10 November 2018.

The referee didn't complete the count so Bellew's final professional fight ended as a TKO defeat to Usyk.

Ricky Hatton lies on the canvas after being knocked out by Manny Pacquiao at 2 minutes 59 seconds of the second round of their IBO super-lightweight title fight at the MGM Grand, Las Vegas, on 2 May 2009.

An aerial shot of Pacquiao looking down on the knocked-down Hatton as referee Kenny Bayless prepares to start his ten count.

Callum Smith knocks out Lenin Castillo in the second round of their light-heavyweight contest at Tottenham Hotspur Stadium, London, on 25 September 2021.

Vasiliy Lomachenko walks away after knocking out Anthony Crolla during their WBA and WBO lightweight title bout at Staples Center, Los Angeles, on 12 April 2019.

In a shock defeat, Mike Tyson is on his knees as he loses his WBC, WBA and IBF world heavyweight titles to James Buster Douglas at Tokyo Dome on 11 February 1990.

away. He doesn't remember a thing and as far as he's concerned it's better that way.

'When I looked at the opposite side of the ring and I saw him I thought, "This is gonna be hard." Look, what happens in a fight is that you don't feel nothing, there's no pain you feel, because it's like a dream, it happens so quick, it's so short, it's like a dream and I know I've trained very hard for it, I know I'm in good shape for it, it's like autopilot, my mind just goes in its own world. I don't remember that fight, I don't remember what happened in that fight. I just got through it, well, I didn't get through it because I got knocked out, whatever, but I don't remember anything in the fight, which is probably the best thing ever that could happen because I don't remember anything, I don't remember the pain and that's why I keep going back and doing it again and again and again, because I never remember it.'

Amir Khan had five more fights post-Canelo, before hanging his gloves up after losing to Kell Brook in 2022. Brook was a final cash-out, with the rest being fights he was supposed to win apart from one more mission impossible against the undefeated Terence Crawford at Madison Square Garden in 2019, a fight he essentially withdrew himself from with forty-seven seconds gone in round six. I would have loved to have seen what would have happened if a Khan of five years or so previous had shared the ring with Crawford that night, but that version of Amir was long gone, his career was deep in act three by then and thankfully he had the good sense to call a halt to proceedings before he got knocked out again.

When I spoke to Amir in Riyadh he was entertaining a come-back, considering 'going back and doing it again', for huge money against Manny Pacquiao, another ostensibly retired fighter. He seemed willing to roll that dice one more time. Fighters like him always will be, it's their tragic flaw. They know the game and they're happy to play.

*

Tony Bellew was happy to play too, happy to spin that same wheel.

'If you're paying, I'm playing. Simple. Yeah, I'll fight him. How much? But I must stress, that was only once I'd become a world champion, my mentality completely switched. I was playing the game for a long time just for the glory. You don't get into amateur boxing thinking about money.'

For Bellew act two ended when he knocked out Ilunga Makabu at Goodison Park and became WBC cruiserweight champion of the world. One swing of his left hand and he'd achieved everything he wanted in boxing in terms of titles and respect. From that moment on he was into act three and it was something he'd been planning and preparing for long since. He knew exactly what, and more specifically who, he wanted.

The man in his sights was David Haye.

Bellew had made Haye take a knee in sparring just before he won one of his three national amateur titles in the early 2000s. Haye at that stage was already a professional and progressing well, tipped for the top, but Bellew got out of the ring that day determined to meet Haye as a pro. His great friend David Price, who had also been involved in that sparring session, thought he was mad when Tony shared his prophecy with him, and didn't pay too much attention to it, it was just Tony being Tony. But once he beat Makabu in May 2016, Bellew pushed the button on Mission Hayemaker. Not many people knew that Haye had offered Bellew a fight at cruiserweight in late 2015 but the Liverpudlian turned the Londoner down, having already agreed with his promoter Eddie Hearn that he would fight Mateusz Masternak for the European title. Haye thought he was crazy, knowing how much more money Bellew could make fighting him than an unknown Pole, but for Tony it was simple: act two had yet to be completed; once it was then he would pursue the fight with Haye full force. In 2016 the two bumped into each other at the premiere of *Creed*, the *Rocky* franchise revival that Tony had starred in opposite Michael B. Jordan.

His eldest son, who was ten at the time, was with him and asked if he could get a picture with Haye. Bellew had no problem with that, introducing Haye to his son as 'the man who wants to beat your dad', to which Haye replied, 'Yeah, I'd knock your dad out.' Tony didn't like that one bit and stored it away, fuel to be added to the flames when he needed that extra bit of motivation. After beating Makabu to win his world title, Bellew wanted to make a defence and chose BJ Flores, a friend of Haye's who'd been with him at the premiere, as his opponent. He knocked Flores out in Liverpool in three rounds and then in his post-fight interview threw down the gauntlet to Haye, who was at ringside, berating and insulting him in front of a large viewing audience. The fight now had to happen and was set for March 2017, at London's O2 Arena, live on Sky Sports Box Office. It was a pay-per-view event and would make both fighters a lot of money. Haye was a star and nothing sells like bad blood between fellow Brits. The fight was at heavyweight too, the sport's glamour division, where sales are always highest, a division in which Haye had won a world title and one in which Bellew had never boxed as a professional.

Tony Bellew had got exactly what he wanted, what he'd been aiming for all those years since that spar. But sometimes people need to be careful what they wish for and the consensus amongst the boxing fraternity was that Haye would demolish Bellew, as Tony recalls: 'Haye does big numbers, I speak an awful lot of shit, and Sky were like, "Let's throw him to the wolves and see if he can survive." I was getting paid five times more than I'd ever earned in my career so I can't complain but at the same time nobody thought I could win. Even my own promoter agreed to take less of a percentage because he thought I was going to lose. Eddie agreed to take less money because he thought I was gonna get fucked.'

I worked on the fight and there was a darkness around it. A mismatch in boxing is not the same as a mismatch in any other sport because the potential consequences are so much more severe, and people were genuinely fearful of what those consequences could be. One of those people was Bellew himself.

'Against David Haye, I signed a will, I made my wife come to the solicitors with me a week before the first fight and I signed the will because I knew he was capable of killing me. I told her he was capable of killing me, he's that powerful, and I knew that because I'd sparred him. She asked me why do it then and I said because it's going to secure us for the rest of our lives, we'll never have to work again, as long as I invest it right.'

He knew what he was getting himself into and Haye was happy to remind him, talking in the build-up about how he was going to put him into a coma, about how the fight would end when he wanted it to, about how Bellew was mere cannon fodder for the entertainment of the thousands who would pack the arena, lured there by the promise of blood and thunder, by the suggestion of destruction and maybe even death.

I remember being nervous at ringside on fight night. It was a strange atmosphere. The only thing I can compare it to is the fore-boding I'd once felt when, after leaving a football ground, I'd turned a corner and found myself in the middle of a stand-off between rival sets of fans, at the point of conflict, teeth bared, their bad intentions choking the street like a fog. I'd run that night; I didn't want to see what would happen next, even less find myself dragged into it. But I was on the safe side of the ropes at Haye vs Bellew, I would merely be an observer, at worst a witness, and I very much wanted to see what would happen next. My nerves were almost entirely selfish. I didn't want anyone to get seriously hurt because that would be bad for business, bad for boxing, bad for Sky and, by extension, bad for me. I wish I could say my concerns were more altruistic but they weren't. I didn't know Tony Bellew at that stage, nor David Haye, not in a way that would cause me to care about their physical health more than the health of my own career anyway, and that's just the honest truth.

Bellew danced in the ring as he waited for Haye to make his ring walk. I remember watching that and feeling sorry for him. He looked like a man whistling past the graveyard, trying too hard to appear unconcerned and convincing nobody, least of all himself. But it wasn't an act. Tony had been visualizing this scene for years, his interactions with Haye in the weeks and days preceding the fight had gone exactly how he'd wanted them to, and he felt like mentally he'd got Haye where he wanted him. He was ready. Trainer Dave Coldwell knew it.

'I knew how dangerous Haye was. But I just knew that my guy had his number. I knew how training had gone. Tony was so aware of the dangers of Haye. He wasn't one of these where he's saying, "Yeah, but he's not gonna knock me out." He was not. He knew, "If I make one mistake, he's going to turn my lights out." And I think when you know that your fighter is aware of that, you know that [their] senses are higher and you know that they're going to follow the instructions to the letter. And when you believe in your fighter's ability, that helps you relax. On that ring walk, that was the most relaxed I've ever been. I remember, I was just leaning against the ropes. I was just really comfortable. And we were both really enjoying Haye's ring walk. It was like we knew what was gonna happen.'

Coldwell knew his fighter wasn't in denial and knew how crucial that was. Bellew had always known that to succeed in the ring he had to be aware of the risks, he had to accept what could happen. That knowledge, that awareness, on that night more than any other, was his superpower.

'I know boxing, it's the only thing I truly understand and know, and if you land on me clean then I'm going down. I have no choice, it's science, it's not my opinion, it's just a fact. I knew one hundred per cent that if he caught me clean I was going to sleep, he was so powerful, but I knew I could make him miss. I was slick enough, I was brave enough, and I also had pop in me own gloves. I just knew

I was gonna win that fight. I look at boxing so different to other fighters because they're so dishonest. I'm realistic in me approach. I know who I could beat and I know who I couldn't beat.'

When the bell went Haye went about his business like a man who knew he had the ability to halt proceedings any time he felt like it. Prowling, stalking, his right hand was straining at the leash like a pitbull, salivating at the prospect of the savagery it was about to inflict. But through five rounds it was yet to sink its teeth into Tony Bellew. Bellew was calm, poised, following his game plan of trying to take Haye into the second half of the fight, where he was convinced his opponent would run out of steam. The 7–1 underdog broke his hand in those early exchanges but nobody knew, so well did he disguise it as he waited for adrenaline to numb the pain.

Then in the sixth something extraordinary happened. Midround, Haye's right foot gives way underneath him and, although he stays on his feet, it's apparent immediately that he has a huge problem. His back foot, that back heel, where the lightning bolt that loads that right glove originates, has betrayed him. His Achilles tendon has ruptured and from that point on David Haye is essentially fighting on one leg. In no other sport would an athlete either be expected or allowed to continue in that state. If Andy Murray had suffered the same injury midway through any of his Wimbledon singles finals then he would have been forced to withdraw, to concede, and not one person in the Centre Court crowd would have even considered there to be another option. But those in attendance at the O2 watch in morbid fascination as Haye fights on, at times an open, almost defenceless target given his immobility, submission of any kind out of the question. He is a barely walking knockout waiting to happen but is never going to oblige that fate, even in such hopeless circumstances. He still believes he can win – all he has to do is land that right hand and victory can still be his. No, there will be no surrender from David Haye, he will swing until the very end, and the crowd are more than happy to watch, I am more than happy to watch. We had all arrived that night expecting to see Tony Bellew get separated from his senses but the most dramatic and unforeseen twist has meant that if anyone is going to get stretched out on his back then it will now surely be David Haye. It is the knockout we have come for and the knockout we want.

Tony Bellew, seeing the predicament his enemy is in, lets his hands go, determined to supply it, but quickly realizes that in doing so he is affording his opponent the only glimmer of hope he has. Haye has no balance and no base to punch from; throwing his trademark Hayemaker is like trying to fire a cannon from a canoe and all Bellew has to do is stay at a distance from which he can see it coming, watch it sail over his shoulder or fall short, then step in and pick off an open target. Eventually, midway through the pen-ultimate round Haye goes to ground under assault and collapses through the ropes. But even now he won't quit. He drags himself back into the ring and beats the count only for trainer Shane McGuigan to decide enough is enough and throw the towel in.

I have never seen anything like it and I may well never witness a scene of such rare drama again. Tony Bellew risked it all and won in every way imaginable, via a narrative unimaginable even by boxing's standards. It was a fight that teetered on the verge of a knockout with every second that ticked by but somehow didn't provide one. But it didn't matter; the sheer anticipation of it was electrifying enough. As I left the arena, my nervous system flooded with adrenaline, it occurred to me that I, along with everyone else who had filed into that amphitheatre or purchased the fight on pay-per-view had been the puppets rather the puppet masters that we, the mob, like to think we are. The fight was sold on the promise of a knockout, and on the suggestion of something worse, and we, all of us, in our lust and greed to see it, had bought that promise. There would be no refunds and, furthermore, we would all pay to see it again fourteen months later, when once again there would be no knockout and once again Bellew would win, this time for double the money he earned in their first fight.

After beating David Haye again in the rematch, act three was complete for Tony Bellew. It had been an extraordinary success. There was still a final act to come, in the shape of his fight against Oleksandr Usyk. It was a fight for which he was, again, very well paid, but after securing his family's financial future against Haye, Bellew was back hunting glory, legacy, more than money. Even though he didn't win that battle, he left the sport having won the war.

In recent years there have been few more difficult or daunting tasks for a fighter than travelling to Japan to take on Naoya Inoue, but that was the mission Jamie McDonnell accepted in May 2018. McDonnell received a very handsome offer to put his – WBA – version of the bantamweight title on the line but it was no cash grab; he and trainer Dave Coldwell accepted the challenge in the belief they could win. The Monster, as Inoue is known, was 15–0 and, having become world champion at light-flyweight and super-flyweight, was now targeting a world title in a third division and had set his sights on McDonnell. Team Inoue had homed in on the Yorkshireman because he had a belt but also because he was a long-reigning and very credible champion who had defended his world title six times, including two outstanding wins Stateside against another Japanese fighter in Tomoki Kameda. If Inoue could beat McDonnell he would win kudos as well as hardware, which was crucial, as fighters from the Land of the Rising Sun set no store in easy touches.

When the offer arrived in early 2018, McDonnell and Coldwell were about to move up in weight to super-bantamweight, an elevation that would allow them another four pounds to add to Jamie's tall angular frame, but the figure offered was too good to refuse for a fighter at any stage of their boxing life, and particularly for one who was thirty-three bouts into a very successful but tough career. Jamie had been a pro since 2005, it had been a long second act, and whilst he and Dave both knew his body had long outstayed its welcome in the 8st 6lb bantamweight division, they also knew that it would take most likely five more fights to earn the same amount of money as he would receive for this one fight, and that's assuming he kept winning and had five more in him. This is boxing, and these are the decisions that have to be made, something Coldwell knew only too well.

'We went there to win. Guaranteed. Listen, we spent three weeks in Dubai and then three weeks in Japan. You're not doing that to go there for a pay cheque or just to give up the title. We know he's dangerous, he's very, very good, but Jamie has got the tools to do this. Jamie's always been big for the weight but you stay at the weight division because you're not the big fish in the promotional pond and you know that title is your bargaining chip. Without that title, you've got nothing, so that's why he stayed at that weight. He should have moved up to super-bantamweight well before Inoue, but we go to the fight, preparation's brilliant.'

I covered the fight, remotely from London. I was in touch with Dave Coldwell during that build-up and I also believed McDonnell could pose Inoue some serious problems and possibly win. The team's ambition and optimism was real and, in my eyes, justified. But in fight week, as the hours ticked down to the first bell, it all went terribly wrong, as Coldwell relates:

'He started using a different nutritionist. And I remember going over to see him on the morning of the weigh-in and the first thing I ask is what weight did he wake up at? And when I was told what weight he woke up at, it was three pounds heavier than the weight he always woke up at. And I just looked at him, the fella who told me what his weight was, and I told him, "We're fucked." I asked, "Why has he been brought in at that weight?" And it turns out he's been brought in at that weight on purpose. I was fuming, I knew we were fucked, I knew it for a fact. We tried to shift the weight but nothing was working, there was nothing left in him and it got to the point where I just looked at him and said, "You can't do this, mate." He said, "No way, I can't lose this title on the scales, no way." And I said, "It's fucking you up, you can't do it."

Making weight, as it's described in boxing, is a science, one that is tailored individually to each fighter. As Coldwell outlines here, McDonnell ordinarily would wake up on weigh-in day a few pounds over his 8st 6lb bantamweight limit and then in the hours before the weigh-in would lose those last remaining pounds, step onto the scales, weigh-in fractionally under 8st 6lb, step off the scales and then immediately begin the process of replenishing and revitalizing a body that in the days preceding the weigh-in would have been denied the calories and fluids that it would usually need. But this time it had gone wrong. McDonnell had too much weight to lose in too short a period of time and, even if he could somehow do it, there wouldn't be enough time to properly replenish a system that had been subjected to too much punishment, too much trauma.

In that scenario the fighter will enter the ring a pale imitation of themselves, a ghost, a far too vulnerable shell. It's a very dangerous position to be in. Coldwell knew this and knew that the only safe thing to do in those circumstances is to not subject the fighter's body to that level of trauma, to either pull out of the fight completely or reduce to the lowest weight they could whilst still allowing the fighter to be robust enough to compete safely. But in boxing if a boxer doesn't fight, they don't get paid, and if they fail to make weight but the opponent agrees to fight anyway, then the fighter at fault will be fined a large portion of their agreed purse for failing to fulfil their contractual obligation. Neither was an option for McDonnell. For personal reasons the Doncaster man needed to get paid in full. He explained this to Coldwell and as the trainer listened his heart sank. I know Dave Coldwell well. Like most trainers, he is an intelligent and empathetic man, and he could see that the implications for his fighter of not going through with the fight were very serious. Dave had a choice; he could either accept the reality of the situation and do everything he could to navigate his man through it safely or he could walk out of the door, knowing that McDonnell would just go through with the fight anyway, without him. There was no choice. It was an impossible situation.

'The mood then changes from, "We're here to win," to "I just want to get him through the fight safe." And that's a kick in the teeth because I'm a winner. I go into things to win. I don't do things to just get through, and Jamie's a winner, a proud, proud champion. But now I know in his head he's just thinking, "Just let me get through this and then financially I'll be OK and then we'll move up [in weight]." So you want to pull him out, but he won't pull out because there's a bigger picture. That's an awful position to be in. So we go to the weigh-in and he's the worst I've ever seen a fighter at the weigh-in. We literally had to walk from the car through the entrance foyer and then he sits down and then had to get back up to go to the scales, gets on the scales, gets weighed in, we then start refuelling and then I remember we went for a walk in the evening and Jamie's walking a few steps in front and I'm just watching his body as he's walking and he's moving like an old man and I said to him, "This is the plan for tomorrow, I just want you to get out of the first round. If you get out of the first round and come back to the corner then I'm pulling you out, whatever happens." I promise you, I had that conversation, I didn't care if he won the first round or whatever, because I'm looking at him and I knew his body wasn't recovering properly. My concern wasn't him getting knocked out early, my concern was him being in the fight later, that's where the damage would be, so I wasn't going to allow him to be in the fight later in, taking punishment.'

I remember watching the weigh-in and being shocked at Jamie McDonnell's appearance, not having been aware of what was going on behind the scenes. It was by no means the first time I'd seen a fighter displaying the effects of dehydration, 'weight drain' as it's called in boxing, but this was another level. He looked, and I do not say this lightly, like a cancer patient, skeletally thin, skin bone-dry and seemingly vulnerable to the merest touch. The next day he would have a merciless, malevolent Monster coming out of the opposite corner at him. I feared for him.

'When we were warming up on the pads in the changing rooms, I could tell he had nothing in his legs. It's the most scared I've been walking to a ring. I felt completely defenceless because if I'd said I wouldn't do his corner it wouldn't have stopped him, he'd have just done it with whoever rather than pull out of the fight. The fighter makes the decision, so that ring walk was the worst ring walk I've ever had in my life. I remember walking to the ring, and I've watched it, and my wife said to me, watching me walk to the ring, you could tell, I looked terrified, because I was terrified. And I'll be honest with you, when he got done with a body shot, I was so thankful. And I remember when he went down, he just looked at me, and he got up, there was another little scuffle and he got stopped. And I was so relieved. I've never been so relieved for a fight to go so wrong, to get beat in the first round, as I was for that.'

Commentating on the fight, thousands of miles away in a voiceover booth at Sky, Matt Macklin and myself were relieved too. Watching Team McDonnell stood in that Tokyo ring as the final announcements were made, you could see how subdued they were; a normally ebullient crew of gym mates and experienced cornermen were all unusually silent. Early on the champion tries to keep Inoue at bay with his jab but halfway through the round the challenger staggers McDonnell with a left hook to the head and then puts him down with a left to the body, a punch that under normal circumstances would have had much less effect. McDonnell stays on his hands and knees in his own corner, staring directly at Coldwell, who is just a few feet away, talking to him, and then on the count of six gets back to his feet. Boxing resumes and immediately Inoue pins his man to the ropes and starts to unload, but he isn't given the opportunity to do real damage as experienced referee Luis Pabon, who knows a depleted fighter when he sees one, steps in and stops the action just as Dave Coldwell appears on the ring apron, towel in hand. It's over.

Jamie McDonnell survived, he lived to fight another day, but there was only one more day after Japan, one more fight before he hung the gloves up. Inoue is without question on his way to the hall of fame. Nobody has come remotely close to taming the Monster, whose fresh-faced, schoolboy looks belie a rare ferocity.

Boxers run the risk of getting knocked out every time they answer the bell. Sometimes they choose to heighten that risk, in turn for a heightened reward, which is what Amir Khan and Tony Bellew did, with mixed results. On other occasions circumstances conspire to make an already hazardous task even more dangerous, which is what happened to Jamie McDonnell and also to Ricky Hatton, who admitted he shouldn't have been in the ring the night he got knocked out by Manny Pacquiao because mentally and physically he, like McDonnell, was in no position to give of his best. But in both cases pride and pragmatism dictated that they had to fight.

As Amir Khan told me, 'We're all prize-fighters, that's what we are.' And if a fighter wants the prize, then fight he must.

CHAPTER SIX

A Duty of Care – Referees

I've said this before and I'll say it again, twice in me career referees have saved me life. The referee on Usyk night because if he lets me carry on, which some referees would have because I was the home fighter, I probably would have been killed. And the Stevenson defeat. I was asleep standing up and Michael Griffin definitely saved me life. It's the punch that you can't brace for that's the punch that does the most damage. And on them two occasions I've been very fortunate that a fighter hasn't been allowed to get that free shot on me. So I'm very grateful and thankful to those referees.

Tony Bellew

O fficials in all sports live their professional lives under a spotlight and the higher profile the sport, the more intense it is. They need protecting as much as possible because the abuse and threats they receive can be appalling and the resulting burden they carry can become crippling. But there is no helping the boxing referee, because whilst the consequences of the swing of a boot can be erased, the consequences of the swing of a fist cannot. Referees stand alone in that squared circle, the sole arbiters of the contest, and the two boxers in there with them can literally live and die by their decisions. It's a weight of responsibility like no other in all of sporting officialdom because only in boxing is it the primary aim of the participants to damage each other, in no other sport is victory achieved via that one basic method. Boxing carries with it a constant, clear and present danger and nothing is more emblematic of that danger than the knockout.

I needed experience, a wealth of it, for this chapter and thankfully I managed to secure just that. The following referees, who were all very generous with their time, between them have been presiding over the professional ring for more than a hundred years, taking charge of over three thousand fights.

Charlie Fitch is from Macedon, a small town in Upstate New York. In his fifties, he's been refereeing professional boxing for more than twenty years. He boxed himself and had one pro bout, in July 1998 at Whistles Pub in Scranton, Pennsylvania, where, by his own admission, he took a beating over four rounds. His wife Tracey informed him after the fight that he'd been so slow she was confident she would have bested him herself, after which he decided to hang up the gloves. Tracey knew how much her husband loved the sport though, and pushed him to become a referee. Fitch was reluctant at first but made his debut at Niagara Falls in 2001, picking up about three hundred dollars for his trouble. His biggest night came in front of 80,000 people at Wembley Stadium in May 2014, when he was the third man in the ring for Froch vs Groves II. Three weeks before that night, before he even knew he would be taking charge of such a huge contest, he refereed at the Whitehall Armory, in Whitehall, New York. The headline act was a fight for the vacant WBA female featherweight title between Ronica Jeffrey and Carla

Torres, and by Charlie's estimation there were fewer than ten people watching by the end. Such is the life of a referee.

Kenny Bayless resides in Las Vegas, Nevada, and has refereed many of the biggest fights of the last few decades. In his seventies and recently retired, he has been involved in boxing as an official for almost fifty years, starting out as a judge on the amateur circuit in 1977 and taking charge of his first fight as a referee in the professional ring in 1991. Bayless refereed his first world title fight in 1994 and has safeguarded all the biggest names in the sport since then. When Manny Pacquiao knocked out Ricky Hatton and Amir Khan was rendered unconscious by Saul Canelo Alvarez, it was Kenny who was in there with them, first on the scene, ensuring they immediately received the assistance they needed.

Marcus McDonnell has been a professional referee for thirty-six years. His brother Jim was a very good fighter who twice challenged for world titles at super-featherweight and Marcus became a referee after going to watch Jim fight at the Royal Albert Hall, where he found himself asked for his opinion regarding who he thought was winning a particular fight. An official from the Board of Control was sufficiently impressed by his ringside appraisal to suggest he consider giving his verdict for real. McDonnell took him up on the offer and has been found in British rings, week in and week out, ever since.

Victor Loughlin, from Glasgow, has been a Board of Control referee for twenty-eight years and, along with Marcus McDonnell, is one of the UK's best officials. He took the plunge after a conversation he had with a professional fighter called Michael Deveney at the YMCA in Paisley. Deveney's description of the vagaries of the judging of boxing contests struck a chord within him and he decided he wanted to make a meaningful contribution. Victor was the man in the middle for Tony Bellew's knockout win vs Ilunga Makabu and Jamie Moore's epic late stoppage of Matthew Macklin.

All knockouts are difficult for referees. From a technical stand-point the official will ask themselves whether the fighter who has just been knocked out should have had to suffer that fate, or whether there was something they could or should have done differently to prevent it? Referees have to assess their contribution in as objective a fashion as they can, because if there are lessons to be learnt then learnt they must be. But whatever their verdict on their own role in proceedings, there will nonetheless be an emotional impact to deal with, because witnessing a knockout is to witness a potentially fatal incident. It is a traumatic experience, no matter how many times a person may have experienced it previously. A type-one knockout is the perfect example of the above dynamic. It is universally agreed that there is nothing anyone, not the boxer, not the trainer, not the referee, can do to prevent it, but that lack of culpability doesn't mean they will emerge unscathed.

Deep into our conversation, Kenny Bayless spoke to me about a fight he refereed in September 1997. It was a contest at light-welterweight, scheduled for ten rounds at the New Orleans Hotel and Casino in Las Vegas between James Crayton and Johnny Montantes. In the fifth round Montantes got knocked out by what Kenny described to me as a third-degree knockdown. (Bayless sep-arates knockdowns into three categories: a first-degree or flash knockdown, which occurs due to a loss of balance rather than a particularly heavy punch and leaves the fighter who has suffered it in full possession of their mental and physical faculties, after which they will be allowed to continue; a second-degree knockdown, which occurs when a fighter gets hit and hurt, where the fighter is dazed and it's clear their coordination has been affected when they get back to their feet, after which they will only be allowed to con-tinue should they satisfy the referee that they are willing and able to do so; and a third-degree knockdown, which happens when a fighter gets hit with a punch they don't see or are not braced for, a type-one knockout punch, after which the referee will immediately stop the fight.) Kenny stopped the fight at once and ushered in the medics but he knew it was bad: 'I could see the pupils in his eyes going up to the top of his head.' Montantes was taken to hospital where it was discovered he had suffered a cerebral haematoma, a bleed on the brain, as that injury is described in boxing. The doctors did everything they could but tragically Montantes passed away. Kenny Bayless was blameless. There was nothing he could have done to prevent the punch landing but that was no consolation. A fighter had sustained a fatal blow, in his ring, right in front of him; it is an event that once seen, cannot be unseen.

'I was a wreck after that. I thought very hard after that about whether I still wanted to be in the sport, I was so hurt by it. I didn't know if I wanted to referee any more. But I got a few calls from some of my officials, consoling me, and the executive director Marc Ratner called me and consoled me and told me, "We've got a fight card in a couple of weeks and you're going to be on that fight card, so get yourself together," which I did. I did well on that next fight and my career continued.'

The fact that Bayless was able to return to the ring, and so soon, is a testament to his character but also an illustration of the acceptance a referee has to have of what boxing is and of what can happen. He witnessed further type-one knockouts, two such being the chilling blows Hatton and Khan suffered at the gloved fists of Pacquiao and Canelo, both of which Bayless recalls with unerring clarity.

'There were two flash, first-degree knockdowns in the first round. Ricky Hatton's the type of fighter that comes to fight. At the end of the first round, when I went over to my neutral corner, I had never had an adrenaline rush in a fight, never, but I did in that fight, because the crowd was so loud and excited after those first two knockdowns, I could feel my heart racing as if I'd just a run a four-hundred metres and I'm standing in the corner and I can feel my heart beating and I'm thinking, "Heart, calm down, because the bell's getting ready to ring and I have to go back out there."

When the bell rang, I'd settled down and I went back out and towards the end of the second round when Manny Pacquiao caught Ricky and when Ricky went down there was a scary moment for me, because of the way Ricky went down, and the same thing's happened to me in a few fights I've refereed, when a fighter gets hit a light switch got turned off, and it was like life left Ricky's body before he hit the ground. I'd done another fight later, when Canelo fought Amir Khan, and when Canelo hit Amir Khan, he went down the same way, like someone had turned the light switch off. And there's a concern that comes with that for us because I've seen fighters go down like that before and never get up, where that fight took them completely out, that one punch took them completely out. So I waved it off, got the doctors in so they could do what they do and I just hope and pray that he's going to be alright. In that situation Ricky Hatton was OK, in the situation with Amir Khan, he was OK, but like I said there's been situations where a fighter's never got up. That's the kind of sport we're in.'

Hatton and Khan recovered and so Kenny was spared the horrific aftermath he experienced after Montantes's tragic passing, but in the moment, in the ring, at the point of the knockout, when anything is possible, the trauma was just as bad: 'You're in a place where you don't know. You don't know what the outcome is and even if he does get up, what is his condition going to be like? How is he going to be as a person for the rest of his career?'

Victor Loughlin was inches away when Tony Bellew knocked Ilunga Makabu out at Goodison Park in May 2016. It had been a firefight, with Bellew getting knocked down in the first round before pinning Makabu on the ropes in the third and mercilessly dispatching him with a left hook. As that left hand landed Loughlin was within touching distance, firmly plugged into the chaotic maelstrom at hand whilst having to try and remain aloof from it in order to process what he was seeing and then decide what he should do.

'I knew that Tony was getting through although he was still hitting gloves, I'm thinking, "Right, how long am I gonna let this go? How many unanswered shots can I let go before I stop it?" It's a world title fight, it's live on the telly, it's a stadium fight, so you've really got to factor all those things in as well, and I've got to give Makabu every chance because I told them both when I went to see them in the changing rooms, "I will give you every chance." But I was probably hovering, waiting for an opportunity, thinking, "Right, this might be coming soon, this might be coming." And then Makabu, as he's avoiding the punches, decides to throw one, to try and take Tony again, and that's when Tony just cleans him out, and I think I was just a couple of feet away and straightaway I knew he was gone. If it had gone on for even a couple more seconds I'd have got in and stopped it, I would say so. I knew right away the punch had cleaned him out and I didn't even take the count, he was gone.'

Unlike Kenny Bayless's experience with Ricky Hatton and Amir Khan, the action allowed Loughlin to identify the strong potential for the knockout, and that that potential was likely to be realized imminently. But for the reasons he lists, he was satisfied that he was justified in allowing the action to continue, that the resulting knock-out wasn't necessarily avoidable. It's fascinating to read the list of factors he mentions, the sheer number of things he feels need to be taken into account, because what it demonstrates is that whilst the health and safety of the fighter is the referee's number-one priority, it is not the only thing they have to consider. It seems unrealistic to expect a person to be able to make what could be a life-or-death decision under such circumstances and I was very curious to know what the feeling was as he watched, poised and ready to intervene, when Bellew landed his left hand and knocked Makabu out.

'It's a bit of relief but also you get scared. Relief in that it's been taken out of your hands slightly. It's slightly been taken out of your hands in a way but then you get a bit scared because somebody getting hit like that is a bit scary. And I've been in a situation obviously where I've had a fatality. Relief maybe isn't the right word, it's more that your part of the job has been taken out of your hands by that punch because there's no argument, you're not taking up a count, the fight's over, that's it. The first thing I think is, "I hope the guy's OK." That's the first thing I think. "Is he OK? Is he getting up from this?"'

Relief: a word that has been mentioned in connection to the knockout in these pages before. We discussed further exactly what it was that he meant, because it occurred to me that the right word to describe his emotions in that moment possibly doesn't exist. He was not, of course, relieved that Makabu had been knocked out, more that it came as a relief that such an intense and demanding situation and one in which his own intervention, an intervention that could have been controversial, was rapidly looming had come to a natural and irrevocable conclusion. I appreciate that describing an extreme occurrence such as a knockout as a natural conclusion may seem strange to some but in the context of a boxing ring, it is just that.

Scared: another word that has been mentioned previously. Knockouts scare referees, no matter how experienced they are. Makabu lay prone on the canvas, unconscious, for a couple of minutes, during which time nobody knew if he would live or die.

Victor mentions above that he has been witness to a fatality in the boxing ring. In September 2016 Victor refereed a contest between Mike Towell and Dale Evans in Glasgow. Towell was knocked down in the first round and then again in the fifth before Victor stopped the fight. Tragically Towell passed away the next day after suffering a cerebral haematoma caused by blows received during the fight. There was nothing Victor could have done to prevent it and no blame was attached to him. But that was of no comfort to him.

'What happened with Mike Towell hit me pretty bad, to be honest. He was on his stool talking to his mum and then he collapsed down and when that happened I knew it was bad. I just knew. And then we get the phone call and I was kind of in bits a wee bit. So I done a disappearing act for a few days and there were some crazy thoughts. I remember Robert (Smith, General Secretary of the British Boxing Board of Control) at the Board and Charlie (Giles, Chairman) were always mega-supportive of me and they said to me that I just needed to get back in the saddle, sort of thing, and I can't remember what contest it was when I came back but it was a TV job. And I always remember looking up at the sky thinking, "What am I doing this for?" Because my family wanted me to call it a day.'

Thankfully Ilunga Makabu recovered, as did George Groves after he was knocked out by Carl Froch in front of Charlie Fitch. Groves recovered incredibly quickly, managing to get back to his feet within seconds of being collapsed on the canvas, but the fight was already over as Fitch had looked into the fighter's eyes as he lay on his back and his experience told him that what he was looking at was a human being who had lost consciousness.

'It looked clear to me that he was unconscious, but because of the magnitude of the fight I wanted to look in his eyes and confirm that he is clearly knocked out, and I bent over, and I see that the eyes are open, but as a referee you get to recognize when nobody's home, their eyes are open but they're not there, and I saw that and once I seen that I said, "OK, this is a knockout, it's over."'

Referees have to be able to recognize when a boxer has been knocked out, and although that may sound straightforward, a combination of a fighter's freakish powers of recovery and a burning desire to continue at all costs can make it difficult. A combatant may be knocked out by a punch, be unconscious as they fall to the canvas, and then find themselves awoken from that state by the jolt of hitting the floor; or they might, as Groves did, somehow be capable of coming around very quickly. However fleeting that loss of consciousness might be, the referee has to recognize it and stop the fight. If a referee can't do that then they leave the fighter very vulnerable and very likely to find themselves knocked out for a second time, an event that could have disastrous consequences. Being knocked out twice in one fight was not a scenario I had entertained prior to speaking to referees, I wouldn't have believed it possible, but, as Fitch told me, although it isn't common, it does happen.

'I think it's less common now in the 2000s than it was in the 90s, 80s and 70s. I think the further back in time we go the more common that was, but now with more regulation from commissions and with safety being paramount, I think it happens less often, but I do think it could still happen. It could happen by accident, by a referee who doesn't realize the fighter was knocked out, or could happen with a referee saying, "Oh, no, I'm OK with that," but they probably won't be refereeing for long.'

This discussion brought to mind the actions of referee Jack Reiss in the final round of the fight he officiated between Deontay Wilder and Tyson Fury, the first in what turned out to an epic trilogy between the two. In the twelfth round Wilder put Fury down hard with a left hand and the Gypsy King collapsed to the canvas, stretched out on his back. He looked to the untrained eye like he was unconscious, like there was no need for the referee to count, just as Kenny Bayless hadn't with Ricky Hatton or Amir Khan. But Jack Reiss did count and, just in the nick of time, with the count nearing ten, Fury rose, as if from the dead, beat the count and boxed out the rest of the round with remarkable alacrity. It was an incredible sight and one of the most famous recoveries in boxing history. People marvelled at Fury's ability to come round from being rendered unconscious by Wilder, rise and rally like he did, and Reiss was praised for giving him the opportunity. But Jack Reiss never believed Fury had been unconscious – had he believed that then he would have stopped the fight. The referee later explained in an interview how his trained eye had spotted Fury break his fall by rolling onto his elbows and shoulders to protect his head from hitting the canvas, how his right leg was up as he lay on his back and how he was moving his hands slightly, in a gripping motion. For Reiss these were telltale signs that the fighter was still conscious, something he confirmed in his own mind when he looked into Fury's eyes.

The fact that a loss of consciousness can be problematic to identify highlights just how difficult a referee's job is. But they are not just required to know when somebody has been knocked out, they are also required to know when somebody may be *about* to get knocked out and intervene before it happens, to anticipate that event and prevent it from occurring. It's a difficult thing to do because, as Victor Loughlin outlined, there are numerous factors in play and whilst none of them trump the number-one priority that is the health of the fighters, they do influence a referee's decision. It's an incredibly fine line that referees have to tread, like walking a high wire but without the luxury of a safety net, knowing the potential consequences of just one missed step. Charlie Fitch is familiar with that responsibility.

'It doesn't take much for these guys to be hurt forever. In regards to knockouts and damage that fighters take, in those world-level, championship fights, there's more risk of them getting hurt than there is for fighters in four, six or eight-round fights, because they've trained themselves, disciplined their minds to fight through being hurt, so that sometimes, nobody even knows that they're hurt except for them, and sometimes I don't think they even consider themselves hurt, they think, "It's just part of the work I do," and they just fight through it. And the guys who fight at that world championship level are more determined to fight on than fighters who haven't got to that level because they've made so many sacrifices to get there. And as a referee you know that, that this is the moment of this guy's life, what he gets paid in his next fight is probably going to be determined by the outcome of this fight. So it's a real balancing act for me as a referee . . . you know, number one is safety, number two is fairness in the ring, that it's a level playing field, then number three though is the reality that this is entertainment, that people are paying to watch this, that people are paying to see people put themselves at risk like that. There's a point where there's like a perfect time to stop a fight. Look at it like a triangle. There's the tip, which is the perfect time to stop it, and there's a little bit to the left which would be a little bit early but still acceptable to everyone that's watching, then the same thing on the right side of the triangle, you know maybe a punch too late but it's still OK. And then you go further down the left of the triangle and then it's "Oh, no, that was too early" or further down the right and that was too late, so I always want to get it on the tip of the triangle, not too early, not too late, I want to get it perfect.'

Fitch, like all referees, is striving for perfection but if in doubt, as Kenny Bayless tells us, an official wants to be to the left of that tip of the triangle, not the right: 'It's hard because some athletes are truly warriors and they want to fight until the very end. What a lot of fight fans don't understand is that we're in a position where we'd much rather stop it too soon than too late because the difference in terms of their long-term health and their career can be astronomical. It could be career-ending. Maybe sometimes they could make it to the final bell but the question is, what's the point? It's much better to stop it and save them to fight another day.'

Fighters want to hear that final bell if possible, even in an obviously losing cause, it's a point of pride; and although referees always want to give them their pride, they cannot do so at the expense of their health. Boxers are prepared to be reckless with their physical wellbeing; they never see any cause as lost and it is that bravery that makes them vulnerable and that the referee must protect them from, as Marcus McDonnell explains.

'In the event of a knockdown you've only got ten to fifteen seconds to make your assessment so you've got to be pretty quick about what you're assessing, and how you assess it is as follows: What has happened previous in the fight? If we're now in round nine of a twelve-round contest and this is the first time you've been put down, you've been fifty-fifty in the fight, you've been put down and you've got up, then I'm going to let you go on, you're fine. But if it's the ninth round and you've been taking a beating for seven rounds, I'm not going to let you go on, this is my opportunity to step in and call it a day. The boxer's not gonna stop, they don't do that.'

Context is key. If all that awaits a fighter is further, one-sided punishment, punishment that could eventually be consummated by a knockout, then the contest must be stopped because it is no longer a contest and a subsequent knockout would be no more than a pointless execution. There is no room in sport for such a cruel and unnecessary spectacle because, although boxers are often referred to as modern-day gladiators, this is not the Colosseum, it is a sporting arena, and just because spectators may want to see a knockout, a referee is not obliged to facilitate one.

Kenny Bayless explains: 'When fans are booing at us because we stopped the fight, they're sitting in the stands with maybe a beer and whatever else and they're paying customers so they get to yell and scream and do what fans do. There are podcasts I do and I do them to educate the fans because they need to be educated that there are two lives in that ring and, being the referee, I'm responsible for both those lives in there and, regardless if I stop it and they don't agree with it, that fighter I saved usually has a wife and kids and my job for the sake of the fans' entertainment is to protect the fighters.'

But it is not just the paying public who sometimes need to be educated – the same can be said for corner teams. During his long career Bayless has perfected the art of subtly signposting to those involved who are failing to see the true nature of what is unfolding in front of them, what that truth is.

'A lot of times the corners want to give their fighters every opportunity to win and a lot of the time they're reluctant to stop it because of that, but at the same time for us referees we're looking at the safety of the fighter. So what we do a lot of the time . . . we use the term "selling the call". I have to "sell the call" to the fans, to everyone, because I'm the only guy that's in there with them and I have to do something to show that at some point I'm going to have to stop it because he's taking too much and he's fatiguing. So a lot of the time what I'll do is when there's a clinch, I'll break them and look hard at the fighter I think is in a little trouble, and I'll keep looking at him to let the fans know and the corner know and the doctor know and everyone who's watching the fight know that I've got a close eye on this guy because he's taking a little too much and fatiguing too much.'

Marcus McDonnell spoke to me at length about how important it is that a referee is capable of supplying this subliminal running commentary, designed to influence the thoughts of the principal players at ringside, in the hope that they will see what the referee is seeing and respond appropriately. Referees always prefer to give a fighter's corner the opportunity to withdraw their fighter and end the contest, rather than do it themselves, but sometimes a corner will prove itself incapable, at which point the referee has no choice but to step in. Marcus mentioned a fight he'd taken charge of just a few weeks prior to our conversation, a fight I'd commentated on and one in which he'd been forced to take matters into his own hands. It involved Natasha Jonas and Kandi Wyatt and was for the vacant IBF female welterweight title. It was a mismatch which, although unusual at world title level, is not unheard of. Jonas was far too good for Wyatt and hit her hard and often from the opening bell. Round after round Jonas meted out punishment whilst barely taking anything in return, and as those rounds passed it became more and more apparent that what we were witnessing was a one-sided beatdown. It was uncomfortable. Anyone could see that the visiting Canadian had no chance of winning the fight and after six rounds it was clear that her corner, having kept her pride intact by allowing her to proceed past halfway, should stop the fight. But they didn't. After seven rounds the need for them to save their courageous boxer, who clearly had no quit in her whatsoever, was staring even the most inexperienced observer in the face and yet still they sent her out for another round. Referee McDonnell, who at this point had no more hints left to give, stopped the fight thirty seconds into the eighth round, stepping in and hugging Kandi Wyatt who, he told me, then quietly thanked him for bringing her painful night to an end. Watching it made me angry. Either Wyatt's corner couldn't see what was happening, in which case they were guilty of gross incompetence, or they could see it but decided to let it happen anyway, in which case they were guilty of gross negligence. It wasn't the first time McDonnell had witnessed such a dereliction of duty but it still left him shaking his head.

'Corners need to be educated. They have that person in the corner for a minute and they need to be talking to them: "How are you? How are you feeling? You OK? You're getting hit a bit too much, are you OK? Have you got any headaches?" But often they don't do that, it's all, "You've got to get back out there, you're gonna win this." And with Kandi Wyatt, I was worried for her, Tasha was beating her up and it was like, I can see it, you commentators can see it, the crowd can see it, but yet the corner are waiting for me to do it when they should have said, "Ref, that'll do." But no, "Because fighters want to go out on their shield," they'll say, but that poor girl took a beating that night. You need people around you that are going to protect you and look after you.'

'Going out on your shield' is a phrase heard often in boxing and is a metaphor for a noble and valiant defeat, one in which a boxer chooses to fight until the very end rather than concede defeat. But historically the phrase is attributed to ancient Sparta and refers to a warrior literally fighting to their death, rather than surrender. I understand what is meant by it but do not find it a helpful device; the temptation for people to lazily roll it out of their mouths without thinking about what it is that they are saying is too strong.

Thanks to Marcus McDonnell's intervention Kandi Wyatt ended her world title fight against Jonas on her feet rather than flat on her back. She exited the ring with both her faculties and her pride intact and that is the kind of exit that referees will always do their best to afford a fighter. Achieving this requires a lot of skill and judgement. Often a referee knows as soon as a fighter hits the canvas whether they're going to allow them to continue or not. If they have been knocked out then the fight is stopped immediately but if it's not that scenario – if, for example, the fighter has been down once, or even a couple of times, already and then they go down again, the fight has turned against them, they're exhausted and not too far away from unravelling – then referees will do what they can to bring a halt to proceedings in a way that allows a fighter to hold their head up high as they walk back down the aisle to the changing room. Kenny Bayless spoke earlier of the need to 'sell the call', in certain instances and this is a variation on that theme because in this scenario the referee isn't selling the call to the crowd or the corner but to the boxer.

He elaborates: 'At that point in time us referees have to make that decision. And we can make that decision when he's sitting down on his stool, which is a good time to make it, or when he's out in the ring and trying to fight back and showing his energy to want to continue.'

Kenny furnished me with a great example of a referee doing all the above. It came from referee Mills Lane and occurred in a fight between Mike Tyson and Trevor Berbick in Las Vegas in November 1986. Tyson was 27–0 after just twenty months as a pro, a wrecker of bodies and a stealer of souls, who was about to fulfil his destiny of becoming the youngest ever heavyweight champion of the world by dethroning WBC champion Trevor Berbick.

That was the script and even though Berbick, a proud champion and good fighter, had other ideas, on the night he could do little to alter the narrative. Iron Mike jumped on Berbick in round one and the champ elected to stand and trade with the baddest man on the planet, as Tyson was known. It was courageous but foolhardy and by the end of the opening three minutes it was all he could do just to stay on his feet. Early in round two he got knocked down heavily. The writing was on the wall and if the same situation had occurred later in proceedings with a few more torrid rounds for Berbick behind it then Mills Lane would most likely have stopped it there and then, but it was early on, Berbick was defending his belt on the sport's biggest stage, and so the referee chose to give him the chance to recover. It didn't prove possible. Tyson dropped his opponent again and at that point Lane would have decided that the fight was over, but rather than jump in and wave it over immediately, he waited and counted. He waited because he could see that Berbick was trying to get back up and get back up he did before, balance and coordination completely scrambled, he fell again. Twice that happened. That would have been the cue to intervene for most referees, but Lane continued to count because he could see that the stricken Jamaican was still determined to rise a third time, which he somehow did, regaining his feet just as Mills Lane reached the count of ten, at which point the referee wrapped him up in a big hug before Berbick's corner team arrived and escorted him back to his corner. It was a great example of a referee giving a boxer every chance to fight and then, upon realizing that the ability to fight and defend himself was no longer there, allowing him to finish on his feet, pride wounded but not destroyed.

I didn't have the privilege of being able to speak to Mills Lane about his handling of Berbick vs Tyson (Lane passed away in late 2022 at the age of eighty-five) but luckily for me Victor Loughlin was happy to talk me through his thought processes during two contests which, between them, elucidate much of what has been examined in this chapter. Loughlin was the man in charge of the 2006 British light-middleweight title bout between Jamie Moore and Matthew Macklin that has been explored in detail in previous chapters. It was a brutal affair, a thrilling encounter that ended with Moore knocking Macklin out in the tenth round, by which point both men were running on empty. Given the pace, intensity and savagery of the battle, it seemed very likely that it was going to end in a knockout and, although that is an easy conclusion to reach with hindsight, that was how it presented in real time. For that reason there was some debate afterwards centred around whether the referee should have intervened prior to that final left hand from Moore and prevented the knockout. Here is Loughlin's analysis.

'I remember the contest being quite tough and I remember seven, eight and nine, those are the rounds I really remember because they were really full-on. Macklin had elements of winning at least two of those rounds, I felt. The ninth round was back and forth and back and forth and at no time in the ninth did I think, "I'm gonna stop this." If anything I was looking at Jamie when he was up against the ropes, he turns away and Macklin's hitting him with shots, and there's no real power in them, but that was a time where I thought, "I'm gonna see how this goes," because obviously I could have stopped Jamie at that stage, I could maybe have stopped Matt earlier on. At the end of the ninth round what I did notice was, when Matt went back to the corner, he had a tired walk. In my opinion it was more of a tired walk than the walk of some-body who had been hurt, when they've been hit with a shot and their legs have gone. And I thought, "I wonder if he's gonna come back out." But once they did come back out I remember Matt was gassed and I could tell he was gassed but he went straight at Jamie and landed a couple of shots and then at one stage he got into a tangle and Jamie kind of pushed him over and when he got up I thought to myself, "You're done, mate." But he kept swinging at Jamie and that's when Jamie cleaned him out. But there wasn't anything in the contest at any stage where either one of them was under so much pressure that I felt I had to stop it because there was nothing coming back. Even at the end Matt tried to throw a shot. So there was no stage at which I would have thought of stopping that fight, to be honest. They were both under pressure throughout the whole contest, they both had their successes and Matt was probably the more aggressive of the two throughout the whole fight, he just kept going for it, whereas Jamie had that tuck-up style. The finish was quite hard but ultimately I didn't see a point where I could stop it, to be honest. Watching it again, there's maybe a couple of bits in rounds seven to nine where each of them was under pressure where you could have maybe justified it, but I think you would have got slaughtered for stopping it.'

Loughlin harbours no regrets about the way he handled Moore vs Macklin. It was a very hard fight that ended in a knockout, which in the sport of boxing can be the natural way of things.

Another fight Victor refereed came in January 2023 at the Manchester Arena between Chris Eubank Jnr and Liam Smith, a fight I commentated on alongside Matt Macklin and George Groves. It was an unexpected grudge match. Smith had been a world champion, albeit in a different division to the middleweight division he and Eubank had agreed to meet in, whilst Eubank, although possessing a higher profile than Smith, had never attained that status. Despite that, Eubank made it his business, as has always been his custom, to patronize and belittle his opponent, making great play of the fact that Smith had been stopped previously in his career whereas he himself had not only never been stopped but also never been put down or even wobbled in the professional ring. Jnr, like his father, seemed to possess a granite chin and, although seasoned observers gave Smith, who possessed the superior boxing skills, an even chance of winning the fight, his prospects of hurting Eubank, let alone stopping him, were rated at zero. The atmosphere in the arena when the fighters ring-walked was as good as any I've experienced. The 'fight we never knew we needed', as I described it just prior to the opening bell, had that feral feel to it that all fight fans crave.

It was a cagey start, with nothing much happening in the opening two rounds before Eubank won the third thanks to a series of uppercuts. It was in the fourth that the fight exploded. Eubank was backed up into his own corner and as he attempted to slip and roll to avoid Smith's attack he got hit and dropped by a left hand he didn't see. He slumped to the floor, taking a seat on the canvas, back supported by the ring post, as if dropping onto an imaginary stool. Eubank, granite chin well and truly cracked for the first time ever, jumped back up to his feet quickly but he was, as I described him, 'all over the place', his legs just about capable of supporting his weight but barely able to obey any instruction from a brain that was barely able to issue any. Victor Loughlin could have stopped the fight there and then and in that split second I voiced the opinion that he may well do just that, before he wiped the fighter's gloves and allowed him to continue. Smith advanced, landed a right hand, not all that heavily but heavily enough to send Eubank down again. He scrambled back to his feet but fell forward into the arms of referee Loughlin, who stopped the fight. At exactly the same time the towel came sailing in from Eubank's corner, his trainer Roy Jones Jnr knowing, just as Victor Loughlin did, that his man was done. It all happened very, very quickly, as it always does in that white heat of battle. This is what Victor recalls about his handling of the situation.

'Say for instance it had been the fourth quarter of the fight, rounds ten to twelve, and it had been a hard fight and maybe something had happened previously, then I would definitely have stopped it. But with that one in particular, one of the reasons I decided to let that one go is I just wanted to be sure because I don't know whether Eubank is the type who can recover, because some guys get clipped, they're all over the place and then the next minute they're right as rain, it's unbelievable. And I always think with that kind of knockdown when somebody jumps up that quick, I think, "OK, so you've made a mistake there, you've actually got up too quick, you should have taken the count." Because [if you get up too quick] your legs aren't with you when you walk across because you've not allowed your legs time to get together. So by jumping up, your legs aren't there and it makes you wobble around the ring rather than taking the eight seconds. The other thing I looked at in that particular contest, I thought to myself, "Does he know how to hold? Does he know how to stay out of the way?" Those are the two ways a fighter can survive it, but deep down I thought to myself, "You're gonna struggle to survive this unless you can do one of those two things."

'I know Smith's a good finisher. When he come back in and hit him again, Eubank bounced up again too quick and fell towards me and at that stage I called the contest off as there was no point then. The bizarre thing was that afterwards he complained that it was stopped too quick. But I think if I'd stopped that contest after the first knockdown there'd have been a big debate, without a doubt. I think you'd have got people saying the referee was spot-on but that you'd also have got a lot of people, and I mean a lot, saying, "You never gave him a chance, he's never been knocked down, yeah, he was hurt but he could have recovered." So you've got all those factors, so with that one, I wanted to make sure. Of course, I don't mean by that that I wanted to make sure he got knocked out, I mean that I just wanted to be sure, to give him a chance.'

Loughlin was prepared to take a chance to give Eubank a chance. The chance he took was that when Smith followed up he could have knocked Eubank down heavily again, just as Breidis Prescott did against Amir Khan when referee Terry O'Connor allowed that fight to continue after an initial knockdown that left Khan in a similar state to Eubank. Victor knew when he allowed Eubank to box on that he might get knocked unconscious, that that was a possibility, but he chose to take that chance because it was possible Chris could recover. By Victor's own admission that outcome was not probable, but it was still possible, and it was only when he could see that recovery was no longer possible that he stopped the fight.

Thankfully Eubank was OK. Thankfully Amir Khan was OK. Had they not been then Victor Loughlin and Terry O'Connor would have found their decisions hard to live with; that would be true of any human being in that situation, but that would not have necessarily made them wrong. Whether or not to take a chance with a fighter's health to give them a chance to recover and maybe come back and win; that is the choice a referee has to make and it's an extremely difficult one.

This chapter has been somewhat circuitous, deliberately so, because the nature of the role of the boxing referee, the decision-making journey they take in the ring, cannot be mapped out as the crow flies. It is a 'sliding doors' kind of an occupation and one in which the counterfactual is ubiquitous. The desire to ponder what would have happened if a different decision had been made is one that will never wane, whatever the circumstances. Often the boldest decision a referee makes is the one that leaves them most vulnerable to that debate and almost always it is made with that number-one, overriding consideration in mind – the welfare of the boxer.

A good example of this in a British ring in recent times came on 23 November 2013, exactly ten years ago to the day as I sit in my study writing this. On that day Carl Froch met George Groves for the first time at the Manchester Arena. George was a huge under-dog but he flattened Carl with a massive right hand in the first round and for the next four or five rounds seemed one punch away from pulling off a huge upset. Froch was on autopilot, just like he had been against Jermain Taylor at Foxwoods, fighting through a fog, waiting for that steamed-up windscreen, as Barry McGuigan described it, to clear. He survived and in the second half of the fight began to turn things around. George was possibly running out of steam and the scorecards, which would have been one-sided at the midway stage, were narrowing. In the ninth round George Groves was under pressure. Carl Froch had the whiff of a big finish in his nostrils and believed he was closing in to apply it, at which point Howard Foster stepped in and stopped the fight, deciding that Groves was on the point of falling apart, that he was too vulnerable and about to get badly knocked out. That was the call he made and it provoked huge controversy. Foster was vilified for it. People wanted to know what would have happened if he hadn't stopped it. Would Groves have made it through that rough passage? Could he have rallied and held on to win on points? But more than anything, whether they care to admit it or not, observers felt robbed of what was potentially a conclusive and explosive finish, they felt robbed of a knockout, and they attacked Foster for not giving it to them. George Groves was incandescent with rage but lived to fight another day.

But Froch vs Groves is neither the only example, nor the best. On 17 March 1990, in Las Vegas, the unbeaten, 24–0–1, IBF light-welterweight champion Meldrick Taylor met the undefeated 68–0 WBC champion Julio Cesar Chavez in a unification bout. The stakes were high. Heading into the final round Taylor was up on two of the three judges' scorecards by a big enough margin that victory would be his as long as he managed to avoid getting stopped, not that he knew that. But Chavez had been hunting Taylor down and the IBF champion, as the HBO broadcast team correctly pointed out, had very little left. He was coming apart at the seams, 'faded and bat-tered' as commentator Jim Lampley described him, and everyone could see it, it was just a case of whether he could navigate those 180 long seconds. His corner team, unaware of the scores, sent their man out to win the round, believing it to be a close affair, which played into the Mexican's hands. A minute in and Taylor swung himself off his feet throwing a left hook. Chavez bided his time, showing all the patience of a trained assassin. With just over a minute to go Lampley offered the opinion that Chavez didn't 'have the stuff to get it done', a statement that appeared accurate. Then, with seventeen seconds remaining, a marauding Chavez knocked Taylor down in the corner with a right hand. Taylor was in desperate trouble but with so little time remaining if he could get up then he would be all but there. He rose at six, unsteady but on his feet. Referee Richard Steele took a long look at Meldrick Taylor and, not liking what he saw, waved the contest off, with just two seconds left on the clock.

It was a decision that, to this day, ignites fierce debate. The fight was basically over; Chavez would have had no time to follow up; a world title unification should not end in such an unsatisfactory manner; why didn't the referee give Taylor the chance to make it through a few more seconds? These were the arguments observers posited against Steele's intervention and which were summarized by Larry Merchant when he interviewed Steele in the ring minutes after making his decision. Steele explained his rationale with conviction and clarity. The clock was irrelevant. In that moment there was only one thing that mattered to him: 'There's no fight worth a man's life. I don't care what it is or how many I do. When I get tired of seeing a guy getting pounded, pounded, pounded, and I think he's had enough, I'm gonna stop it.'

Kenny Bayless was a ringside inspector that night and was in the changing room with Taylor afterwards. He saw a severely dehydrated fighter, a fighter who vomited blood due to lacerations on the inside of his lip (doctors estimated he'd swallowed two pints of his own blood during the twelve rounds), a fighter who had orbital fractures over both eyes, a fighter who had nothing left to give and very possibly no capacity left to soak up any more punishment.

Richard Steele ensured that nobody would ever know what would have happened should he have allowed Julio Cesar Chavez to unload on Meldrick Taylor for even one more second. He knew what Taylor stood to gain but he also knew what he could possibly lose.

He wasn't prepared to take that chance, so he made the call and didn't give a damn what anybody thought about it.

It was a brave decision.

It was the right decision.

CHAPTER SEVEN

A Duty of Care – Trainers

> When you've boxed from the age of eight, like I did, you learn respect for your coach and you trust and respect them like a father. It's like Mr Miyagi and Daniel LaRusso. You never answer back, you never question what he is doing. 'Wax on, wax off. Why am I doing this?' 'Just fucking do it.' I'm getting pissed off doing it but I'm not going to argue or question it because I have that respect and that's what I've always been like with Rob.
>
> *Carl Froch talking about his relationship*
> *with trainer Rob McCracken*

L ike so many things in boxing, the nature of the relationship between a boxer and their trainer is, I believe, unique in sport. Carl Froch always referred to Rob McCracken, who trained him his entire professional career, as The Guru. Froch trusted and respected him 'like a father'; so much so that when he was inducted into the International Boxing Hall of Fame in Canastota, Upstate New York, in the summer of 2023, an honour afforded to precious few British fighters, Carl didn't take his wife Rachael with him to share the experience, he took McCracken.

The Mr Miyagi and Daniel LaRusso referred to in the quote are characters from the 1984 film *The Karate Kid*. The teenage LaRusso, upon moving to a new city, is bullied viciously by the high school big-shot Johnny Lawrence. His situation is dire and looks unlikely to improve until he finds a mentor in Miyagi, a Japanese man in his sixties. Miyagi teaches Daniel karate, in order that he will be able to defend himself against Lawrence, but also as a means of teaching him how to confront his fears and find his self-belief. The karate instruction is delivered via the relentless repetition of a series of mundane chores such as painting, waxing and sanding and, although Daniel doesn't initially see the point of it, he buckles down, trusting the process and the man who has devised it. Miyagi is a father figure, a psychologist, a best friend, and ideally that is the type of relationship a trainer needs to have with their fighter and exactly the type that is often to be found. The one aspect of Froch's synopsis that would be disputed by some is the notion that the pupil should obey the teacher unquestioningly. Some trainers prefer to work with boxers who do question them, who won't 'wax on, wax off' without understanding the reason behind doing it. Billy Graham is one such trainer: 'A lot of trainers prefer fighters who don't overthink, who like to be told what to do, who don't question it. I liked to be questioned, I preferred people like Matt Macklin and Ricky Hatton who were intelligent enough to be able to under-stand everything and also to know the reality of it, that this is boxing and that's the way it is.'

The closest useful comparison that can be made, in my esti-mation, with regard to the necessary bond and dynamic between boxer and trainer would be with those at play between the golfer and their caddy. Mentally, golf is a demanding sport due to the sheer amount of time available to a player to ponder what they should do next. In most sports, athletes make decisions at breakneck speed, operating on instinct rather than as a result of prolonged analysis, and they find a sense of release in surrendering to that spontaneity. In golf the paralysis that can result from introspective over-analysis is a very serious danger and that is where the caddy is vital. They have walked the course, gauged the conditions, mapped out the contours and calculated the yardages, and are able to furnish their player with all the information they need to help execute a successful shot before handing them the correct club, retreating to a safe distance and watching what unfolds. But the execution of said shot only has a chance of being successful if the golfer trusts their caddy, if they believe what the caddy is telling them, so that when they stand over their ball and draw that club back, they are able to commit to their swing, a mechanism grooved over hours and hours of repetitive practice, with confidence and conviction. If that trust isn't there then at the top of their swing, in that fraction of a second before they shift momentum and drag that clubhead down towards the ball, confidence and conviction will evaporate to be replaced by doubt and apprehension. The caddy cannot play the shot, just as the trainer cannot stay in the ring and throw the punches when the bell goes, but in each instance their proximity to the action and the regularity with which they are able to offer counsel gives them an influence and a responsibility that is not afforded to non-participants in other sports. But the comparison is imperfect because, whilst the stakes for a caddy are high, they are not as high as they are for the boxer's trainer. After all, while misreading the line of a putt or failing to anticipate the effect of a sudden, unexpected gust of wind can seriously damage a player's chances of winning, they are errors unlikely to damage their health. Making that distinction is in no way intended to trivialize the level of responsibility borne by individuals in other sports, it is made simply to illustrate that the boxing trainer has to ride an emotional rollercoaster like no other, and there is no getting off.

'There's nothing worse than a changing room when you've been beat by knockout because the room is just deafening silence. There's a numbness. It's horrible. Sat here talking to you stokes loads of memories, feelings, sickness, morbid fucking changing rooms where you're thinking, "Just get me out of here," but no one wants to make the move to get out. It's like a fucking wake. The fighter's there like the fucking corpse and no one knows what to say or make the first move to pack a bag to go or whatever. It's just horrible. Absolutely horrible. Them tears and cries of fighters. They haunt you, they absolutely haunt you. I can hear them now as I'm talking to you, the fists through walls, wives and girlfriends trying to console them. But the highs. Wow, that energy. That electricity of that win and that moment and that changing room. It could light up the UK, the energy, it's just another level. I've always tried to have the relationship that I don't care whether they're twenty-two or thirty-two, that really they're still an amateur boxer at age eleven or twelve and it's your responsibility to bring that child back from an amateur show back to the doorstep in the evening. And the guilt. I've seen the parents. They're looking at you like, "What happened?" And it just absolutely kills you, I hate it. It's the worst feeling in the world. You're so helpless. It's horrible, such a horrible feeling. But like I say, the wins . . . career-defining fights, when you've won, you're like, "Fuck you and fuck everyone else, we've got the win."'

This description of the emotional turmoil of the knockout for a trainer comes from the lips of Joe Gallagher, one of the UK's most prolific and successful trainers of recent years and a man who invests every ounce of himself in his profession and the boxers he chooses to work with. His vivid vignette lurches from one extreme to another. The low, the high, the low and back to the high again. Despair, elation, guilt, vindication, the crippling burden of responsibility that comes with having another person's life in your hands, it's all contained within those lines. It's an incredibly demanding role and one that takes its toll on a person. A trainer has to know exactly what their fighter is capable of, mentally, physically, emotionally, spiritually. That connection must be there because if it isn't then bad things can happen. If a trainer doesn't know the boxer in their charge on that level, or if they become blinded to the reality of a situation by their own ambition and determination to win, then that boxer can end up seriously damaged or dead. There's an old adage in boxing that states that a brave fighter doesn't need a brave corner, meaning that when you have a fighter who will do whatever it takes to win, who will not submit under any circumstances, then the last thing they need is someone in charge who is prepared to just keep sending them out there, round after round. There are scenarios which demand a trainer's intervention. Peter Fury, who guided nephew Tyson to his 2015 world heavyweight title win against Wladimir Klitschko and who now trains son Hughie and undisputed world super-middleweight champion Savannah Marshall, outlines such a scenario.

'If your fighter's getting outclassed and taking a beating then you know, don't you? Why send them out there and get them properly brain-damaged? It's not what you're there for. You're not there to be a brave man with someone else's body. You're not fighting, you're there to protect the fighter, so that's what you do. I know when a fighter's in hot water and getting beaten to pieces. If you feel there's no chance of winning then you pull them out.'

But in order to give their fighter the best possible chance to win, sometimes corners do have to be brave. Sometimes they have to force that child they're responsible for bringing back to their parents' doorstep to find that extra bit of resilience in the eye of the storm, to give them the opportunity to ride out that storm and come through the other side. Teddy Atlas told me he is always at pains to try and explain to his fighters that the agony they experience when they're under fire and beginning to feel like it's all too much for them, that it is fleeting, that it will pass if they can just hold on, whereas the regret they'll feel if they quit, if they submit, will not. Billy Graham spoke of the need to persuade fighters 'to do unnatural things to win because you want them to fucking win and they want to fucking win'. 'You can't be squeamish,' Graham said, and therein lies the excruciating inner conflict that comes with life leading a corner in boxing. Where does that boundary between squeamish and reckless lie? As Joe Gallagher explains, there's no map, no calculator, no method that can be employed via which responsibility can be abdicated or shared.

'There's a very fine line. You've got to understand what your fighter is capable of or not capable of. And if you've got to ask them to do something that he's never ever done in his career before, never done in the gym, then why do you keep him in there? You've not got the power to turn it around. You've not got it. This kid is not gonna blow up any time soon and we're beginning to get into a highlight-reel knockout situation and he shouldn't be in there. It's very hard. There's a lot of pressure on a trainer. They're out there for three minutes and in them three minutes, they can have good moments, bad moments, they can be winning two minutes and thirty-five seconds of it, then have a bad twenty seconds, and the pressure you can then feel in the arena . . . all of a sudden the oxygen has been sucked out of the ring. All of a sudden your fighter can't breathe. You've got to tell them the right thing, there and then, and you're under pressure and you can sense the crowd and the walls are closing in and you can feel them walls closing in as a trainer. That pressure to say the right thing within forty to fifty seconds is huge.'

The forty to fifty seconds Gallagher refers to here is the amount of time a trainer has between rounds to communicate with their fighter. One of the great privileges of covering and watching boxing is getting to witness those crucial seconds, to listen in. It can be incredibly intense and it's at its most intense when a fighter comes back to the corner hurt and hanging on, that's when you can see those walls closing in. I've watched from my commentary position on many occasions, just feet away, as a trainer looks into the eyes of a person whose physical wellbeing he is responsible for and makes an almost instant assessment of what that person is now capable of. The clock is ticking and the trainer has to be able to reach through that fog that shrouds the senses of a hurt fighter and find them, connect with them and bring them back into the here and now. It's quite something to behold. Their tone and expression has to be calm yet urgent, robust but reassuring, any hint of panic and that fog will thicken and become impenetrable. But before they know it the minute between rounds is over and at that point a decision has to be made, a decision they'll have to live with if the worst happens; do they put the boxer back in harm's way and risk their health or stop the fight and shatter their dreams? As stated previously, these are not decisions that are demanded of coaches in other sports and not circumstances to be found outside of a life spent in the emergency services or armed forces.

It's very difficult and the decisions trainers make are subject to extreme outcome bias. If they send a hurt fighter back into the breach and they manage to survive, turn the fight around and win, then the trainer is a genius. But, on the other hand, if they answer the bell for the next round only to get promptly knocked out then the condemnation of the decision will be swift. Nobody can expect any trainer to foresee a type-one knockout, that would be impossible, it's the type-two knockouts that haunt a cornerman. As we sit in his cottage, having moved inside from the patio, I ask Billy Graham if he felt he should have removed Matthew Macklin from the line of fire against Jamie Moore. He takes a little bit of time to answer. In the room, opposite me, propped up against the glass of his conservatory wall are a framed pair of Muhammad Ali shorts and an empty snake tank. The tank used to house a grass snake given to him by Sean O'Hagan, father and trainer of world featherweight champion Josh Warrington. Billy loves animals. He once shared a Salford flat with a monkey and an iguana and will without hesitation tell you that he prefers animals to people. But boxers are not included in that collective. He loves boxers and cared deeply for all his fighters. Like his animals, they relied upon him, they trusted him and he accepted that responsibility willingly, onerous though it could be.

'That's one of the fights what disturbed me, that fight, because I could have pulled him out and I found it hard, dealing with it, the fact that I didn't. With hindsight it's obvious that I should have but the fact of the matter is that I knew Matt had the power to take Jamie out. Matt was always one punch away from knocking him out and I knew that and that's how I justified it and I've talked to Jamie about it and he made me feel better because I have problems with that fight. But like I said, Matt was always one shot away and he did have that kind of power to knock Jamie out, and if he'd done it then leaving him in would have been seen as a great bit of corner work. It's terrible.'

In my opinion Billy Graham judges himself harshly. I would argue that even with the benefit of hindsight, it still isn't obvious that he should have pulled Macklin out of the fight. An experienced and very capable referee in Victor Loughlin could have stopped the fight but didn't because he also still felt that Macklin was capable of winning. Outcome bias, the temptation to judge all decisions based purely on their outcome, is an unfair and unhelpful road to go down. Furthermore, there are also scenarios in which a trainer still does not stop a fight even when they do feel confident a knockout is coming. Dave Coldwell, as discussed in chapter four, knew Tony Bellew was in serious trouble when he rose from his stool for round eight of his fight against Oleksandr Usyk but he didn't feel he could stop the fight because of what was at stake, because it was for the title of undisputed champion and because with it being Bellew's last ever fight there was no other day to save him for. Thankfully, and Coldwell was thankful for it, Usyk applied a swift and decisive finish and saved him from having to pull Bellew out, something he would have done if he'd adjudged that the Ukrainian had started to inflict a sustained and irreversible beating on his fighter. Bellew's opinion on the matter was that Coldwell knew that he was never under any circumstances to throw the towel in and that should he do so their friendship would be fractured to the point where it could never recover. But that would not have stopped Coldwell from doing it if he had thought it needed to be done, and that would be equally true of any competent cornerman.

But although Coldwell may have been thankful the ending was mercifully clinical, the aftermath was still brutal: 'We'd had a great run, the Makabu fight, and we'd never lost together. That was the end. That was the end of the book. That was the last page of the book. It was the worst ending. And it didn't matter what happened in the first six rounds; that last bit, that last fifteen seconds of the fight, that was the worst possible ending. So it kind of like crushed everything and you're deflated, you're upset. You're absolutely devastated. It doesn't matter that you've lost to a special fighter. Doesn't matter. It doesn't matter. Still now I'm talking about it, it doesn't matter. It absolutely crushed everything. I love Usyk. I'm a massive fan, but because of how that that made me feel, I've still to this day never had a photo with him. I see him regularly and you know I get on with him really well. You know, he comes over to me to speak to me but it's still . . . it still hurts. I've never watched the fight all way through.'

Coldwell spoke in chapter four of having 'no regrets' and although I believe him, because in this hard business and with a fighter like Bellew the way the fight ended was the only way it could realistically have ended, I do wonder if he ever ponders what might have been if Bellew, having been badly hurt at the end of that sixth round, had been willing and able to follow his trainer's advice to 'take a round off and don't punch until you feel your legs are back' rather than go out swinging in the seventh. I suspect he would love to be able to turn the clock back and explore that counterfactual because navigating a fighter through rough waters, giving them the right advice and getting them to follow it when they're hurt, that is the business end for a trainer, that is where they are worth their weight in gold and that is where that trust kicks in.

That is not to say that Bellew didn't follow Coldwell's advice because he didn't trust him – he trusted him implicitly, but in certain cases, and this was one, even a very experienced fighter can reach for the panic button and once that button has been pushed it overrides everything else. 'When you start fatiguing mentally, you start making the wrong choices. And that's when you start pressing the panic button a little bit, doing things that you shouldn't be doing and that you know you shouldn't be doing, but you do it anyway because you think, "I've got to get him. I've got to slow him down. I've got to get rid of him because my tank is running low." You're not thinking, "Well, if I get through this then I'll get a second wind," you're not thinking that. You're thinking, "Shit. I'm feeling it now and he's cranking it up. I've got to stop him cranking it up." But you can't stop him from cranking it up. It's a level of panic, because your judgement is completely clouded. And you're making the wrong choices. If you're calm and you're cool and you're relaxed even when you get caught, you can get through it. But when you're not clear thinking, and when that doubt comes into your head and you're feeling your energy levels go, you're in trouble.'

Bellew had reached the point where he could no longer think clearly, his instincts took over and the fight ended the only way it could, with his trainer powerless to prevent it. But there are many cases in which a trainer is able to talk a fighter down from the ledge, cases in which the fighter is still thinking clearly enough to make the decision as to whether they want to continue or whether they want to quit. Quit is a dirty word in boxing and once a fighter is labelled as a quitter then that stigma is hard to shed. Fellow pros will talk about someone 'having quit in them' as if it's some kind of virus which lies dormant in the bone and sinew, ready to invade the system once the mercury at ringside rises above a certain level. A traditional view is that the bravery required to keep going, to do whatever it takes, is something that a person either has or doesn't have, something that cannot be taught. 'You cannot put in what God left out,' is a phrase I've heard often and the belief that there are certain required minerals that an athlete needs to have from birth is one that is commonly held across the sporting landscape. But is that belief valid or is it merely a convenient excuse that coaches in any sport can reach for if they cannot get their athlete to respond to a situation in the required manner? If a fighter quits in the boxing ring, if they go down and stay there, although not seemingly badly hurt, if they simply stop punching and wait for the referee to stop it, if they feign an injury, if they tell their corner they can't do it any more, if they go down and then deliberately rise just too late to beat the count – is that solely due to an innate deficiency on their part? Or is the trainer also to blame for not being able to recognize what could be about to happen and talk them out of it, make them believe that they can continue, that they do have what it takes, that the bravery they need is in there? My belief (which others have shared) has always been that a good trainer can teach bravery, that they can locate that seam of courage buried below the surface and skilfully mine it. This isn't possible with just anyone but with boxers it is because they are, by definition, brave and that seam of courage is there, waiting to be mined.

Jamie Moore was a brave fighter and is now a trainer. He trains top professionals at the Moss Side Fire Station gym in Manchester, about a ten-minute walk from the famous Champs Camp that Joe Gallagher works out of, but he also coaches youngsters, children who are at the very start of their boxing journey. These kids don't stride through the gym doors oozing aggression and confidence, most are riddled with fear, panic writ large when they spar for the first time, wide eyes ready to well with tears when they get hit for the first time. Many of them seem certain to quit after their excruciating first session and many do exactly that, having discovered that the boxing ring isn't for them. But many don't and the ones that do come back, and they're often the ones you least expect to see again, return because that seam of courage is there. How plentiful it is and how easy it will be to reach, nobody can know at that point, but it's there. According to Moore:

'I've said this loads of times down the years. I'm just guessing that thousands of years ago, we [fighters] were the stupid bastards who got sent out hunting for food. Because you're stupid enough to do it. You know what I mean? Like we wasn't the smart ones who set traps and stuff like that, we'd go out with a spear and go and try and kill something. So there must be a reason why. Like when you first go to a gym as a kid and you get punched in the nose for the first time and it bleeds. We cry. Why? What inside you says, "I'm gonna go back and do that again." It's a competitive mindset. It's something built in our genes which goes, "I'm not having him beat me, I'm going to go back and do it again." And that's what I mean about it being teachable because at that stage, you know, you've got something inside which is teachable and it's bravery.'

It remains teachable when a fighter reaches professional level. Moore used to train a boxer called Tommy Coyle. 'Boom Boom' was his nickname and, by the time he retired, this extremely likeable Hullensian had earned himself the reputation of being a true warrior, a real-life Rocky Balboa, someone who got knocked down plenty of times but who never stayed down, who was ready to go to war at the drop of a hat. Fight fans adored him because although he wasn't the best fighter out there, he gave it everything for their entertainment and when he came up short, he would dust himself down and go again. He was brave and vulnerable and beloved for being both. But Coyle needed help locating that aforementioned seam of courage. Jamie told me that Tommy had come into the gym one day in 2014, early on in camp for a fight against an Argentine called Daniel Brizuela, and as he sat on the ring apron wrapping his hands, he mentioned that he'd watched Moore's classic encounter with Matthew Macklin the previous evening and asked his trainer if he thought he'd be capable of walking through the fire in the same way that Moore had against Macklin. Jamie replied that nobody can ever really know how a person will respond in an extreme situation like that until they're in it but that in his opinion, yes, he did think Tommy had it in him to bite down on his gumshield and go to that place. Fast-forward six weeks and the two of them are at the Ice Arena in Hull and deep in a torrid fight against Brizuela. Coyle had been down in the second round and then again in the sixth. Right at the end of the sixth he got sunk by a body shot in his own corner, made that dreadful gasping winded sound, looked at his trainer and shook his head. He wanted out. He wanted to quit.

But Moore wasn't about to let that happen: '"Get up," I said to him. So he got up and took a big deep breath and it looked like he was going to cry and the bell saved him. So he sat on the stool and I said, "Look at me. Remember that conversation what we had six weeks ago?" I said, "This is that fight now, can you do it?" He just nodded his head but he was like feeling sorry for himself. So I slapped him across the face and said, "Can you fucking do this?" and he said, "Yeah," and I said, "OK then, stop feeling sorry for yourself."'

Moore knew what to say to his fighter and, just as importantly, he knew how to say it.

'You can't be squeamish but you can't scream and shout either. You've got to know your fighter. Because with Tommy you need to put your arm around him, to give him a cuddle and make him understand. And then once he was on the same page, then you can say, "Right, fucking come on now." But you had to get him on your side first. There's some fighters you need to give a bollocking to straightaway, some need that cracking of the whip, so you've got to understand your fighter. So there was no quit in him that night, after we had that conversation, but he nearly made the decision to quit. And then he ended up turning it around. He got put down again in the eleventh round but his attitude was different.'

Coyle won the fight. After being down three times by the end of the sixth, he knocked Brizuela down once in the eighth, twice in the eleventh whilst going down himself in that same round, and then stopped his opponent in the twelfth and final round. It was utter mayhem and on that night 'Boom Boom' was born. Having walked through the fire once he knew he could it again and Moore now had a different problem, which was convincing him that just because he could do it that way, it didn't mean he should always choose to, that sometimes it was better to box, to hit and not get hit. Coyle's final fight came at Madison Square Garden, New York, a true Mecca of boxing, in June 2019 where he opened a show topped by Anthony Joshua vs Andy Ruiz with a scheduled twelve-rounder against former world champion Chris Algieri. It was a tough fight. I commentated on it from ringside and after a good opening for Coyle the tide started to turn around midway and there was no sign he could turn it back. At the end of the eighth, after a punishing finish to the round for Tommy, myself and Matt Macklin, who was working with me, wondered, as Jamie was walking his fighter back to his stool, whether he'd let him out for another round. He didn't. He'd seen enough. He'd witnessed his fighter grow from being on the verge of quitting against Brizuela to being incapable of making that decision; from being in a position where his instinct was to consider saving himself to one in which he needed saving from himself.

'He's trained himself to not quit and at this point he'd got the reputation of being one of the ballsiest fuckers you'll ever meet in your life and he'll never diminish that reputation, so he'll go out on his shield no matter what, so he needs saving from himself. He's not gonna win the fight so why the fuck would I leave him in there? I remember afterwards, loads of people kept patting me on the back going, "Fucking brave decision, that was a great decision." It was easy for me. It was an easy decision, because of our history and my knowledge of the situation.'

Moore plays down his own part here where he describes Coyle as having 'trained himself not to quit'. The ability not to quit, that courage, that bravery, was in Tommy Coyle but it needed a good trainer to extract it, to locate that seam and mine it for all it was worth. 'Boom Boom' went from a fighter who was on the verge of quitting in the face of a very possible knockout to one who would rather get knocked out than quit. People say that can't be taught but, with the right raw materials, it can.

A trainer's role, with regard to the knockout, is not simply to protect their fighter from it though. Yes, they want to ward off the temptation of Muhammad Ali's Near Room, but equally they want to cause the fighter in the opposite corner to succumb to that temptation. Knockout power, the ability to deliver that telling blow, that punch from the gods, is another good example of something that people will often claim is a natural ability, not something that can be taught, and whilst it's true that some pugilists will have naturally heavier hands than others, just as any person can possess more natural aptitude for any task than another person, it most certainly can be taught. Billy Graham explains why, and how.

'I hear people say that this or that is natural and you can't teach it. Like you can't teach people to punch. That's bollocks, because you can teach a fighter to punch. Because the mechanics of boxing, that's my game; balance, distance, the mechanics, all of that, that's what I've got an aptitude for. But they have to be athletic enough. Not everybody can do it. For example, I could never teach anything to one of my fighters, teaching him the mechanics of punching, he just couldn't do it, he wasn't athletic enough, his anticipation wasn't enough. But somebody who understands mechanics and is athletic enough, and has the right anticipation and speed, can be taught to punch. Take a footballer, I think they'd be easy to teach because they've got great balance, they're connected to the floor, always, because your feet have got to be in position, it all starts from the floor, so a footballer would be easy because it starts from there, the hand is just the hammer at the end of it. So if someone's a decent fucking coach and the person is athletic enough then you can teach it. Everything can be improved but the one who's born with it, without having to think about it, he's in front anyway. You've got to have the minerals but if you've got the minerals then you can be taught the mechanics of boxing.'

Peter Fury likens the fist to the conker on the end of a string. Without the string the conker isn't going to do much damage; it doesn't weigh much, if you had a stick or twig of the same weight then you wouldn't achieve much by hitting someone with it. But attach the conker to a string and you've got a serious weapon if you can get the distance and leverages and all-round mechanics of swinging it right.

Someone who knows for certain that a fighter can be taught to knock people out is Andy Lee. Andy was a very good international amateur who went on to become a world champion at middleweight as a professional. He is now a trainer, passing on what he learnt from his trainers to his own fighters. As an amateur, representing Ireland, he won a silver medal at the World Junior Championships and then as a senior qualified for the 2004 Athens Olympics, where to his bitter disappointment he lost in the second round. He was a very skilful fighter but not a puncher, which is not unusual in the amateur ranks. The main difference between amateur and professional boxing was then, and remains now, the fact that to win a fight in the amateur ranks a fighter does not have to damage their opponent – the emphasis being on hitting the target, rather than hurting that target, on landing a scoring blow, much like in fencing, rather than trying to decapitate someone. What that means is that amateur boxers often don't fully commit to punches, instead choosing to pull off the punch almost as soon, if not slightly before, it lands, so that they don't get caught with a counterpunch and concede a scoring blow themselves. When a fighter turns professional they then have to be capable of making that shift in mentality and style which sees them commit to the punch, to planting their feet and driving through the target, to being willing to risk being hit hard in order to hit their opponent hard, because pro boxing is the hurt business and if a fighter wants to succeed in that arena then they have to accept that. If a boxer doesn't want to accept that and is unwilling to make that shift then no matter how skilful they may be, at some point they will get found out and it will be a brutal experience when they do.

As Andy told me, he never knocked anyone out as an amateur, he stopped hardly any of his opponents, but he'd still attracted the attention of professional boxing's ultimate knockout factory, the Detroit Kronk gym, presided over by the legendary Emanuel Steward. Steward, one of boxing's all-time great trainers, was all about the knockout and it was to the Kronk, to that infernal, subterranean boxing blast furnace, made famous by the likes of Thomas 'The Hitman' Hearns, that Lee headed when he hung up his Irish amateur vest. Steward had been following his progress since his silver at the World Juniors. He wanted the Irishman, he was going to teach him to be a pro, and at the Kronk that meant teaching him to knock people out. Lee knew what was expected of him from the very first day he walked through the door of the gym to be greeted by the banshee howl of 'fresh meat' issuing forth from the lips of Cornelius 'K9' Bundrage (a future IBF light-middleweight champion). Respect had to be earned and it was earned by knockouts.

'My first pro fight I went the distance and I became paranoid that I wasn't a big puncher and that I wouldn't get knockouts and, being in the Kronk, probably the worst thing you could be was a non-puncher, because everyone was getting knockouts and because of the priority they put on getting knockouts. Like, if you won, it was "OK, you won" but if you got a knockout you were probably getting a high five and a pat on the back.'

If skilful points wins were your currency, which they had been for Andy his whole boxing life up until his arrival in Detroit, then your money was no good at the Kronk. Steward and his fighters engendered an atmosphere where self-worth in that ring was defined by the ability to dominate the opponent and win by that most decisive method, an environment where a fighter's ego would demand of them that they be capable of doing it. Professional athletes – and this becomes truer the more elevated the level they operate at – largely sustain themselves with a diet of praise and embarrassment. If they succeed, they are fed praise by their coaches, by their contemporaries, by their gym mates, and if they fail then they are left to stew in their own embarrassment, unable to bear it, desperate for the next opportunity to cast it off and replace it with that praise they crave. It was a baptism of fire for Lee but he was a very willing student.

'With Emanuel he would teach me, first of all how to set up a knockout, by using the jab, changing the pace and the speed of the punching and using the jab to blind them or distract them; get them used to seeing something, the shape and look of your body or your hand and the way it's going, and the next thing, to change it at the last second, and punch with a different speed. That was how we would get the knockouts, it was about setting the knockout up, hitting the guy with a punch he couldn't see or wasn't used to feeling. Emanuel put a lot of emphasis on locking the elbow, wrist and fist, and really driving through with it. Full extension but especially locking that wrist and the elbow, driving through with the hand.'

Before too long 'Irish' Andy Lee was a knockout artist and the owner of one of the most feared right hooks in boxing. It was a dramatic transformation and one that developed even further when he teamed up with a new trainer in Adam Booth following Steward's passing in 2012. Booth, who trained David Haye throughout Haye's most successful years, was also a man steeped in the psychology and mentality of the knockout.

'With Adam it became something different. I was a lot more powerful when I was with Adam because training with him I was more athletic, I was more conditioned, I was more of an athlete with Adam and I became a pure power machine, and although the knockouts came from shots they didn't see, it was more because of power. With Adam the emphasis was more on power, and sinking into your legs, bending your knees and really twisting. Like swinging a baseball bat or a golf club: first the hip, then the shoulder, and at the last second it's the hand.'

Two trainers, with two different takes on achieving the same thing. The common denominator? Repetition. Practice makes permanent and therefore if an athlete's practices are good then it's astonishing what can be achieved, as Andy Lee explains: 'Repetition is an amazing thing, physical repetition and also mental repetition, because subconsciously you're so much quicker than you are consciously. For instance, when I knocked out John Jackson, which is one of my most famous knockouts, I threw the punch and then I had the thought to throw the punch. The punch was first, then the thought. And if you watch the knockout, I walk away and I actually check it happens. But you can only do that through repetition, to make it instinctual. You have to dress it up. If you watch my fight with Carl Daniels I threw a hook to the body, hook to the body, hook to the body and then at the last moment came up with a hook to the head. A change of pace and a change of rhythm can have a devastating effect.'

Repetition allowed him to train his own instincts, to embed a new 'natural' response, proof positive that with the right basic ingredients and an open mind, a willing student can be taught almost anything by the right coach.

But not everyone agrees that the ability to knock your opponent out can be taught. One person, and he's by no means the only one, who falls more on the nature rather than nurture side of the argument is former unified heavyweight champion of the world Anthony

Joshua. I caught up with Anthony at the press conference to announce his fight versus Otto Wallin, which had just been officially set for Riyadh, Saudi Arabia, two days before Christmas. The card had been named The Day of Reckoning and AJ had just been sharing a top table with long-time rival Deontay Wilder, who would fight that same night. Joshua told me that in his opinion knocking someone out was 'a natural gift, either you've got it or you don't'. I would argue, though, that Anthony is the perfect storm of nature and nurture. He always had the basic ingredients. As Billy Graham described it, he's 'one who's born with it', and so 'without having to think about it, he's in front anyway'. In that regard his argument that 'either you've got it or you don't' is a valid one. But he is also someone with a phenomenal ability to learn, that is the reputation he has, and the timeframe within which he has managed to achieve what he has in the sport proves that reputation is deserved. Those natural tools therefore have been enhanced by the coaching he has received and rendered more deadly than they would have been without it, with the technically correct, textbook way in which he delivers his punches, I think, bearing that theory out. Deontay Wilder, on the other hand, delivers his punches very often with the kind of unorthodox technique that, it can be argued, couldn't or indeed wouldn't be taught. That's not to say Wilder's trainers have had no impact on his punching – after all, a hallmark of a good coach is knowing when not to interfere, when to leave well enough alone – but of all the boxers I've seen live, the Bronze Bomber, as the Alabaman is known, is the most natural puncher, the most natural knockout artist of them all, a subject he addressed at the press conference.

'I have the ability to knock a man out with a single punch and this is something that's been with me all my life, it's not something that's just been developed. That's what I come to do, you know, that's my only mission I come to do. When I look at the heavyweight division, you know, a win is a good thing, it's just like basketball, I can shoot twos, I can shoot threes, but there ain't nothing like a dunk.'

The nature versus nurture debate is a fascinating one and a good place to finish this discussion of the trainer's impact on the knockout. Their role in general, and the role of the corner on the night of the fight, has always fascinated me. In my opinion, what separates a good trainer, a good corner, from an average one is the ability to see things as they actually are, rather than how they would like them to be, and for their decision-making process to be founded in that reality rather than an alternative fantasy. That realism will give them the opportunity to make the correct decision, to do what they believe to be the right thing rather than the easy thing, regardless of the potential repercussions. As Joe Gallagher pointed out, there is an enormous amount of pressure on boxing trainers and often there is not the support available to them that there possibly should be. The level of responsibility they have to accept is more, it could be argued, than a person should be expected to tolerate, but that is the nature of the job and there is no real way to change it, as boxing requires decisiveness above all things. Hesitation or, worse, panic can be fatal and, as impressive as it is to witness a well-run corner, it is just as alarming to see a disorganized one. It's a distressing sight to see a fighter sat in the middle of chaos, deafened by the white noise of numerous voices, their tired body and mind being even further exhausted by the tumult that surrounds them.

The trainer has a big impact on the knockout but the knockout also has a huge impact on them. It seems to me that a boxing trainer has a love-hate relationship with the knockout, that their feelings towards it are similar to the feelings of craving and revulsion that torture an addict. It also seems to me that, like any addiction, it takes more than it gives, that emotionally the knockout leaves the trainer in deficit, not profit, with the feeling of elation that a win can bring wiped out by the self-loathing that can be provoked by a defeat. They feel responsible when it happens to the person in their care and that responsibility, that culpability, whether justified or not, weighs heavily.

That weight would be too heavy for me, that much I do know.

CHAPTER EIGHT

Fear

> Fear is like fire. You can make it work for you: it can warm
> you in the winter, cook your food when you're hungry, give
> you light when you are in the dark, and produce energy.
> Let it go out of control and it can hurt you, even kill you.
>
> *Cus D'Amato*

F ear.
  Every person in the world feels it and every person in the
world needs to learn how to handle it. Fear of failure can at
best hinder ambition and at worst destroy it. Fear is closely aligned
with ego because often what people fear about failure most of all is
the embarrassment, the humiliation that can accompany it. This is
particularly true of athletes. To be a successful athlete is, by definition, to be a winner: success cannot come in any other form. Even
in a team sport, where individual achievement can still stand out in
defeat, that outstanding individual will yearn for a winning environment, a winning culture, and will seek one out if it cannot be
created where they are. In chapter three I discussed my belief that
in the early 2000s, elite sporting culture was dominated by an

attitude that to even celebrate winning was akin to failure, akin to an acceptance that success was an aspiration rather than an expectation. It is also my belief that in more recent years there has been a rebellion against what I would describe as this culture of fear, with coaches instead attempting to create environments within which players are encouraged to concentrate purely on the execution of their skills and to do so unencumbered by concern for the outcome of that execution and therefore free of the fear of failure.

It is both a courageous and ambitious ideal but one that has been applied with significant success by Brendon McCullum, the coach of the England Test cricket team. Cricket is a detailed and complicated sport and unusual in that it is made up of a one-on-one duel between batter and bowler conducted within the framework of a team dynamic. Detailed knowledge of the sport is not necessary here, suffice it to say that it is not a landscape in which there is any place to hide for its practitioners; they attend to their business completely exposed, mistakes and shortcomings glaringly obvious. As a player McCullum captained New Zealand. He was extremely good, with his play characterized by his positive approach, by his willingness to take risks if he felt the reward on offer was sufficient, to weigh up the percentage chance of success of a certain action in the split second available to him to do so and to then commit without hesitation to that action. It's exactly what he did in the 2015 World Cup final in which he captained his country against arch enemies Australia, one of the biggest possible occasions for a Kiwi sportsperson. Failure was unthinkable, as he explained to the *New Zealand Herald*.

> All my life I had dreamt of that moment. As a child, I played it out against mates day after day, and as a man, I practised for it with an almost eerie certainty that one day it would come. I mean, the World Cup final, against Australia, at the MCG on a hot and sunny day and I was captain of my

country. I won the toss, chose to bat and walked out to open the innings. It cannot get any better. I took first ball and the plan was to set the tone. I was more ready for this than anyone outside my closest circle of friends and family could begin to understand. I was facing Mitchell Starc, the quickest and best bowler in the tournament. I was excited but not overexcited; in fact, I reckon I was pitch-perfect for anything Starcy might throw at me.

Determined to make a statement, in the first over of the match he swung at the third ball he faced, missed and was dismissed. It was the cricketing equivalent of getting knocked out on the grandest stage but he refused the figurative sackcloth and ashes of shame and humiliation that an athlete had traditionally been required to wear following such a failure, telling a Sky Sports podcast: 'I got back in the dressing room, sat down and just laughed. You know why I laughed back in the dressing room? Because I forgot the only single thing that really matters. I forgot to watch the ball. Yes, it was a bad shot, but it wasn't a bad idea, no way. If I had watched the ball and hit it well, the tone would have been set. But I didn't. After a lifetime of dreaming about exactly that moment, I messed it up. So I laughed – otherwise I'd still be crying.'

'You can't have regrets,' he said; 'It is what it is.' It is that attitude that McCullum now instils in his players as a coach and those players buy into it because they know that the man preaching that gospel to them had gone through what should have been the worst possible experience any player could have, the kind of experience from which often there is no full recovery, but that he survived it. The New Zealander wants his players to understand that the fear of the worst happening is worse than the experience of it happening. Only when they understand that, can they remove that debilitating obstacle from their psyche and perform to the best of their ability. The performances that McCullum's side have produced since he took charge of the England team in early 2022 and the results that have accompanied them have proved that his approach works.

Can such an approach work for a boxer? Can a boxer operate unhindered by the potential consequences of defeat? The answer is no. Fear is a fighter's constant companion, like a stream bubbling away in the back of their conscious mind, sometimes as still and serene as a millpond, at other times a churning foment. It is always there, it needs to be there. Cus D'Amato, mentor to Mike Tyson and one of boxing's foremost philosophers, recognized its value: 'Every fighter that ever lived had fear. A boy comes to me and tells me that he's not afraid, I'd send him to a doctor to find out what the hell's the matter with him, because this is not a normal reaction. The fighter that's gone into the ring and hasn't experienced fear is either a liar or a psychopath.'

'A liar or a psychopath.' That is an intriguing line. A psychopath would not prosper in the boxing ring. Their lack of empathy and awareness and their too-dominant ego would not allow for the acceptance a fighter needs to have of the possibilities of life in the ring. A psychopath would not be able to achieve the compartmentalization that sees a fighter accept and admit to themselves that they could be knocked out whilst remaining mentally steadfast that it will not happen. The ability to lie, more specifically to lie to themselves, however, is crucial to a fighter's prospects, for it is that ability that enables them to walk that fine line between self-confidence and self-delusion that they have to tread, that allows them to reconcile themselves with the two sides of the same coin that are bravery and vulnerability, knowledge and denial. That is what this chapter is about. It is a deeper exploration of the mentality of those who sign up to life in pursuit of the knockout, of how they handle fear and nerves and of the tools and coping mechanisms they use to help them navigate such a contradictory existence.

As D'Amato states in the chapter's opening quote, 'fear is like fire', and fighters need that fire because boxers cannot operate unencumbered by the fear of failure: the stakes are too high for that approach to be viable. Getting knocked out is not the same as swinging and missing a ball in a cricket World Cup final or producing a double fault on a tennis court at match point at Wimbledon. The consequences of losing in the ring have to be respected, they have to be feared, but, as D'Amato says, that fear can not only be shackled, it can also be employed to a fighter's benefit. An individual must be able to do this, but, as Carl Froch describes, it takes time and dedication:

'I was a really nervous amateur. I felt like crying sometimes, I felt like hiding, I remember going to the toilet before I walked to the ring and I'd be on my own and I'd be thinking to myself, "If I just didn't come out of the toilets now, if I just jumped out of that window and nobody saw me again, what would happen? I'd be alright. Why am I doing this to myself." As a kid, I'm talking ten, eleven, twelve years old. And then you slowly get confident but you're always nervous because you can't stop the adrenal gland from releasing adrenaline and when that adrenaline gets pumped into your veins, you feel your stomach churning, your legs go weak, you start shaking and you get scared, and it's fight or flight then. It's a natural reaction, it's how you cope with that reaction and how you deal with it and I made nerves my friend. And that was psychological, that was success breeding confidence, so I was nervous but I was full of confidence from my training, from my previous wins. And my whole pro career, I was ridiculously nervous, every fight, but I backed myself because I trained so hard to make up for the nerves, so I was confident I could put in a performance.'

Froch has always been very honest about his relationship with nerves. It would be easy to assume that someone like him, given how astonishingly tough he was in the ring, emerged from the womb bombastic and bullet-proof, invincible self-belief stitched into every fibre of his body and soul, but that assumption would be wide of the mark. Nobody is born like that. How a person comes to handle fear and nerves, how they get comfortable being uncomfortable, varies from person to person and at this juncture I am going to introduce new characters who will inform the discussion.

Johnny Nelson, who featured briefly in chapter two, is a former world cruiserweight champion. He won the WBO title in 1999 and then defended it a record thirteen times before retiring undefeated as champion. Recently awarded an MBE and for a long time now a prominent member of the boxing media, he gives the appearance of a man to whom athletic success came naturally, easily even. But his path to that level of success seemed non-existent when he started out. He lost his first three professional fights, at which point most people would have quit. He had no self-belief, but with the help of his trainer and mentor Brendan Ingle, he found it, bit by bit, which allowed him to tame a debilitating fear of being humiliated and hurt, and channel it in a positive way.

Fabio Wardley, at the time of writing, is British and Commonwealth heavyweight champion, a man who knocks people out but who thus far has not been knocked out, indeed he has yet to lose, in any boxing arena. His route into professional boxing came via four unlicensed or 'white collar' bouts, as they're described, so not for him the traditional schooling of the amateur boxing gym. That background has led people to question him, me included, and contributed to the 'impostor syndrome' that he admits is and will probably always be part of his psychological make-up.

Anthony Yarde is a two-time world title challenger at light-heavyweight. Like Wardley, he turned professional with very little experience and, also like Fabio, has found himself questioned, doubted, throughout his career. Yarde, and trainer Tunde Ajayi, have always chosen to go their own way, to believe in their own method, a method which has often been at odds with the traditionalism that exists in all sports. Anthony has fought for world titles twice, going in deep against Sergey Kovalev and Artur Beterbiev, both devastating punchers, and giving a good account of himself both times, collapsing with exhaustion in the eleventh round against Kovalev in Chelyabinsk, Russia, and getting stopped on his feet by Beterbiev in London. Yarde and Wardley are both knockout fighters, with thirty-nine of their combined forty-one wins coming via that method.

Karriss Artingstall and Lauren Price are GB Olympians, who are now in the early stages of their pro careers at featherweight and welterweight respectively. As amateurs they achieved an awful lot, with Price winning literally every major title in becoming European, Commonwealth, World and Olympic gold medallist, whilst Artingstall claimed silver at the Europeans, bronze at the Worlds and then bronze at the same Tokyo Olympics. They are both undefeated as professionals, with Price already having become the first woman to win a British title. They are also partners, sharing their journey, walking that hardest road in sport together. Prior to their boxing careers Lauren had won world titles in kickboxing and earned full senior international honours in football for Wales whilst still a teenager, whilst Karriss had served in the British army.

The first thing a fighter must do is properly examine their fear, characterize it, make it real, give it a face and a name. As Nelson points out, it's no use closing your eyes and pretending it's not there, hoping, like a child playing hide and seek, that if you can't see it, then it can't see you: 'You've got to run with it. If you run away from it then it'll catch you. You have to face your fear. You have to be your fear, and I know that sounds stupid but you have to be part of it. Because no matter how hard you try and distract yourself and not think about it, it's going to creep up, no matter what you do.'

Fabio Wardley knows that feeling only too well. There is no ignoring it: 'It's funny because for me it's there all the way through camp. If you have a bad training session, if you have a bad sparring session, you think to yourself, "Am I actually any good? Am I out of my depth? Is this a step too far? Am I not all I'm hyped up to be?" And with me in particular, because I'm on the run I'm on and I'm undefeated and stuff and people are saying, "You're so good, you could do this, you could do that," that leaves so much more room for pressure and doubting yourself when you have those little moments which you always get in a camp, of doubting yourself and thinking, "Oh no, maybe I'm not everything everyone's saying I am." That's when the kind of fear will set in and it's funny because no matter how much good you do in a camp when you're training for a fight, the bad things always stick with you ten times more.'

That inner voice cannot be allowed to remain unanswered. There must be a dialogue, a type of Socratic dialectic, out of which a rationality emerges which allows him to move forward. He continues: 'If I double down on it too much and sit in it, that's where myself and a lot of people really spiral and get in your own head too much. It is that feeling of acceptance, "OK, I'll figure it out." The only way to really combat it is to think about the wins you've had and think about when you've had these doubts in the past and these conversations in your head and then think to yourself, "OK, well, things haven't gone well in camp in the past but I did pretty well there." It's like evidence to yourself that, "OK, actually, stuff goes wrong but so far you've done well to figure it out, so there's nothing to say you can't do that again." It's a repeated cycle, a conversation that doesn't seem to go away.'

He knows that the conversation will be repeated, it's a continual exercise, but if that same rationality is able to be applied to every dialogue then that inner voice, whilst never a comfort exactly, can serve as an essential safeguard against complacency.

'In terms of your training that fear helps, like a lot of people have said, it helps you a lot. It helps you for the duration of your camp. You might think, "I can't be fucked to go to that session today," but then you think, "But what if you lose?" And then you think, "OK, I should go and do that." If you use it right, it can carry you through in moments where maybe you'd slack off. Maybe in situations where the stakes weren't so high . . . if I was practising for a table tennis match or something then maybe I would skip a couple of sessions because you'd think, "Oh, well, maybe I'll lose but I won't be sparked out asleep on the floor." It's a different beast.'

Fear of failure and of its ultimate expression, the knockout, serves as the catalyst during training camp, an environment in which the athlete can control what they do, where they can measure their performance and take comfort and confidence in that performance. For Anthony Yarde it is during that period, during training, that the mental and physical fortifications he will need come fight night are built and they need to be as strong and as true as he can make them.

'You build up an alter ego, you have a mentality, "I can't be knocked out, I can't be knocked down," similar to the famous Mike Tyson speech, "I refuse to be hurt, knocked down or knocked out, I can't lose, I refuse to lose." It's like an alter ego. So I feel like it starts with mentality and when you realize that you can be knocked out it boosts how seriously you take the game or how hard you train. Every time you spar, every time you're in preparation for a fight, the possibilities are the same, so it might cross your mind [that you could get knocked out] but it's your job to channel it, you have to channel your mind, channel the nerves, channel the fears and possibilities.'

At some point during a fighter's preparation, though, that mentality has to shift. A fighter needs to make the transition from a situation where they are using the fear of losing, of possibly getting knocked out, to motivate them during their preparations, to one where failure is not entertained, where there is no acceptance of it as an option. Simply put, fear fuels a fighter to prepare as thoroughly as they can, which in turn allows them to keep the feelings of self-doubt, that Fabio Wardley referred to, under control, because when that first bell goes there is no room for anything other than total commitment, confidence and conviction.

Fighters can choose to make that transition in different ways. For Karriss Artingstall it is more of a gradual mental process rather than the flicking of a switch. I caught up with her and Lauren Price in Bournemouth a couple of weeks before Christmas where Price was boxing on the undercard of hometown hero Chris Billam-Smith's first world title defence against Poland's Mateusz Masternak. We'd all been in the same place over the summer, on which occasion we'd been treated to glorious weather and all the best that a seaside town in full bloom can offer, but in winter they are different places, riding out the rough off-season months like a boxer tucking up and trying to survive those torrid rounds when the fight has turned against them. Lauren had just weighed in and we didn't have long as it was an opportunistic strike on my part, but in the few minutes we had there was time for the thorny issue of fear to rear its head whilst the palm trees outside were lashed by the wind and rain.

'It's a weird one. I've heard fighters say, "I've never dreamt of being beat," and this, that and the other. I'll put my hand up; every opponent I get in with I'm like, "What if they do this? Or what if they can do that better than me? What if?" Do you know what I mean? I always go through them scenarios in my head but then by the end of the scenario I'll be thinking, "But they won't do it because I'll do this better." There's not a fight I've been in where I haven't thought, "This [bad thing] could happen." But then you put your foot down and you're fighting that battle in your head; the thought comes into your head and you've got to accept it but then fight it off, sort of thing. I do a bit of work with a psychologist and it's freeze, fight and flight, the three Fs, so you either freeze in a situation, or you can run away from a situation or you can fight it head-on, but it's a balance because obviously you don't just want to fight it head-on because you're just gonna start rushing your work.'

Carl Froch referred to the fight or flight conundrum, a classic scenario that everyone, boxer or not, can relate to. It's usually treated as a binary choice but, interestingly, what Karriss is saying here is that fight has to be tempered by flight to a degree, because blind aggression will serve no useful purpose. Lauren added her own thoughts at this point, describing the required formula as being 'fire in the belly but ice in the mind', describing how a fighter has to always focus that necessary aggression, how there has to be a thought process and balance behind it, otherwise all that will happen in the heat of battle is that they'll rush in 'all hells blazing'; and therein lies the path to ruin. They both agreed that the biggest challenge for them in boxing is achieving that mental equilibrium, that if their mentality is correct come fight night then that's when they know they will perform.

Johnny Nelson preferred a more extreme, back to the wall, method: 'You've got to go in with a kamikaze mentality. Prior to the fight, that's where you can make or break yourself, but in the ring, that's the wrong place to be if you're scared. So you've got to get yourself into a kamikaze mentality, where in your mind it's shit or bust, by the time you've got into the ring. Every world title defence I had, I had to be the last one out of the dressing room. I'd tidy away my clothes, my shoes, and before I went out, I'd clear the dressing room and I'd look at myself in the mirror and I'd tell myself, "I'm not getting fucking knocked out." I've got to build up every wall to make sure that doesn't happen. I did that for every world title defence; it was my way of trying to ensure that if I got hit with a hard shot, that it wouldn't render me unconscious. It was scary but at that point there was no turning back.'

Tony Bellew reminded himself as he walked to the ring for his fight against David Haye of the need to stay focused every second he was in there or his opponent could knock him out. Nelson and Bellew needed to feel that razor's edge of fear right up until the last possible moment, whereas Anthony Yarde takes a different approach, one where, preparations complete, he will then allow himself to surrender to a very particular type of serenity, a serenity rooted in the knowledge that he has done all he can do, that he has held up his end of the bargain.

'I don't feel nerves on fight night. Never. I thank God that that's part of my demeanour. My mentality is that the fear or the nerves come in my training. When I feel like I'm training as hard as I can, that I'm doing that bit more, going that extra mile, it's because of fear. Then once I'm like, coming to fight day, you're here now, you're both in the ring, so I'm not going to let fear take over my experience, my experience of being a professional boxer, fighting for a world title, my experience of maybe possibly winning a world title. So I enjoy the moment and have complete confidence in myself.'

The mental transition being discussed here, from a recognition of all possibilities to a narrowing of the focus that excludes all but one possibility, with that one possibility being victory, is a classic case of compartmentalization (described in chapter four as 'a form of psychological defence mechanism in which thoughts and feelings that seem to conflict are kept separated or isolated from each other in the mind'). Different situations require different thoughts and feelings and the boundaries between them must be solid; any blurring of them will obfuscate and obstruct to the point of self-destruction. As Johnny Nelson explains, the ability to compartmentalize is non-negotiable, there is no other way.

'Every sportsman and sportswoman has to do it and if you're not capable of doing it then you've failed, you're done. You've got to put your fears, your doubts, into one compartment and you've got to put your determination, your confidence, in another compartment. Because if you don't that's half the battle lost. You've got no choice, you've got to do it because if you don't do it, you can't do it. Most fighters understand that and that's why you've got to be selfish, you've got to be a proper wrong 'un, to think of yourself ahead of your wife and kids, your friends, you've got to be able to do that because you'll only go so far if you can't. As a fighter you've got to be arrogant enough to think that in your weight division out of the 7.8 billion people on the planet, no man on earth can beat you. That's how you've got to think.'

Standing across the ring from their opponent, fighters tell themselves whatever it is they need to tell themselves. But whatever that is, they must believe in it. Fact, fiction, delusion, it doesn't matter. In that moment, perception is reality and their perception must be that tonight is their night. As Yarde says, belief is everything: 'Someone's not going to put one hundred per cent effort into something if they don't believe in it. That's a fact. You have to have the mentality that this is impossible [getting knocked out] and even if you've been knocked out before you have to believe that ain't ever happening again. It's a mentality. Because some people, you know, they can lie to themselves, and that's why I say a lot of it is ego and that's why controlled ego, and the same with controlled aggression, controlled pride, anything that is controlled can be a good thing, if you use it right. They say stubbornness is bad but if you use your stubbornness in the right way it can be a tremendously good thing. I can be very stubborn and I try to use it in my boxing; not stopping before the other person. Or ego, you know, thinking, "I'm the best." It's a mentality, an ability to channel what can be seen as negative attributes and make them positive attributes and make them work for you. If someone has ego then they're less likely to go down, they'll take longer to wear down because their ego's telling them, no way, this is not happening.'

But it does happen. Fighters do go down, they do get knocked out, they do get beaten. What happens when that happens? How do they react to it and recover from it? I've spoken to numerous athletes about this down the years, across a number of sports, and if they give an honest answer, which they're not always in a position to do, or not always willing to do, then they'll tell you that their attitude to defeat is a philosophical one, that losing is an occupational hazard and that although they'll strive with every sinew to avoid it, it can never be removed from the equation. Anthony Yarde gave me a succinct explanation of his own outlook.

'My belief is literally that it's gonna be what it's gonna be anyway, regardless of whether I'm fearful or confident, the result, nine times out of ten, is gonna be what it was always gonna be anyway, based on the preparation, so there's no point being nervous, it's a waste of time.'

This attitude often surprises people, and it is true to say that it is more unusual in boxing than it is in other sports, but what this philosophy states and what Yarde is saying is not that the outcome is and always has been predetermined and therefore his own attempts to influence proceedings are futile, but that come fight night the part of proceedings that he has had control over, namely his training, is complete and now all he can do is answer that bell, perform as best he can, accepting that whatever happens as an result of that is whatever happens. In that ring, the margins between victory and defeat can be very fine and that is life on the front line of elite-level sport. In short, defeat must be considered unthinkable, but it is not impossible; that is the reality, and all competitors accept that. In defeat Anthony Yarde stuck by his philosophy. He said very little and, although obviously bitterly disappointed, he made no excuses. It wasn't his night against Kovalev or Beterbiev, but his night would come; that was his attitude.

But this approach doesn't work for everyone because when it comes to recovering from a defeat ego again can take over and dictate that a palatable reason be found for failure; and the list of palatable reasons does not include the concession that the opponent was better. As Billy Graham told me, 'You have to be capable of lying to yourself if you're a fighter; there's nothing wrong with it at all, it's a necessary evil, I suppose.' In the immediate aftermath of a defeat a fighter will often give a very honest appraisal of what happened, but that version of events often has a short shelf life. When Chris Eubank Jnr got dropped and stopped for the first time in his career by Liam Smith, something he never thought could happen, initially he shook Smith's hand and said that 'he caught me with a great shot'. He was gracious. But mere minutes later, back in his changing room, his perception had changed. A great punch became a lucky punch and then metamorphosed from a punch into an elbow. In no time at all his version of events had transitioned from him coming up second-best on the night, something that can happen to anyone, to him being the victim of an illegal blow, rendering his defeat invalid. When Deontay Wilder got taken apart by Tyson Fury in their second meeting in February 2020, a first defeat for the Bronze Bomber and a brutal one, when interviewed in the ring his response was, 'Things like this happen, the best man won tonight.' But that narrative did not linger long. Soon enough, different, outlandish reasons were found, graduating from the weight of his ring walk costume to allegations of glove tampering. Both Eubank and Wilder also claimed that they had been perfectly capable of continuing and that the fight should not have been stopped, a perception that was not grounded in any kind of reality. It was bewildering to listen to at times but both men were doing what they needed to do to take those first steps towards rehabilitation following a crushing loss; they were selling the defeat to themselves.

It is a well-trodden path for fighters post-defeat and one Johnny Nelson has watched numerous fighters tread: 'To be a fighter you've got to have an arrogance, you've got to believe you can beat everybody on this earth in your weight division, so that is a ridiculous arrogance you've got to have. So if something goes wrong then you have to have the arrogance to say, "No, no, that happened because of x, y and z." You've got to have that because this is a sport where if you don't believe in yourself, if you get in the ring and you're half sure about yourself, then you'll get found out and it's a painful way to get found out. So it's a coping mechanism. You've got to fool yourself. If you lose you've got to justify the loss in your head. If you lose and think, "I'm not good enough," then you're finished, you're in the wrong game. You've got to be like a narcissist and ignore the truth and ignore the facts that are in front of you and you've got to convince yourself the reason why that happened, why it didn't turn out in your favour. You've got to be able to lie to yourself, you've got to be able to justify everything that happens to you and pick out the positives and ignore negatives, make excuses for the negatives.'

The higher the level a fighter is operating at and the higher the level of their own expectation the more common this is. Anthony Yarde was a heavy underdog in the two world title defeats mentioned above, up against two vastly more experienced, established world champions, and that made for a different dynamic to the one other defeat he's suffered, which came prior to the two mentioned when he was still unbeaten and lost on points at Commonwealth title level to Lyndon Arthur in a fight he was expected to win. It was a close fight and one that he thought he had won, but the judges at ringside decided otherwise. He found it hard to take and from the moment the decision was announced he questioned the validity of the result, and still does so to this day, although with slightly less vehemence than in the immediate aftermath. But his response to that defeat remained consistent, as it did with the two other reversals, and that consistency would have been critical to his recovery. However a fighter chooses to explain an undesirable outcome to themselves, that individual has to be able to live with it, to get as comfortable as they can be with what for them is the most uncomfortable and inconvenient thing of all.

Like Nelson, Yarde has watched with fascination at times as boxers have gone down the rabbit hole that can be selling defeat to themselves: 'It's happened so many times. You've seen it where somebody might say something in an interview and then a couple of months down the line they might say something else because they've had to rewire their thinking to change what they feel, and sometimes it's a positive and sometimes it's a negative. So at the end of a fight someone might still be positive, "Oh you know, things happen, I'll get back in the gym," and then you might hear that person a few months later and their tone's different, their morale's different. But for some people it's opposite, so I think it does depend on the individual and the mentality of that person. Because boxing can take its toll on people; you've got this ego, this belief in yourself, and then the person gets knocked out, what's that going to do to someone's spirit? How are they going to respond to that? To the embarrassment. Now they might be fearful of it happening again. AJ [Joshua] would in my opinion be an example. Before he suffered a loss or got knocked out, he was a knockout artist, so powerful, he was committing to his punches, but from when he took that loss versus Ruiz, he was never the same, ever, and I feel like it's taken time for him to have confidence in throwing his punch again because when he threw that punch against Ruiz he got countered and he ended up being dropped by him. So since then, when he goes into the ring, every time he throws that punch it's almost like PTSD, he's worried about what's coming back. And that's not saying that he's not mentally strong or anything like that, it's just that the human brain will remind you of a traumatic experience. Being mentally strong and being able to deal with things, it's not for everybody, you can't teach it, I don't believe.'

There is an alternative to selling the defeat, to seeking out that reason, or reasons, for defeat that satisfy the ego and allow a person to move on, self-belief seemingly repaired. Ironically it involves explaining a reversal by resolutely not attempting to find a specific reason behind it. 'Everything happens for a reason' is a phrase that often issues forth from the mouths of fighters. As a response to a specific event I've always found it to be problematic, constituting, in my mind, an abdication of responsibility, a refusal on the behalf of an individual to examine their own contribution to a failed enter-prise, and an attitude that is unlikely to be helpful in the longer term. On this Yarde agreed.

'It's almost like you're questioning reality: "Oh, it's OK, everything happens for a reason.' Because in the beginning that ego's there, "I can't lose, it's impossible," and then they lose or get knocked out and then it's "everything happens for a reason". It's a cushion. It's not an excuse but it's a way maybe of keeping their sanity, and that's a result of a high ego, I think, that's always believed and told themselves that they're the best; if they get beat then mentally you don't know how that person is going to react. In the past with boxers you've seen boxers take one loss and they're never the same again because mentally they can't recover from it. Naseem Hamed, you know, when he fought Barrera, after his loss he was never the same fighter; Ricky Hatton, when he lost to Floyd, he fought Pacquiao, he had to retire because maybe his ego and his belief changed and if it's not dealt with properly it can be dangerous.'

It's pertinent here that the two fighters Yarde mentions, Hamed and Hatton, were undefeated for a long period, during which they scaled the highest heights of their chosen profession, as did Anthony Joshua. Their success had been such that defeat became increasingly unthinkable and therefore when it did arrive it was that much more difficult to deal with. There was no physical, tangible satisfactory reason or combination of reasons to be found that could justify it and so a more ethereal approach had to be taken.

Despite my reservations above, I do believe, having discussed it with numerous parties, that 'everything happens for a reason' can be a helpful navigational tool (especially in a career as unpredictable as that of a professional boxer), if employed as a philosophical overview, as an ongoing course of treatment, if you will, rather than as a cure for a specific ailment. Matt Macklin has always used it as such and it's easy enough to see how he has made it work for him.

'We're all growing, aren't we? If you think at thirty what you thought at twenty then you've wasted ten years, haven't you? When you're older, you have more wisdom, or at least you should have, if you learn from experiences. You've got to go through it. You've got to trust where life's taking you, the process. You're at A, you want to get to B, but you don't know what way you're gonna get there. There's setbacks, there's lessons learnt, it's never how you think it is.

You get there in the end but you didn't get there how you thought you were gonna get there because no one's really envisaging the losses, we're just thinking positively. But there are gonna be losses. What's that famous quote? "Success is going from failure to failure without losing enthusiasm." You've got to have that in you to be successful in anything.'

The word ego is one that has recurred in this chapter and that was inevitable. Ego plays a huge part in life and in an elite sporting career in particular. It is both extremely powerful and alarmingly delicate. Damage to the ego is what fighters are most afraid of – many have testified to that in these pages – and recovering from it can be very difficult. But could it be that boxers are afraid of the wrong thing? I believe them when they tell me that they're not afraid of the physical impact of getting knocked out, that it's the emotional toll of the embarrassment and shame of being so comprehensively defeated that cuts them. I believe them when they tell me that they'd choose death over any form of dishonour. But what I've never understood is why a fear of damage to the ego should be so much more of a motivating factor than an aversion to damage to your physical being, to your body. Can a balance not be struck between fear of the humiliation of being knocked out and the fear of the medical trauma of being hit so hard on the head that the brain shuts down, or do they have to be mutually exclusive?

Johnny Nelson argues: 'It depends if you're thinking about them [the people watching and their reaction] or yourself, and I was thinking about me. The embarrassment of it happening wasn't my worry, the fact of it physically happening to me was my worry. So my mentality was probably different to other fighters because I was thinking about the trauma, the physical effect it had on me. I didn't want to get killed. So when fighters say they didn't think about that, I did, I thought about it every day. That was my main fear. If as a fighter you don't have the intelligence to look at what you're doing and what can potentially happen and don't give a shit about it then you're an idiot. I don't care about getting embarrassed; I don't want to get killed.'

Anthony Yarde has a similar view. He is prepared to do whatever it takes to prevail over his opponent in that ring and, had his trainer Tunde Ajayi not stopped his fight against Artur Beterbiev, he would have stood and fought until the bitter end. He has no doubt that if that is what it takes to win, and at world title level it often is, then that is what he will do. But he says that doesn't mean that a fighter shouldn't still be concerned with self-preservation, that that shouldn't have a bearing on how they approach things.

'They say that a nervous fighter is the best type of fighter because he's got more of his wits about him. An over-confident fighter can be in danger because they're over-confident; he might get caught with a shot because he's not very wary of the things that could happen. And it don't matter who I've been in there with and who I get in there with, I'm always wary about getting hit, I don't like getting hit, and I think there's a culture in British boxing and Mexican boxing of being able to take a punch, and I've never really bought into that because of the dangers of what can happen physically when you get knocked out, or the potential for what could happen after you retire. I just don't feel there's anything good about getting hit, about taking a shot to give a shot.'

Fear is a great motivator. It can be inspired by many things and debating which of them is the most beneficial is an interesting exercise, although ultimately it is up to the individual which source they choose. But what is clear is that fear is necessary in boxing. A fighter must feel it. If they don't, then, as Cus D'Amato said, they are 'a liar or a psychopath' and I don't like the chances of either of those two in the prize ring. I'll leave the last words in this chapter to Fabio Wardley, the only undefeated fighter to be quoted in this book. He doesn't know what it's like to lose, to get knocked out, although he accepts that it could happen, that in all likelihood it *will* happen.

'Yeah, I've considered it, I've definitely considered it. It's a funny one for me because I've never experienced it in boxing at all. I thought about this quite a lot after my last fight because I had limited white collar and I won them all and all of my pro fights I've won so everything boxing related, I've never actually lost and it's actually quite a weird feeling. They rise together because obviously winning a fight, you get better and you get more accolades and people are more impressed with you and bigging you up more and all of that stuff, but so does the other side of it because it's like you've rolled the dice again and you've won, you've hit sixes, but I've got to roll the dice again in three or four months, I might hit snake eyes and I might go south.'

I was ringside for that last fight he mentions, in Saudi Arabia, where he put on a very good performance to stop David Adeleye and add the Commonwealth title to the British belt he already possessed. He's rising higher with every win, like a hot-air balloon fuelled by the plaudits and praise, feeling like he's in control but aware of the constant jeopardy, trying to enjoy the view whilst not looking down for fear of seeing how far he has to fall. That's what I imagine it must be like, the journey he's on, but when that bell goes there's no time to think about any of that, it's back to that most basic of scenarios.

'It's such a singular thing as well, there's no fluff or excess to it, it's just you versus another man, fighting it out. At its core that's really what it is and it's a very simple thing, very simple mechanics, but it feels so exhilarating to be in the middle of. I've been in the middle of fights and I've been clipped really hard and you're in the middle of a fight but you're still in your own brain, having a conversation with yourself. I remember getting clipped really hard by Molina [Eric] and I had to back up and go back across the ring and I pulled myself back and I remember being in my own head and being like, "Don't fucking lose this here, this is not good, move, do this, do that, don't get in trouble, we know you're hurt, keeping moving, do this, do that, alright, fuck it." I remember there was a switch in my brain that went from defence to offence that went "Fuck it, throw back". I remember I was doing stuff and in my brain that's where I consciously am, and it's funny to me how you can be in that situation and still be having a full-blown conversation with yourself in your own head.'

Fear, nerves, apprehension, whatever label a person gives it, can be a tremendous motivator, maybe the most powerful of all, but only if it can be harnessed and put to work in a positive way. During the build-up to a critical life event, be it a fight in the professional boxing ring or an exam, a job interview, an audition, whatever it may be, fear can drive a person during their preparation, help them find that extra level of commitment they need to ensure that they arrive on the given day in a position to give of their very best, with the doubts and insecurities that accompany any crucial performance quietened by that knowledge that they have done everything they could have done to secure a positive outcome. This is how boxers harness that fire that Cus D'Amato speaks of in the chapter's opening quote and their ability to do that is born of a realistic approach, of a willingness to confront their fear, an acceptance of what could happen, an awareness of how things could go wrong. Complacency, in any form, is the enemy. But when the event itself arrives, when the bell tolls and it's time for action, from that point onwards there is no place for fear, it no longer serves a useful purpose. At that stage that mental shift that fighters have spoken of has to occur, that narrowing of the focus that visualizes only success and allows only for thoughts and actions geared towards that end. The ability to make that mental transition from preparation to performance, to achieve that compartmentalization, doesn't guarantee a successful outcome, but an inability to do it will almost certainly precipitate failure; more specifically, failure garlanded with regret, which is the very worst kind.

CHAPTER NINE

Are You Not Entertained?

> You have disdain for the crowd. You get up there and it's like you're a performing monkey. But with boxing what you've got to do is think for you, you've got to think not about why they're there but think, 'I'm making money, I'm getting paid for this, because I want to do it. I'm using you, you're not using me.' The majority of people who pay money want to see blood, want to see somebody get knocked out, and nine times out of ten they get that.
>
> *Johnny Nelson*

The title of this chapter is a line uttered by Maximus Decimus Meridius, Russell Crowe's character in the 2000 Ridley Scott epic film, *Gladiator*. Maximus asks this question as he stands in the middle of a provincial amphitheatre having just soaked the sand of the arena with blood, satisfying the lust for savagery of the assembled crowd.

'Are you not entertained? Are you not entertained? Is this not why you are here?'

Maximus has disdain for the crowd and they love him for it, chanting his name as he makes his exit. But he needs the arena because it is his only way to survive and his only route back to Rome. It is a complicated relationship.

The boxing ring is not the Colosseum. The two are often compared and, although I understand the comparison, they are not the same. The relationship between the man in the arena and the audience, the voyeur, however, does bear comparison. Codified boxing, boxing as we know it, is now 133 years old and for a good portion of those 133 years, people have been questioning whether society should grant a platform to pugilism, that practice of fighting with fists, with the intent behind that practice being to harm.

During that period boxing has been banned in some countries. In Sweden professional boxing was illegal between 1970 and 2007 and in Norway it was outlawed between 1982 and 2016. But both of those countries still produced fighters during those years and the sport still existed, albeit underground. The governments of both countries relented in the end; the human desire to fight and to watch people fight prevailed. The attraction of boxing, of that one-on-one fistic duel, is undeniable, whether society cares to admit it or not, whether individuals are comfortable with that or not. I have seen the way people react to a knockout at ringside and I know how I react to one myself. I know how I reacted when I witnessed my first knockout as an eight-year-old. I enjoyed it and I have never had any problem with that fact, that I was entertained and that I continue to be entertained by the spectacle. I do not believe that taking enjoyment in said spectacle is any kind of comment on my character, that it by definition marks me out as a person lacking in compassion or empathy; indeed I believe that quite the opposite is true, that my familiarity with the act and its potential consequences allow me to be as empathetic to the plight of an unconscious boxer as it is possible to be. I also believe a significant proportion of those who insist that they never could and never would allow themselves to partake of the watching of such an activity are not reluctant to subject themselves to it because they know they would hate it, but because they are afraid that they might like it and therefore discover something they would find unedifying about themselves.

In the *Confessions* of St Augustine of Hippo, written in the late fourth century, St Augustine tells the story of how a friend of his, Alypius of Thagaste, a man of strong moral beliefs that precluded any affinity with the violence of the Roman arena, was, nevertheless, persuaded to go by some acquaintances and, after insisting on keeping his eyes closed at first, he eventually relented and allowed himself to take in his surroundings. This is how St Augustine described his reaction:

> As soon as he saw the blood, he drank it in, with a savage temper and he did not turn away but fixed his eyes on the bloody pastime, drinking in the madness, delighted with the wicked contest, drunk with blood lust, he was now no longer the same man that came in but was one of the mob he came into of true companions of those who had brought him there. Why need I say more? He looked, he shouted, he was excited and he took away with him the madness and it stimulated him to come again.

I recognize this kind of reaction. Not in myself – as previously stated, I've never harboured any troubling inner conflict about watching people fight – but I have seen it in others. Alypius' conversion to the spectacle of the Colosseum, which, incidentally, did not endure, is an extreme reaction to an extreme spectacle. Boxing, although extreme by modern standards, does not approach the savagery of the Roman amphitheatre. There is another quote which I think speaks to the attitude of a modern audience a little better and it came from the famed escapologist Harry Houdini

(1874–1926): 'I knew, as everyone knows, that the easiest way to attract a crowd is to let it be known that at a given time and a given place someone is going to attempt something that in the event of failure will mean sudden death.'

The potentially fatal gamble and the jeopardy of the spectacle of that gamble; that, I believe, is the appeal of boxing in today's world. Nobody wants to see anybody die in the boxing ring and nobody attends boxing with that expectation, just as nobody went to see Houdini in the hope that he would fail in his latest brush with death and perish. People want to see fighters fight, they want to see them try and knock each other out, but they also want to see them both escape from that ring without serious, lasting damage, and in that sense boxing is more akin to escapology than gladiatorial games. But it must be remembered that the jeopardy is real, it is no trick, deception or illusion.

I do also believe that the dynamic of the knockout and the attraction it holds for certain people can be misinterpreted. Critics of the sport berate boxing enthusiasts on account of what they believe is their predilection for violence and a desire to see a human being damaged. But boxing is a sport, and an extremely skilful one at that, and the knockout can also be viewed as the ultimate demonstration of sporting skill. This has long been a point of frustration for Billy Graham.

'People who don't know boxing or don't follow boxing get it wrong. When someone gets knocked out, you're not marvelling at what's happened to the fighter who's been knocked out, you're not celebrating his demise, you're marvelling at what the other guy has managed to do, because it's beautiful. That's what you love, seeing that happen. People who don't watch boxing or follow boxing think you must be a twisted, violent bastard because you're enjoying watching this guy get knocked out, but it's not that, you're not gloating on anyone, you're just marvelling at how good someone is. But people who are against boxing don't get that.'

But that is not to say that it is still not a shocking thing to witness, because it is. One moment a person is indeed marvelling at the skill, the beautiful brutality, that has just effected the knockout, but very soon that admiration can morph into fear.

The most dreadful example of this rapid juxtaposition that I have experienced occurred at Tottenham Hotspur Stadium on 25 September 2021. The bill was topped by Anthony Joshua vs Oleksandr Usyk, yet another huge night for British boxing. It was a magnificent scene; 65,000 people packed into a new sporting amphitheatre. On the undercard Callum Smith, a former world champion at super-middleweight, now building towards winning a world title at light-heavyweight, was fighting Lenin Castillo. Castillo, a 33-year-old Puerto Rican, was a solid operator who had challenged for a world title before, coming up short against a very good boxer in Russian Dmitry Bivol but lasting the distance. It was a fight Smith was expected to win, with the idea being that he would plant a flag in the sand at 175lb by doing a better job than Bivol had done. This is often the way of things in boxing; it is a sport which lacks straightforward metrics, there are no times or distances to compare, such as there are in track and field, for example, and therefore one of the few ways to try and rank competitors is by comparing their performances against common opponents.

The fight occurred midway through the card so the arena wasn't full as Smith and Castillo walked to the ring on a dry and warm north London evening, but there were enough spectators in position to provide the constant background hum unique to stadium fights. I was on commentary alongside Matt Macklin. We'd both always enjoyed watching Callum Smith. He possesses a bit of everything in that he's a technically correct boxer so pleasing to the purist but also wields the raw power to do real damage, as he'd previously demonstrated by knocking Luke Blackledge clean out with a left hook in another of his fights that we'd commentated on five years previously.

The first round was quiet but then in the second, with just under a minute gone, lightning struck. It happened at the far side of the ring to us but at the moment of impact, the action was side-on, so we had a very good view, a view I can recall more clearly than any other knockout I've ever seen. As for why that is the case I could not tell you for certain; all I know is that it left an imprint that has never faded, and it is not an imprint that was enhanced and embedded in the days after the event by my watching replays as I chose not to do so. I don't even know if the footage would have been available in the immediate aftermath. Sky Sports, who I was working for, didn't show the knockout again on the night and have not done so at any point since. There are replays available online now, one of which I watched a few minutes before writing this, as I wanted to check if my recollection was clear. It was the first time I had watched the knockout back and the picture I have always had in my mind's eye, that freeze-frame that has stayed with me, of Callum Smith's right hand landing, is practically pixel perfect. I was expecting my recall to be faulty, as the human memory can be a fascinatingly imperfect thing, but on this occasion it was photographic. As I say, I don't know why my memory of this one is so clear, because I have rewatched numerous knockouts for this book for descriptive purposes and I have found quite often that they hadn't materialized quite as I had remembered – but that was not the case with this one. Maybe the obvious seriousness of it precipitated a more violent mental impact. I don't know.

Smith lands a perfectly executed right hand, the textbook mechanics of it masking its inherent savagery, and Castillo starts to fall. Smith follows up with a left hook which doesn't land, but it doesn't need to. Castillo plummets to the canvas, stretched out with his legs seemingly welded together and pointing directly towards us, gloves hovering over his chest, head slightly raised. I couldn't tell in real time if his eyes were open or not, and it's still difficult to tell watching it back, but from the angle of his head, it appears as though he's looking down the length of his body towards his feet. It is instantly and abundantly clear that it is a bad knockout. But then something happens that I had never seen before and have never seen since. His left leg starts to twitch. It's not a violent, jerking motion, more a convulsive tremor, but it is an unmistakably involuntary physical action, the product of a nervous system that has just been dealt a horrific blow. I distinctly remember thinking that we could be watching a human in his final throes.

Matt had a similar feeling: 'I've seen a few knockouts where it's been horrible, where it's sent a shiver down your spine and made your blood run cold and you get a horrible feeling in your stomach. That was one. I seen Martin Concepcion knock out a guy in the Midland final in the amateurs, a guy called Terry Adams from Birmingham. He knocked him out cold and his leg was shaking, not as bad as Castillo, but it was moving. I knew Terry Adams, and I liked him, and it was scary. And I've seen a few bad ones down the years.'

Referee Bob Williams wasted no time in declaring the fight over and calling in the medical staff. Callum Smith, who had turned away in celebration as Castillo fell, was alerted to his opponent's serious condition by his older brother Paul, a former professional fighter himself, who quickly jumped into the ring. The two brothers, along with everybody else, could now only watch and wait and hope and pray that the worst was not going to happen right in front of all our eyes. Silence engulfed the stadium like a thick dust settling in the wake of a volcanic eruption. An eery silence, heavy with foreboding. My tone in commentary shifted from a percussive pitch to a measured melancholy. I reverted to radio reporter mode, purely describing what's happening in the ring, carefully selecting what I think it is that people watching need to know and being very careful not to issue any statements surrounding the state of Castillo's health that could subsequently prove to be incorrect. There is no room for any interpretation of events in a situation like that. I may see what appear to be signs of recovery, such as a movement of a limb or the opening of the eyes, but I cannot then declare that as proof positive that the danger has passed because I cannot be sure of that, I am not qualified to pass judgement on that; all I can do is relay what I can see.

Over on the side of the ring where Castillo was lying, with a better view than us, was promoter Eddie Hearn, the man who has masterminded this entire spectacle.

'The reaction from Castillo when he went down was a classic sign of someone who could be in a bad situation. Whenever a fighter goes down and his leg starts twitching, it's a neurological response to what's happened, and that's never a good sign, so at that stage I'm thinking, get oxygen on him.'

Oxygen was very quick to arrive. On duty that night as part of the medical staff was Dr Neil Scott: 'We had a complement of medical officers at ringside, I think there were four. Myself and one of the anaesthetists were in the medical room finishing off some of the post-contest assessments. Fortunately there was a huge telly on and we could just about see this knockout coming, so we started making a move towards the ring and then obviously by the time we got to the ring this chap was on the floor and essentially was fitting. And, I mean, we were all quite anxious, particularly myself and one of my consultant colleagues I work closely with, purely about the fact that it was back at Tottenham Hotspur's ground, just because of the history that it carried. That's just human nature, isn't it, but of course when this starts unfolding in front of you . . . I mean that night, the care that boxer got in the ring and the evacuation was absolute textbook, it was absolutely streamlined, but sitting here now the hairs on my arms are standing up thinking about that night because that was . . . you're in an environment where you shouldn't really be practising medicine, that pre-hospital environment, and that's a scary place because essentially it's just you, your immediate group around you, and whatever equipment you've got because you haven't got anything else. It's a very, very small speciality that really only incorporates the emergency helicopter and car services. It's scary. It doesn't matter how well trained you are. I mean, I go to A&E, I put emergency airways in, I open people's necks, but I'm doing it within the hospital environment and I've got a lot of backup mechanisms in place, I'm not in the middle of the pitch at Tottenham Hotspur.'

The 'history' that Neil mentions here refers to the September 1991 fight at the White Hart Lane, between Chris Eubank Snr and Michael Watson that ended with Watson suffering a serious brain injury, from which he thankfully was able to make a recovery, but which caused a much-improved level of medical procedures and protocols to be introduced as standard at ringside in the United Kingdom by the British Boxing Board of Control.

Away from the middle of that pitch, sat in a TV truck in a dusty car park across the road from the stadium, staring at a bank of TV screens, was Sky Sports boxing director Sara Chenery. She witnessed all of this unfold and it is her job to decide what the watching world sees and doesn't see, when something like this happens. She decides what it is necessary for the viewing audience to witness and what that same audience must be protected from. It is a big responsibility.

'That's one that's really stuck in my mind. And I think what was interesting was that it just kind of came from nowhere. That's one of the ones that's slightly different to the Froch–Groves one. It just came from nowhere and they're the ones where you know it's finished, you know it's over, there's no question and those for me . . . I think I probably hold my breath in those moments. I'm quite an empathetic person and I've worked on boxing since 1996, a very long time, and I've directed a lot of fights. And in that moment you just want them to be alright and we have such a responsibility to show the right thing. So we're on one of our jib [overhead] cameras. Castillo goes down, and it's the leg twitch, as soon as you see that leg twitch, and Ricky Hatton had it against Pacquiao, and as soon as you see that leg twitch, the camera starts to come out and then you have to give it that moment. But then obviously the fight's off and all the paramedics and everyone come in and Smith goes to celebrate and then he thankfully realized as well and was very respectful. It was like a shock. I think everyone was just so shocked. It was absolute silence in the truck.

'So I will be quite firm at that time. I'll say, "We're staying here. We're staying on this camera. Everybody quiet." And then I'll say straightaway or reiterate to the camera operators in the ring to get out of the way if anyone, any of the medical staff, needs them to and a couple of them, especially the low cameras, will move just so they're out of the way. Then the first thing we do is mix to a camera that's just a wide angle of the ring. You can see everyone rushing in, so we're telling the viewers who can see that everyone's coming in, that he [Castillo] is getting the help he needs and then I'll be looking at everything else. So often you'll get a camera shot that's zoomed into a tight shot of someone having oxygen or something like that but straightaway, I'll say, "I don't want to see it. I want to know they're getting assistance but I don't want to see a beautiful shot of it." So they'll get out of the way because people get sucked in and my job is to make sure we take that step back.

'The pace of everything slows right down and I'll be widening shots out so that people feel they're still seeing what's going on in the ring but they're not actually seeing anything, they're just seeing that someone's getting attention. I remember keying through to you and saying, "Just do radio-style commentary," at one point. I don't think we've ever had one that bad, certainly not that I can remember. Hatton–Pacquiao maybe, but we've never had one that bad. So as soon as you then take over and do that radio-style commentary, I will then do my best to help you, and prompt you to mention the obvious things such as the fact he's getting all the medical attention he needs, that the best safety protocols are in place and all of those sorts of things, because people at home, like we all were in the truck, and we work on it all the time, would all have been holding their breath. It was a deep, deep silence.'

I remember the wide shot Sara mentions, that visual has stayed with me. I remember flicking between looking at the ring and the screen because what appears on the screen is what people can see at home and my job is to speak to those pictures but also to make them talk, by adding detail my eyes can see but that, in that instance, the camera lens couldn't magnify due to the respectful distance that needed to be kept.

Sara continues, 'You just never want anything like that to happen and I think people at home are going to be just as shocked. My job is just to slow the pace down, go from one angle that's wide to another angle that's wide. We put in a shot of the Smith brothers, who often are quite passionate, and they're all sat there with their dad really quiet and respectful. Everyone's seeing what's happening. Smith himself goes to the corner and bends down and crosses himself and you put in a line about him saying a quick prayer for Castillo. I think all of that just really showed how serious it was, but how everything that could happen, with regard to the care he [Castillo] was getting was happening. Everything that needed to happen was happening and we have to make sure we illustrate that. Had Smith been celebrating and going crazy, I wouldn't have shown it. I try and save someone from that because sometimes in the moment, the fighter who's won doesn't realize they [the opponent] are hurt and it looks so bad. I'm always thinking, "Hold on a minute, how does it look? Does it look bad?" Because you're trying to save them from themselves because clearly nobody ever wants anybody to get hurt. And we know when a knockout like that happens that we're not going to show it again. We don't need to see that again. We don't want to see it again. It's about telling the story. It's slowing the pace down.

'Many years ago when I first started working on boxing, somebody said to me, "Never forget their parents are watching at home, their friends are watching at home," whoever it might be. A lot of family members don't watch at ringside. They'll be watching it at home. So we have that responsibility to our viewers because we don't want to make people feel anxious watching something but we need to give them the information so they don't think, "Oh my God, what's happening?" There's a balance and you need to fill a vacuum. You want to comfort people. I think people were in shock and we were in shock and anyone watching at home would have been in shock whether you knew the fighters or cared who won or lost. There was the punch and then that thud and then the leg. All bets are off at that moment and we just have to make sure that we tell that story respectfully. And that continues afterwards as well because we then go to the studio chat and we had Eubank Jnr with us and the first question Anna Woolhouse [Sky presenter] asks is about how no one ever wants to see that because that's the thing that people struggle with, the fact that you're trying to hurt them but you don't want them to be hurt. It's such an odd thing, isn't it? We want to live and breathe every punch and we're all in that moment, but then when something like that actually happens the tone completely changes.'

This account of the impact of the knockout vividly illustrates the shock value that it possesses and how that value, that currency, never gets debased, no matter how many a person sees. Sara Chenery has seen more live knockouts than most people but each time is almost like the first time and I'd say that's true for the majority of people who work in boxing; it's certainly true for me. It's impossible to become inured to something so serious.

That does not mean though that everybody treats the knockout in the same fashion. On the night described, on the table next to me was an American commentator, working for a different broadcaster, and his treatment of the knockout, in terms of the vocabulary he used and the type of energy he afforded it, was different to mine. It was more graphic and, I would say, less sensitive. That is not a criticism, merely an observation, but it does illuminate what I find to be an interesting comparison between British and US boxing coverage, namely that in general our colleagues Stateside, for whom I have total professional respect, are less squeamish when it comes to what they will and won't say and will and won't show. Sara Chenery has seen the difference at first hand for many years.

'It's a different culture. We've done Anthony Joshua fights where they've shown replays we haven't of our own stuff. When Hatton got knocked down against Pacquiao, when he went down they were US pictures but we had two cameras, one massive long lens, and one on his family at ringside. And when he went down they had this overhead camera shot. And this camera just kept getting tighter and tighter and Ricky's leg was convulsing, so I cut off it to his family at ringside, and I got criticized for it at that time: "What did you cut off it for?" And it's because I just couldn't stay on that camera any longer, as it was getting tighter and tighter. We went to the family shocked at ringside for six, seven seconds just to give us that breath and then we went back to it. Because at that moment you're thinking, "Are they going to die on telly? Are they going to die?" And there was nowhere to go. When you're directing something, you have to come back out and just let people just take a breath, and think, "What's the right thing to do here?" That's how we approach it.'

I pass no judgement here regarding who is right and who is wrong, I just find the difference interesting, as ultimately that difference comes down to what the broadcasters' experience tells them their audience expects to see, what they feel entitled to see, and it would appear UK and US viewers are different in that regard. Another aspect to take into account when it comes to what appears on our screens is that the spectacle of the knockout is more alarming when you witness it in the flesh at ringside, than when viewing it on a TV screen. I know from my own experience that this is a true statement and one that Thomas Hauser, one of the most experienced boxing writers of his generation agrees with:

'TV cosmetizes the violence. When you're watching a fight on TV, or even from most seats in the arena, you tend to experience it almost like you're watching a video game. You tend not to understand what is happening to these men. Now, if you're sitting in the press section and you're close enough to see the faces, and the pain and anger and fear, it becomes more real.'

Thankfully Lenin Castillo recovered that night. He lay in the ring for a long period, whilst the crowd inside the stadium increased in number as the situation developed and word spread; fans drawn in from the concourses to the potentially tragic, unfolding event, like moths to a flame. At ringside logistics were managed with great efficiency. There was no sense of panic emanating from anyone involved in the boxer's care and once it was felt Castillo was in a position to be removed from the ring, the bottom rope was taken out and the stretcher he had been delicately shifted onto was slid out onto a gurney and he was taken to the waiting ambulance and subsequently to hospital. As he left the scene, nobody watching had any way of knowing what fate might befall Lenin Castillo, but before too long the bottom rope was restored, the canvas was brushed and the next pair of fighters made their way to the ring. The show went on, as it always must.

Were people entertained by what they had seen?

The dictionary definition of entertainment is as follows: 'the action of providing or being provided with amusement or enjoyment'. Amusement wasn't in evidence at Tottenham Hotspur that night, but enjoyment? People may not have enjoyed the aftermath but they enjoyed watching Castillo get knocked out, they took pleasure in witnessing that moment, of that I have no doubt.

Sara Chenery is part of the entertainment industry that delivers boxing to the public, as am I. Is she entertained?

'I think what's interesting for me is, I didn't like boxing as a sport, but I liked directing and then I started working on boxing in 1996, and if you could say, "boxing doesn't exist", I'd say it's probably a good thing. But it does, and you can't go back in time. So it exists and for me it exists in its best environment and its safest environment. And there's something amazing about the dedication, the training and then the other side of boxing. I spent a lot of time at the Wincobank [Brendan Ingle's gym in Sheffield] with Johnny Nelson and Naz [Naseem Hamed] back in the day and the good that it does for those kids and all of those good stories that we've told, it's got such a positive side as well. It's a way of life, not just a sport. It's a wonderful sport handled in the right way. And I think that that's what we always endeavour to do.'

Boxing is a sport grounded in conflict. As a concept, the fight started life as a means of conflict resolution. In that sense it is a straightforward dynamic, particularly when there's a knockout, but the inner conflict it provokes in those who stand on the periphery, in those who do not take part, is much more difficult to resolve. I asked Dr Neil Scott how, having taken the Hippocratic oath, an oath that requires those who swear it to 'do no harm', he manages to reconcile that with facilitating a sport in which his role as a physician is not to prevent harm, but to allow it and then respond to it. Had he found a way to be at peace with that?

'I wouldn't say I'm OK with it but you have to accept it. I do get a lot of colleagues ask me, "What's wrong with you? Why are you into boxing?" But we're drawn to this sport, aren't we, because of what it delivers and it will never be safe but you sit there at ringside trying just to make it as safe as you possibly can and I don't think you can say any more about it than that, because otherwise you're just not being honest with yourself. I sit there and I know a couple of my very senior colleagues sit there, and you're edgy, and you know when someone's concussed and you know that things are starting to turn in a direction that from a medical perspective are not great. But the rules of the sport in this country are the rules at this current point in time and as medical officers we respect them and you just have to be there with everything in place to make it as safe as possible.'

As a promoter Eddie Hearn is looking to make fights that will end in a knockout because the knockout is boxing's money shot. He is in the hurt business and has never been under any illusion about what that means: 'We all know what the sport's about. We know it's a dangerous sport and we respect the sport but ultimately it's a prize-fighting sport and there's no point in dressing it up: fans like to see knockouts. They don't like to see skill over twelve rounds and a points decision. Hardcore fans can appreciate that but it's not the reality for the mass audience.'

Hearn is right. Those 65,000 souls didn't flock through the Tottenham turnstiles to watch contest after contest in which boxers bewitched and charmed their audience with displays of balletic grace and subtlety. That was not why they were there. The promoter has a vested interest, of course, a financial stake in the game, and, as discussed, knockouts are good business, but what about others in the boxing business? How comfortable are their ringside seats? Thomas Hauser says, 'You tend to have cognitive dissonance when you're watching boxing, which is the disassociation between what you tend to know is right and wrong and how you're experiencing it. On a practical level we understand that somebody is being beaten badly sometimes, or beaten unconscious in front of us; I've been at ringside for two fights where fighters died, but as a fan you either find a way to get past that or you stop following the sport.'

Tris Dixon, former editor of *Boxing News* and author of *Damage: The Untold Story of Brain Trauma in Boxing*, has seen his tolerance of what he finds himself watching change down the years: 'I'm permanently conflicted. And the things I appreciate most now in a fight are very different from the things I used to appreciate most. I was at the first Ward–Gatti fight [a brutal fight] and I don't know if I'd have the stomach to be ringside for that now.'

Given the research he did for *Damage*, a terrific piece of work, it would be surprising should it not have altered Dixon's view. Indeed, of all the people I know, if ever anyone would have had reason to turn away from boxing, to decide it was no longer something they could justify an involvement in, it would have been Dixon. But he didn't turn away. He still loves the sport.

For observers, though, it pays not to get too close to fighters, as Hauser knows: 'If you have a personal relationship with one of the fighters, it becomes more real. I remember sitting in the press section for Lennox Lewis versus Mike Tyson. I knew Lennox reasonably well at that point, and my heart was pounding as those two men walked down the aisle, literally. I was very invested emotionally in that fight. Lennox won so it was very satisfying for me. Had the tables been turned and the result would have been reversed I would have been devastated.'

There is no deeper emotional investment in a fight than watching a loved one. I've always thought that to watch a partner, sibling, parent, son, daughter, must be excruciating. Ricky Hatton elaborates on this given his son Campbell is now a professional fighter: 'It's worse being a father watching your son than fighting yourself. When you're in the ring yourself you can do something about it but when you're watching your son out there ... it's horrible for a father to watch his son knowing what a hard game it is. Knowing I've got knocked out before, I've seen friends get knocked out and it's heartbreaking. So when I'm watching me son and the thought that the day could come when he gets knocked out, it's very, very worrying for a father.'

Mick Hennessy is a boxing promoter. Like Ricky Hatton, he knows the sport inside out, but that doesn't help when it comes to watching son Michael Jnr and teenage daughter Francesca, who are both now professionals: 'When it's your kids in there, you kind of like know them inside out and you know what their strengths are and what their weaknesses are. It's quite a nerve-racking situation. I'm usually very, very calm about everything, even in situations where you're in the trenches and things are going wrong, left, right and centre, I'm normally very calm, but it is something I find very, very difficult, the nerves, especially on the day of the fight.'

As for Mick's wife, Mrs Hennessy, she can't bear to watch: 'She normally stays in the hotel room and doesn't watch it or listen to it and just waits for the result basically. She struggles in a big way. She gets very, very nervous and we've actually found that it's better for her not to be there. She waits for the call.'

Marcus McDonnell's mother took the same approach when it came to her son, Marcus's brother, Jim. She would never go and watch Jim fight, and so wasn't there the night he got knocked out by Azumah Nelson at the Royal Albert Hall: 'He couldn't see the left hand coming and he got knocked spark out. It was absolutely horrible because he was out, they took him out on a stretcher. We were in the changing room and I was there and my brothers were there . . . watching someone you know and you love getting hit . . . It's hard watching someone you love, it's really hard. My mum would never watch it, we'd have to phone her up and tell her the results, she would never watch it, and he was on live on the BBC and things like that but she would never watch it. I never wanted him to fight Azumah Nelson, because Azumah was one of the best, he was like granite, and I said, "Jimmy, you ain't got a punch that's gonna stop him but he's got punches that are gonna stop you." It was a nasty knockout and I'm thinking, "Oh my God, is he dead here?" Because he was on oxygen and got carried out on a stretcher. So that was close to home.'

Mia Billam-Smith, wife of WBO cruiserweight champion Chris Billam-Smith, told me after his last fight, 'He loves a tear-up and I hate it. I always say to him after every fight, "Stop getting hit so much." For us it's really, really hard to watch. I've only missed one [fight] and that was in lockdown when it was fight camp, behind closed doors, and now it's a bad omen if I don't come. I watch between my fingers and I'm extremely anxious but I have to come now. Me and his family come, we respect the opponent, we clap them when they come in and then we just, obviously, hope for the best.'

Karriss Artingstall and Lauren Price have to watch each other box and both find it excruciating because although on the one hand they each know how diligently the other has prepared and how very capable they each are of defending themselves, the flipside to that coin is that they are painfully aware of how badly things can go wrong. Broadcasters are understandably keen that they box on the same night, it's promotional gold to have them on a bill together, but having done it once it's not something either wants to do again, as neither can properly concentrate on their own fight for worrying about the other's contest.

Artingstall and Price know the risks, all fighters do. That might sound like an obvious statement but it is a fact that often seems to escape boxing's detractors, many of whom like to cast the sport's practitioners as unintelligent, uneducated, pitiful souls who, ignorant of the potential consequences of plying their pugilistic trade, are conned into putting their lives on the line for public entertainment by sneering, malevolent moneymen who will happily exploit them for financial gain. It is true to say that boxing history is littered with fighters who have indeed found themselves used and abused on the business side of things, but the vast majority are aware of how the sport works, they understand their role and, as Johnny Nelson pointed out in this chapter's opening quote, have to ensure they profit from doing something that they want to do, because, make no mistake, fighters do want to fight, that desire to fight is in them.

But why do they want to fight? Why do they think it is that the spectacle of watching two people fight still holds such an appeal for the viewing public, most of whom will never set foot inside a boxing ring? What is their attitude to the people who pay to see them stripped to the waist, gloved up and set upon each other? The following testimonies give a variety of responses to those questions.

Billy Graham has a complicated relationship with boxing, for him it's a thin line between love and hate: 'I definitely don't stick up for boxing. I've got this line, that the only good thing about professional boxing is that it gets people like me out of poverty, so if you banned boxing, all you're doing is taking another way out of poverty for working-class people. That's the only good thing you can say about it because what else is there that's fucking good about it? The only other thing is: I remember what it was like to want to fight, to want to go in the ring, which most people would think is the worst thing in the world, walking out in front of all these people, taking the risk of getting knocked out, and embarrassed, because they don't understand what that urge is, how much you want to be in there, how much you want to do it, they can't understand that. But as an ex-boxer I know what that urge is like.'

Andy Lee knows what that urge is like, to want to knock his opponent out: 'There's nothing more empowering – and it's probably a bad reflection of the fighter – than to dominate another man to the point where you knock him out and stop him, to show your dominance really, it probably goes back to primeval, primordial days of when we were warriors or when we were apes even, asserting your dominance over somebody by knocking them out. There's not many places in society where that can happen any more but in the ring it does.'

David Haye is convinced that society not only wants that place to exist but that it also needs that place to exist, that society is healthier with boxing and other modes of combat available to people as a legal, organized activity, than it would be without it: 'It's a natural, human instinct to watch fighting, to watch combat, to watch two men who were born to fight each other. A lot of men have that in them, it's buried deep down in many of them, and society softens a lot of men so they get their buzz from fighting through other people. Deep down in every man, if their life depended on it, if their family's life depended on it, they'll step up and fight, but we live in such a soft society today that the majority of men never have a fight. My kids have never had a fight – actually, my daughter has, my two sons haven't. It's not a thing that happens in society now. You used to have boxing in schools, you used to have a lot more amateur boxing clubs, kids used to fight but now they stab each other. It's a different world now so people stay well away from combat and I think people get their outlet for combat through watching boxing, UFC, kick-boxing, Thai boxing, there are so many different forms of combat, karate, bare-knuckle fighting, people want more fighting because it's a natural thing for a human being, particularly men, but now women are starting to see the benefits. I think the more fighting the better, as long as it's controlled, rules, referee, the medical side of it's good. It's better than going down the pub, killing your brain cells getting pissed every night.'

Matt Macklin works in the media and so sees, week in and week out, the appetite the public has for boxing. He understood it when he was fighting and he understands it now. Like Haye, he doesn't believe there is anything untoward about it and, like me, he doesn't believe that the desire to watch boxing signals an automatic lack of compassion on behalf of the viewer: 'Everyone's got that bit of bloodthirstiness in them, you have to admit that because otherwise why are you watching two guys knocking lumps out of each other, knowing that one could get knocked out? Why do you cheer when the knockout comes? It's because everyone's got that little bit in them. But that can very quickly turn to fear and concern when it's one of those particularly bad ones. Because as much as everyone's got that bloodthirstiness in them and they're entertained by it, nobody wants to see anyone get actually hurt. Yeah, they want to see a knockout, but then they want to see the guy get up and be OK, nobody wants to see anyone get hurt permanently. But when you see those particularly brutal, bad knockouts you all of a sudden go from this entertaining, exciting highlight reel "wow" to a situation where it gets a bit too real and it can be life and death.'

As a fighter, and one whose stock-in-trade is the knockout, Fabio Wardley does not feel he can with any validity criticize people for craving a spectacle he so very much wants to supply: 'As humans I think that's something we all have. You drive past a car crash, all of us slow down because we want to see what happened. We're always chasing those iconic moments: "I remember where I was when this happened or when that happened." Especially in boxing because the stakes are so much higher, so there's so much more anticipation. Before a really big knockout, there's like this pause where the rest of the room thinks, "Shit, that happened," and then everyone goes mental and everyone keeps paying to keep chasing that kind of buzz, but we as fighters, we're chasing it as well because whatever feeling the supporter or fan is getting watching me or someone else do that, the feeling for me actually doing it is a thousand times bigger, and then I'll turn around and look at the crowd and everyone's on their feet and shouting your name . . . there's no drug like it.'

'There's no drug like it.' When boxers talk about what it feels like to fight, to win, to knock somebody out, they can often sound like addicts. 'You feel like a god and a powerful one at that,' were the words Deontay Wilder used to describe to me the feeling of inflicting a knockout. I have experience of my own with addiction and find it to be a problematic condition to define. Wikipedia describes it as a 'neuropsychological disorder characterized by a persistent and intense urge to use a drug or engage in a behaviour that produces natural reward, despite substantial harm and other negative consequences'. The NHS, the National Health Service in Great Britain, adds to this definition, saying that 'addiction is most commonly associated with gambling, drugs, alcohol and smoking, but it's possible to be addicted to just about anything'. Does boxing exist therefore to allow boxers to indulge their addiction to fighting in order that another section of society may indulge their own addiction, that is watching it? On face value this appears to be a troubling thesis, but the extent to which a person will be troubled by it is determined by the extent to which they buy into the perception I described previously that boxers are unwilling victims, that they are unaware of the 'substantial harm and other negative consequences' of plying their trade. I do not accept that perception and I never will. Boxers are not victims and do not see themselves as such. In elite-level sport, if an athlete is to be successful then, at the very least, a level of obsession with their chosen sport, a willingness to sacrifice almost anything in pursuit of victory, is essential. All elite athletes subject themselves to 'substantial harm and other negative consequences' because the lives they are required to lead are extreme and have a huge impact on their mental, emotional and physical wellbeing. In my opinion, therefore, it would be true to say that all professional sport involves indulging the practitioners' addiction and their willingness to indulge in it allows the viewing public to indulge theirs, namely watching it. Sporting excellence comes at a cost, and whilst it is true to say that boxers run the risk of paying a higher price than other athletes, the example set by elite-level performers in terms of the dedication, perseverance, self-belief and self-respect required is of value to society.

Spencer Oliver got knocked out at the Royal Albert Hall in May 1998. He was twenty-three years old, making the fourth defence of his European super-bantamweight title. He was expected to win and then look to challenge for a world title. The Omen, as he was known, was a very popular, likeable character and he was good to watch; he had the world at his feet. But in the tenth round, in front of a live TV audience, he got knocked out and his world as he knew it collapsed around him.

'I vaguely remember getting on the scales the day before the fight and I vaguely remember travelling to the Royal Albert Hall, although I'm not sure if I really do remember that or if I've just pieced that together in my brain afterwards. Then I remember waking up in a hospital bed two weeks after the fight. When I woke up, I remember looking up and the doctor asking me if I knew who all the people around me were and I thought I was still in the dressing rooms, I thought I was at the Albert Hall still because that's the last thing I remember. And I was thinking, "Fuck, I must have got knocked out."'

He had been in the operating theatre for three hours, during which time a blood clot was removed from the right-hand side of his brain. Ninety-eight staples were used to reattach the part of his skull that had had to be removed to allow the doctors to save his life. He had to learn how to walk and talk again. In the very early days of his recovery nobody wanted to tell him the full extent and implications of his injury, they were too fearful of his reaction, and Spencer only realized his career was over when he finally saw himself in a mirror, head shaved like a tennis ball, one side grotesquely swollen. He needed to know what had happened.

'I decided I needed to watch the fight because I needed to regain my memory from the fight. I sat down and watched it and from the moment I pressed "play" on the tape I cried from the moment it started until the moment it finished and I've never watched it again since.'

Five months later he was watching Sergey Devakov, the man who had knocked him out, fight in Manchester, defending the title that the Ukrainian had taken from him. He had already started the next stage of his life and was watching from ringside, working as a television pundit. I find it incredible that he was able to make that transition so quickly because boxers very often cannot bear to be around the sport in the immediate aftermath of their career coming to an end. I have heard many describe retirement as being like a bereavement, a loss that can take a long time to come to terms with, and in Spencer's case that loss was exacerbated by its suddenness and prematurity. But remarkably that did not turn him away from the sport.

'If anything I think it made me want to be around the sport even more, which is an insane thing to say because a lot of people ask me the same question, including my own mother and father: "How do you still love the sport that nearly took your life?" But actually, it give me an amazing life and I don't know nothing else and I still want to be involved in the sport.'

He has been involved ever since. I've known Spencer for a long time, we've worked together for years, and he's one of the most resilient, ebullient characters a person could ever meet. I had never really spoken to him about the circumstances in which his career ended, there had never been any need; in boxing everyone of my generation knows his story and he's aware of that fact. What was it, I finally asked him, about boxing that meant he couldn't turn his back?

'It's that beautiful brutality of the sport. There's something really appealing about watching two people go at it, going toe to toe, looking for that knockout. There's something really magnetic about watching something like that and obviously the end result is you want both people to get up, walk out, have a cuddle like they do, because it's the ultimate gladiatorial sport and when a fighter fights another fighter they get that bond, that thing that will stay with them forever, because only they've shared that moment in that ring. But there's something weird about watching boxing in that where there's that brutality surrounding it, it's very magnetic, there's something about it that sucks you in.'

Despite everything that happened, he is still entertained.

CHAPTER TEN

The Night of the Perfect Knockout

> Colosseum vibes.
>
> *Carl Froch*

F roch vs Groves II was the most eagerly anticipated all-British showdown in a generation. Their first encounter, in November 2013, delivered a fractious build-up and then, when the bell went, incredible drama and controversy. Groves hit Froch with a right hand in round one, as he predicted he would, which knocked Froch heavily to the canvas. For the next few rounds the IBF champion was in survival mode but began to turn the tide back in his favour in the second half of the fight. In round nine, with the contest on a knife edge, referee Howard Foster stopped the fight with Groves still on his feet. In Foster's opinion George was an open target, unable to defend himself effectively, and on the brink of being knocked out. It was controversial and a rematch seemed inevitable from the moment the stoppage came. George was outraged and flew to New York to petition the IBF in person, whilst

Carl was adamant the referee had made the right decision. Controversy, outrage and indignation combined to make the public's appetite to see the pair of them fight again insatiable and so Wembley Stadium was booked and 80,000 tickets were sold. A young Anthony Joshua was on the undercard, early in his professional journey following his London Olympic success. A golden era in British boxing was about to be ushered in and at its dawning was Froch vs Groves II.

This chapter looks back at the night Carl Froch closed the book on his long and storied career by supplying the perfect knockout. The man himself, with a little help from his cornerman Mark Seltzer, his promoter Eddie Hearn and referee Charlie Fitch, takes us behind the scenes and into the ring to give us the inside story, through the eyes of the Cobra.

Mark Seltzer – *We got up, did our little routine. We always went to the newsagent, bought the local papers to see if he had any coverage in there, which Carl keeps. We set off for the morning walk. As we're walking, there's like a little green, outside where we're staying, and there were four or five photographers hiding in the hedgerows. 'What are you lot doing here?' 'Oh we're trying to get pictures of George Michael coming out of his boyfriend's flat.' We told them they were out of order and should leave him alone and sort of moved them on and then they started taking pictures of us – one of them realized who it was who'd told them to move on. So we were then jogging and ended up jogging for about fifteen minutes, until we got back to the flat.*

Eddie Hearn – *I went to see Carl at lunchtime because Carl is the most unconfident, insecure fighter you've ever met, which is bizarre, unbelievable. I walked into his flat In Highgate Village and I sat down and we were having a cup of coffee, three hours to go until he was going to the venue, and he went, "What do you think about this fight then?" And that's what he would always say to me, "What do you think about this fight?" And I said, "This is what I think. That first fight you overlooked him. You're on another level, he cannot compete with you, do you understand?" That's how you had to talk to Carl. He was so nervous, Carl. I was in my mid-thirties, I knew nothing really, and there I am having to reassure a hall of fame fighter.*

Mark Seltzer – *Darren from Matchroom came to pick us up. Carl actually had a sponsored truck with a Cobra on it and all that. It wasn't the most comfortable ride but he pledged to the sponsors that he'd use it for driving around to all the press stuff. So the photographers were there and there was a film crew so we drove off in the truck, probably for about a hundred metres, then switched, got in with Darren and went off to the fight.*

And now over to the man himself.

I went through the back through the service entrance but I remember getting out of the car and taking a little walk round to have a look out onto the pitch and AJ was actually fighting, he was finishing some kid off, and I remember hearing the roars, and it wasn't even that busy, and I remember thinking, 'Colosseum vibes'. The noise dissipates into the air in a stadium, it doesn't bounce off the ceiling like it does in an arena, and that's when the nerves started to kick in a little bit. I could feel my heart pounding in my chest and I started to feel a little bit nervous.

I got to the dressing room and the drug-test man was there straightaway. I was like, 'Can't we do this after?' And he said, 'We can do but I'll have to stay with you,' and I was like, 'Well, I need a sleep, I've got here early.' So I got my kit and went into the changing rooms and I went to a physio room, which was quite small, because I wanted to lie down, not so much sleep, just gather my thoughts, because I knew it was my last fight, you see, I knew during the camp: 'I don't want to do this any more.' I felt myself, during the camp, a split second behind in the sparring and thinking that I was seeing shots and not landing them and seeing shots coming and not getting out of the way of them, so I knew I was kind of on my way down.

I was sitting there in the physio room with the lights out, totally black, and the geezer was moaning about the lights, saying that we needed to keep the lights on because he needed to be able to see me. I told him he could put his phone light on if he wanted to but that I needed to get some sleep. I just wanted to sit down and meditate for half an hour, forty-five minutes. I like to do it, I like to sit there and concentrate and gather my thoughts and I remember lying there and visualizing the ring and visualizing round one and taking the centre of the ring, and not looking at Groves the whole build-up, until the first bell goes. I don't want to see his fucking face, I was so wound up from the first one. I'd done so well ignoring him and I'd been speaking to Chris Marshall, the psychologist, to not get involved in any bullshit beforehand because if I get wound up it affects me in a negative way. In the first fight with Groves I was that fuming and this time I needed to remain calm and focused and concentrate.

So that's what I was doing, And when I was lying there, I wasn't really falling asleep, your heart's beating and when you're picturing the ring walk it's like you're there, it's meditative and they're quite vivid; the images that you get and the emotions you get are actually kind of real.

About an hour beforehand I woke up or came out of that meditative state. In the changing room beforehand Wayne Rooney came in and that made me realize the fight's coming close now.

Charlie Fitch – *A memory that stands out for me was doing the dressing room rules. Both fighters were at that level of focus that world championship level fighters have. You could see both were confident without being over-confident. So when I was doing the rules with Carl Froch, I felt from watching the first fight there was some fouling from both fighters, so I stressed to both fighters that I wanted a clean fight and Carl Froch, I think he was having his hands taped at that time and he wasn't really looking at me, and when I said that to him, he just kind of looked up at me, and just stared right at me and didn't say a word. And then I just continued on with the dressing room instructions and when I got out I remember thinking to myself, 'This could be a rough fight.' I interpreted that look as him saying, 'I'm going to do what the fuck I want and you're just going to have to deal with it.'*

And then it's like, 'Six minutes, you're on.' And I'm a big Eminem fan so I always think of that song, 'Six minutes, Slim Shady, and you're on.' And then it's like, 'Bosh, switch on, it's ring walk time. "Cometh the hour, cometh the man"; there's no backing down, time to go.'

Mark Seltzer – *The ring walk. We discussed the music earlier in the week. I said he should do Queen: 'We Will Rock You', as Queen had a lot of history at Wembley, so it started with that and went into a mix of 'Welcome to the Jungle'. I'm getting goosebumps now just thinking about it.*

I faced my corner the whole announcement, never looked at Groves once, I ignored him, faced the corner post. And then after we did the announcements, we were called to the centre of the ring and that was the first time I clapped eyes on Groves, in the centre of the ring with the referee giving his instructions. I touched gloves and smiled at him and showed him my gumshield. It was a like a new design gumshield and Groves wanted it and I got it and the guy said he wouldn't let George have one now I'd got one. For me that was a little win. George said he didn't even know but I think he did. And then it's: bell goes, round one, centre of the ring, behind the jab.

First seven rounds I felt like it was a slow, boring one, but this is good because he's moving so much. I'm in the centre of the ring and he's circling. I knew he was going to box and run, he likes to keep out of the way and box, and he had nowhere to go and our game plan was to sit in the middle of the ring, not take a step backwards and when he comes, meet him and put him on his back foot. And that's what I did. To the spectator, to the layman, there was nothing really happening, but to me in there I remember thinking, 'He's not hitting me with anything and although I'm only hitting him with the odd jab, the odd little exchange, I'm backing him up, putting him in the corners, he's getting out of the corners, circling, he's moving loads, his feet will be killing him, his legs will be getting tired, and every time I got near him I'd try and put a couple of body shots in, a couple of head shots. But I'm just thinking, round five, round six, round seven, this is beautiful, he's starting to slow down.

By round seven, I'm thinking, 'Right, it's the second half now.' The first half, it's anyone's, he could have been winning, I could have been winning, he'll say he was winning six-nil but it didn't matter to me because in my head I'd done the job I needed to do, backing him up, putting him in the corners, not taking a step back. I could feel him slow down in round seven. Every time we came together I could feel him slowing down. Before the knockout came I can remember throwing a check hook, right hand, and I missed but I thought, 'That's the shot.' He was moving that way because he was looking for the left hook; he'd told everybody he was going to knock me out with a left hook. He was looking for that left hook so he was going to his left and dropping that glove, which was low anyway. So before the knockout: against the ropes, backed him up, got in close, hit him with a little jab, then two big body shots, really hard, my feet were set on the floor, sinking them in and feeling his ribs on my knuckles and I thought, 'They're hurting him,' and then he backed up to the ropes towards the corner and I thought, 'Right, he's gonna go to his right now.' And you're not thinking about too much but you just kind of know, it's automatic, it's just happening. He put himself in a position where he's against the ropes so I threw a little feint, got him to react, and then it's check hook, right hand, and that right hand could not have connected any cleaner and as soon as it hit him I remember feeling it go down my shoulder and thinking, 'Fucking hell, I caught him sweet, right on the chin.' Because when you land you're not sure where you've hit him, on the top of the head, the shoulder . . . I saw him drop and I thought, 'Fucking hell, that's a great shot, probably the best shot I've ever landed.' Because I threw the check hook my body was coiled to my right side so everything then exploded like a golf swing or a tennis shot or a big fucking right hand from the Cobra. And I remember when it landed thinking, 'Fucking hell, if he gets up from that I'll be in for the big finish here and it'll look great. I wasn't thinking, 'Stay down,' I was just thinking, 'Keep cool.' I'd been there a few times and when I saw the ref wave it off I just thought, 'Game over.' I wasn't thinking too much, I didn't get too emotional, I was that much in the zone, it was just seek and destroy and when the knockout came I just kind of knew it was coming.'

Eddie Hearn – *For Carl to produce that knockout in that moment on the biggest night of British boxing at that point, it was unbelievable. I just jumped out of my seat. I jumped out of my seat and then made my way over to the step and then got in and his brother got in and his family and it was just like unbelievable and especially because of the rivalry. I think you may never get a better one, because very rarely when you build a moment like that, an occasion like that, do you get an ending like that.*

THE NIGHT OF THE PERFECT KNOCKOUT

Mark Seltzer – *I had a great view. I was looking through the bottom rope, straight across to the other side, where it happened, and it was like you knew it was going to come, it was just a matter of time before Carl engaged fully. It was the perfect knockout, it really was.*

I don't think until you wake up the next day you understand actually what you've done. You wake up the next day and you still think you need to go on a run, you think to yourself, 'Have I done it?' Two weeks after sometimes you wake up and you think, 'Have I had the fight? Yeah, I've had the fight, of course I did.' Because your mind's in a mad space. But once it was stopped I just thought, 'Yeah, I've done it,' like I'd done it thirty-odd times before.

I went to the Hilton hotel [after the fight]. My mother was there, a few of my friends and family were there. And I was just thinking, 'I just want to get back.' I didn't want anything to drink alcohol-wise. My brother was there, having a good time with Wayne Rooney, and then I was like, 'I'm getting out of here.' I went to drink a pint of Guinness and I couldn't drink it, I had three or four sips and thought, 'I'm already dehydrated, alcohol's going to make me even worse and give me a headache.' I got back to the apartment that I'd rented and I couldn't sleep. I think that was the realization, when I got back to the apartment and it was just me and my brother and one of my friends and I was just like, 'I want to go home now, I've had enough.' It was four, five in the morning and it was starting to get light and I just wanted to go, to get back to Nottingham. I never saw my wife or my mum, or anyone, they were at the Hilton and I did give them a cuddle and kiss and they said well done, great night or whatever.

So we jumped on the motorway and the drive back from London to Nottingham was in a G-wagon, a 6.3-litre fucking machine that we'd had just for that week with Team Froch on the side. On the motorway we had a massive convoy of fans behind us. My brother, massive twat that he is, was 0–140 in about five seconds, bosh, and then all the crowd would try and catch us up. So they'd all come behind us and then Lee would be off again and I was like, 'Fucking hell, slow down.' Everyone who was at the fight was following me back to Nottingham. So we had that fun journey on the M1 back to Nottingham, got home and then it was like, 'That's it, mate, it's all done and dusted, finished.' It was a bit of a comedown but obviously I've been smiling about that fight for years and milking it. I'm still milking it now, the 80,000 thing. I have the craic and I wind people up but it meant so much to me to get that win in my last fight. Maybe if I'd lost, maybe I'd have fought again, to try and satisfy myself and do something different but it's like, that was it, I did what I did and it was so conclusive, there was no argument. The first fight was controversial in a lot of people's eyes and it had to be settled, it had to be done.

CHAPTER ELEVEN

Knockout Truths

> You can come back from a knockout, but it depends when that knockout comes.
>
> *Steve Bunce*

When it comes, how it comes and at whose hands it comes.

Three factors that define how long and hard the road back from the knockout will be.

At first glance the knockout may appear to be the ultimate expression of dominance, the most emphatic possible demarcation between victory and defeat, between success and failure, between winners and losers – which, after all, is what sport is about, is it not? But whilst that may be true for observers, for the practitioners, the men and women in the arena, it is not that simple. Time and again I have heard the words of Theodore Roosevelt quietly echoing in my ears whilst in conversation with contributors:

It is not the critic who counts; not the man who points out how the strong man stumbles, or where the doer of deeds could have done them better. The credit belongs to the man who is actually in the arena, whose face is marred by dust and sweat and blood; who strives valiantly; who errs, who comes short again and again, because there is no effort without error and shortcoming; but who does actually strive to do the deeds; who knows great enthusiasms, the great devotions; who spends himself in a worthy cause; who at the best knows in the end the triumph of high achievement, and who at the worst, if he fails, at least fails while daring greatly, so that his place shall never be with those cold and timid souls who neither know victory nor defeat.

There are no cold and timid souls in these pages but there are no immortals either, just human beings attempting to do superhuman things, willing to confront their fears, willing to compete in an arena in which the stakes are high, in which success can never be guaranteed and in which the consequences of failure can be severe. There have been tales of triumph, but triumph of the most honest kind, untainted by any form of triumphalism but instead underpinned by humility, born of an acceptance that success and failure are merely two sides of the same coin. Carl Froch was never knocked out but he accepted that it could have happened to him. George Groves did get knocked out, as did Ricky Hatton and Amir Khan and Matthew Macklin and Scott Welch and David Haye and Tony Bellew, but none of them allowed the knockout to define them, they all found a way to get past it, to move on. I have seen fighters knocked out for the first time whilst writing this book and, although it remains a spectacle that both exhilarates and sickens me, it doesn't sadden me in quite the way that it used to because I know now that the resilience of a fighter is such that I can allow myself, with reason, to be optimistic about their prospects of recovery.

I am not fooling myself, though, that the knockout is not still the event described so vividly by Teddy Atlas in chapter two, that it is not that ultimate sporting cataclysm, because it is, and it always will be. Atlas described it as an extinguishing of hope, but amidst the darkness did still allow for the prospect of light: 'The end. Over. No hope. And we should always have hope. But with the knockout there is no hope, for that moment at least. There's no coming back. There's no putting the lights back on.'

'There is no hope, for that moment at least.' That split second, when a fighter's field of vision fades to black, that is a bleak and wretched moment; but, except in the very worst and thankfully most rare cases, the lights do come back on and a path to recovery does show itself, shadowy and difficult to see though it may be, hidden by what must seem like an impenetrable gloom.

It can take time but fighters can and do recover from the knockout and the more I immersed myself in the subject, the more I read and watched and looked and listened, the more I realized that, at its core, the knockout is a story of survival and recovery. Those are its dominant themes, the axis about which the narrative of this discourse has rotated. In boxing, the ability to survive is the cornerstone around which everything else can be built. If, on any given night, a fighter doesn't manage to survive, if they get knocked out and defeated, then they will have to find a way to recover. It's a simple contract and it's that simplicity that makes life in the ring more relatable than it would first appear.

Some knockouts, however, are harder to recover from than others and, as stated at the beginning of the chapter, the scale of the task can, to a degree, be calculated by the when, the how and the who. Examination of that trinity does, I believe, allow some useful conclusions to be drawn on what is a multifaceted subject.

These conclusions were fine-tuned courtesy of a conversation I had about the knockout with Steve Bunce. Steve, a fulminating force in the boxing media landscape for longer than he would probably care for me to mention, was the final person I spoke to and leaving him until last proved to be a fortuitous decision because when we sat down, I discovered he'd been pondering the knockout and its different strains over the course of the previous few days for an article he'd written for *Boxing News*. We were on the same page immediately and he engaged with the subject with the enthusiasm that it had been my great good fortune to witness in every person who had been kind enough to spare me time.

We started with the 'how'. He agreed that the pure type-one knockout, the punch the victim doesn't see and isn't braced for, can happen to anyone. In the moment it cannot be survived but it can be recovered from, and that recovery will be slightly easier if the fallen fighter has managed to get back to their feet, if they have effected some kind of physical recovery in the ring, like George Groves and Amir Khan did. If a person has been rendered unconscious for a significant period, as Ricky Hatton was by Manny Pacquiao, then it can be a longer road back. Type-two knockouts, 'exhaustion knockouts', as Steve termed them, although potentially very damaging physically, are more straightforward to recover from mentally because there is a ready explanation available to the fighter for their happening and also because the fighter can take pride in the performance they put in, even in defeat. Matthew Macklin was able to move on from his knockout against Jamie Moore because he knew what went wrong in that he had set too high a pace and underestimated Moore, mistakes that he could ensure weren't repeated in the future, and also because he had proved beyond any doubt to himself and everyone else that he was willing and able to push himself to the limit and beyond in pursuit of victory.

At this point Steve tabled what he believed to be the most difficult category of knockout to recover from: namely, the knockout that the victim never imagined happening. These fighters never imagined it, he clarified, not because they lived in that perilous land of denial where they refused to entertain the prospect of defeat; they accepted they could lose, they just never believed they could lose in the way that they did. He posited Ricky Hatton as an example. Hatton, he said, was aware that he could, and almost certainly would, lose at some point, but that defeat would arrive in the form of a points decision, very possibly a contentious one. What Hatton had never envisaged was getting beaten up, dropped and then knocked out in the fashion visited upon him by Floyd Mayweather, or getting obliterated in double-quick time by Manny Pacquiao. His world came crashing down because, after having achieved so much and having gone undefeated for so long, he couldn't countenance defeat on that scale. Simply put, he had allowed himself to equate the unthinkable with the impossible.

It was exactly this that Steve had been examining in the few days that led up to our conversation, the reason being that the previous weekend he had been ringside in Phoenix, Arizona, to watch Sunny Edwards, the undefeated, 20–0, IBF flyweight champion from Britain, take on an 18–0 WBO champ Jesse 'Bam' Rodriguez from the USA in a unification bout. I had spoken to Edwards about the general prospect of defeat myself, a couple of years previously, not long after he had won his world title, and he told me that he accepted the fact that he would almost certainly lose during his career, that as a world champion he was operating at the very highest level and that given his desire to fight the best opponents available and secure more titles, he would, at some stage, find himself in a close contest that didn't go his way on the scorecards. I'd asked him if he thought it was possible he could get knocked out or stopped, and he did concede that it was possible that he could get caught by that perfect punch, that was something that could never be ruled out, but it was clear to me that he had such confidence in his own formidable skill set that it wasn't conceivable to him that he could find himself comprehensively dominated by an opponent. But in Phoenix that is what happened to him. Rodriguez damaged Edwards's left eye, fracturing the orbital bone, early on and never let up, forcing Grant Smith, Edwards's trainer to pull his man out after nine rounds.

I saw Sunny a few days after his fight, in the lobby of the hotel I was staying at. I was back in Saudi Arabia, this time for the Day of Reckoning, the colossal, mainly heavyweight bill that had been arranged for the final weekend before Christmas. He had flown out to support his friend Lyndon Arthur, who was fighting on the card, and he was already in the early stages of his recovery, his rehabilitation. I commiserated with Sunny on the loss and found him keen to discuss it. The injury, he told me, had been crucial as it had basically robbed him of his vision in his left eye, an impairment that against a boxer of the skill and ferocity of Rodriguez was always likely to prove decisive. Bones get fractured in boxing, he was well aware of that, and whilst he wasn't therefore claiming that sustaining a fracture was unlucky in and of itself, he did feel that the timing of it had been somewhat cruel; after all, he'd been hit hard before and nothing had been broken. Boiled down, his take-away was that if his eye hadn't been damaged so badly, so early in the fight, then things could and would have been different, but on that night that was what happened and there was no point crying about it, and he'd been proud of the way he'd dug in and carried on and fought until his trainer had decided he should fight no more. He wanted the rematch, he told me; next time the story would have a different ending. I found him convincing, in that I believed that he believed what he was saying, that he had quickly found a way to sell the defeat to himself, to take that all-important first step on the road to recovery. It will be a while before there is proof positive of a successful recovery, though. That will only be displayed when he next finds himself in the eye of the storm.

I knew from my own studies that Steve was correct in what he was saying about how problematic the unimagined knockout, if we can term it as such, could be. I had heard his theory corroborated in the conversations I'd had myself, but there had been another fight on that Phoenix card that had caused him to zero in on another category I had not previously considered in as much depth;

namely the 'when'. Peter McGrail took to the ring in Arizona as an undefeated professional, having won all eight of his fights. The Liverpudlian was tipped for the top after moving into the pro ranks following a very successful international amateur career. I'd watched him a lot and shared the optimism that surrounded him. Fight number nine was going according to plan, he was winning comfortably against Ja'Rico O'Quinn, and then in the fifth round, with his opponent pinned in the corner, McGrail stepped in to unleash a left hand, walked onto O'Quinn's right glove and was knocked out cold, the referee counting him out as he lay on his front under the bottom rope.

It would be a knockout, Steve felt, that would prove difficult to recover from, not because of how it had happened, although of course that did present problems, but mainly because of when it had happened. Peter had been knocked out by someone he was supposed to beat, and early in his career, before he had significant experience to fall back on or significant success to take confidence from. It had got Steve thinking and, try as he might, he could not come up with an example of a fighter who had been knocked out cold like that, that early in their career, who had then been able to recover and go on to achieve great things. I couldn't think of an example either. The one that most people I have asked the question of since have reached for has been Amir Khan's reversal against Breidis Prescott. Although it qualifies on one front, in that it was relatively early in Khan's career, it is disqualified on the grounds that Khan wasn't knocked out cold. He was flattened twice but on both occasions he got back to his feet. It is a grim thought that there could indeed be a scenario in which the knockout can permanently dim the lights on a career. I hope it does not prove to be the case for Peter McGrail, and that he emerges as the exception to what would appear to be a sobering rule.

The manner of the knockout, the 'how', matters, as does the timing of it, the 'when', but so, I believe, does the 'who'. The identity of the person who delivers that telling blow can affect the process of recovery. Boxers sometimes talk about how their chosen profession, and what it requires them to be prepared to do to each other in the ring, is strictly business, about how it is not personal, but defeat in the boxing ring, especially by knock-out, is deeply personal. It represents an emasculation, a violation, an evisceration that can precipitate an identity crisis, and that crisis can be exacerbated or alleviated depending on the fallen fighter's relationship with their assailant. Ricky Hatton's enmity towards Floyd Mayweather hindered his recovery, for example, whereas Tony Bellew's admiration for Oleksandr Usyk aided his. George Groves and Carl Froch loathed each other in equal measure. Their antipathy towards one another was genuine and continued long after they'd both settled their affairs in the ring, only ending five years later when Groves up hung his own gloves. Matt Macklin and I spoke to George just a few weeks after he'd announced his retirement. The three of us were working on a Sky show together and also on the team that day was Carl Froch. It was the first time the pair of them had voluntarily shared the same space since their fighting days and it was fascinating to watch them revolve around each other. It seemed almost confusing for them to start with, as if they didn't know how to behave now they were both former fighters and their rivalry finally was obsolete.

George said, 'It took years for me to come here today and have a pleasant conversation with Carl Froch, and him as well, I'm sure he'd admit that, because it was real and it's there. It's kind of what makes it worth it to a certain degree because that's what I love about boxing. I loved the authenticity of it because ultimately it is like no other sport in that it's civilized, to a certain degree, but it's combat, the excitement of one man punching another man. You get excitement in other sports but nothing will compare to boxing because of the emotion involved in it.'

Emotional and personal, authentic and real, that is boxing, with the knockout being the most emotional, personal, authentic and real aspect of it.

My discussion with Steve came at ringside just a few hours before the aforementioned Day of Reckoning got underway. The schedule was dominated by six fights in the heavyweight division and headlined by Deontay Wilder vs Joseph Parker and Anthony Joshua vs Otto Wallin. The idea was that Wilder and Joshua would both win and then finally, after a prolonged courtship, make good their engagement the following March. It was my final fight week of the year and the final one before my deadline for the completion of this book. It proved to be an appropriate assignment, illuminating, as it did, many of the scenarios and themes that have been explored above.

One of the other fights featured, outside of the heavyweights, came at cruiserweight – for the vacant IBF world title – where Jai Opetaia, reckoned to be the number one in the division, met Ellis Zorro, a 17–0 south Londoner. It was a huge step up for Zorro, who, prior to accepting this most formidable of challenges, had been campaigning at fringe British title level. I feared for Zorro because he was up against an exceptional opponent, a man with ice-cold ambition and unambiguous intent running through his veins. In my view, the best possible scenario for Ellis would see him compete with Opetaia for four, maybe five rounds, enjoy some pockets of success, before being pulled out of the fight by his corner once his superior opponent started to get on top and inflict damage. Unfortunately that wasn't what happened. With just a few seconds remaining in the first round Opetaia threw a long left hand from the southpaw stance, caught Zorro, who was trying unsuccessfully to pull out of range, and knocked him out. The Londoner collapsed onto his back, his neck landing squarely on the bottom rope, and there he settled: spreadeagled, gazing across the ring through glazed, sleepwalker's eyes. Referee John Latham looked into those empty eyes and stopped the fight. Zorro lies firmly in that category of fighter previously discussed; an undefeated fighter, early in his career, on the rise, working hard, grinding, dreaming, believing. Will he recover? Only time will tell, but I am hopeful that he can. He was back on his feet in time to stand in the middle of the ring with Opetaia and hear him announced as the winner by first-round knockout, which exhibited a level of physical recovery at least. I saw him at the airport the next day and to look at him I would never have known he'd been in a fight. I would have loved to have asked him what he remembered about the whole episode and how the experience had left him feeling but decided against approaching him. He may have been receptive but equally he may well not have been and I felt it would have been impertinent to ask.

Later in the night came the ring arrivals of Deontay Wilder and Anthony Joshua, two fighters who have, in recent years, had to navigate the full, gory gamut that the fight game has to offer. Joshua, having won Olympic gold in London in 2012, became a world champion just under four years later and a unified champion not long after that. He was a phenomenon, the ideal vehicle to transport boxing from the red-light district to the high street. AJ sold out UK stadiums, regardless of the opponent, and in 2019 was poised to conquer America. But on 1 June at Madison Square Garden in New York he was humbled by Andy Ruiz. I was ringside and watching Joshua getting dismantled by Ruiz was wild, there is no other word for it. To his credit Joshua took the immediate rematch and won on points six months later, but the theory had persisted since his Manhattan mauling that he had left a piece of himself in the Garden that night and had never been the same since. Back-to-back points defeats at the hands of Oleksandr Usyk had done nothing to disprove that theory, despite the obvious excellence of his Ukrainian counterpart. Indeed, Joshua's actions at the end of their second fight, which saw him seize the ring interviewer's microphone and pour his soul out onto the Saudi Arabian canvas, did, in the eyes of many, confirm its veracity. The 2012 golden boy had now lost three times, with each defeat dulling his lustre. He was human after all, something that came as an unpleasant and unacceptable surprise to a lot of the people who had previously supported him. His post-Usyk reboot, which saw him win twice, once on points and then by knockout, did nothing to convince his detractors, who by then were more convinced than ever that he had lost the ability to commit to the knockout, to roll the dice. I had my doubts too. I've always been an admirer of Anthony Joshua, what he has managed to achieve in the relatively short period of time during which he has been boxing has been extraordinary, but it occurred to me that it was entirely possible that he could have lost for good that eye of the tiger, that sniper night vision that formerly had travelled everywhere with him, safely stowed in his kit bag.

I've also long been an admirer of Deontay Wilder. A 2008 Olympic bronze medallist, he had originally taken up boxing as a nineteen-year-old to earn money to support his daughter, who had been born with spina bifida. He quickly discovered he could knock people out, any time, any place, and from any angle. Thirty-two opponents came and went, inside the distance, before he won the WBC title. The Alabaman defended it seven times, all early nights, before running into Tyson Fury, at which point things took a turn. Their first meeting ended in a draw but in their second fight, the 6ft 9in Gypsy King demolished the previously invincible Wilder, knocking him down twice and stopping him in the seventh round. It was a thorough, comprehensive beating, from beginning to end. He subsequently offered up a litany of increasingly bizarre excuses and, as they did with Joshua, the critics questioned his ability to rebound and refind his former identity as a man who won in the most dominant fashion possible, so much so that there was no great appetite amongst the pugilistic public to see Wilder and Fury fight for a third time. But the trilogy fight was what Wilder wanted and he was happy to take legal proceedings to ensure he got his opportunity to right such an intolerable wrong. Fury vs Wilder III took place in October 2021, in a Las Vegas that was still returning to its full, gaudy effervescence following the pandemic. Getting into the USA was difficult for the UK press but by fight night there were plenty of us in attendance and we were treated to one of the most dramatic heavyweight fights of all time. I watched in wonder as Wilder walked straight back into the fire, without fear or hesitation, and went toe to toe with Fury, putting him down twice in the fourth round, having been down in the third himself, and then swinging until his last fighting breath, which came in the eleventh when he was counted out after collapsing through exhaustion. It was awe-inspiring and, although it was Fury who had won, it was the performance of Wilder and his willingness to still risk it all despite what had happened the last time the two had met that left me speechless. Like Joshua, he lost two fights in a row against the same opponent, but unlike Joshua, nobody was questioning Deontay Wilder. He had proven once and for all that he was prepared to go out on his shield, to do what the paying public demanded of him as a prize-fighter, and for that reason he was beyond reproach, whereas Joshua, having succumbed to Usyk on points (and therefore, it was perceived, tamely by comparison), was a fair target for criticism.

Two fighters, Wilder and Joshua, who had such relevant common experiences but who were regarded very differently. They even shared their most recent opponent in Robert Helenius. They had both knocked the Nordic Nightmare out but the method by which they had done it had, once again, illustrated the difference between them rather than highlighted the similarities. A year after completing the epic trilogy against Fury, Wilder returned to the ring and after just two minutes and fifty seconds, with his back to the ropes and standing tall, with his feet together, hit Helenius on the forehead with a short right hand and knocked him out. His feet were both off the ground at the point of impact. It was pure Wilder:

unorthodox, unteachable, flying in the face of all boxing logic. Dr Neil Scott told me it was extremely difficult, borderline impossible, to knock somebody out with a straight punch to the forehead, but Deontay did just that. His win and, crucially, the method of it, was received as evidence that the Wilder of old, the man who had willingly stormed no-man's land against Tyson Fury a year earlier, was still in operation, that the freakish power he'd always possessed still resided in those gloved hands. Whilst it was certainly evidence of the latter, it did not fully support the former supposition as it was impossible to tell what he had left in the tank on the basis of 170 seconds of action.

Joshua dispatched Helenius with a well set-up and perfectly delivered right hand in the seventh round. From a technical standpoint it was a far superior punch to Wilder's but it wasn't as well received. The fact that it had taken until the second half of the fight to arrive was heralded in some quarters as further evidence that the former two-time unified world champion was still gun-shy, conservative, cautious, hesitant, all of the things that Wilder wasn't and all of the things that a top heavyweight could not be. Anthony had been widely criticized following his previous win on points over Jermaine Franklin for not supplying the knockout and was then still criticized when he did provide one. He couldn't win.

The perception of the two boxers when they set sail for the Middle East and their Day of Reckoning was therefore very different, despite all their similarities. People were pleased to see them both on the same card but questioned why they weren't fighting each other. Wilder was quick to suggest that that had been what he had wanted but that Joshua had been the one unwilling to oblige, and people were just as quick to believe him. I was in their company regularly during fight week and was struck by their different demeanours during the days building up to their fights.

Wilder wasn't just different to AJ, though, he was a different man to the one we had come to know, not the man he used to be, and the man that we, the press, were used to. In days gone by he had a brought a sinister edge to proceedings, tastelessly vocalizing his desire to furnish his record with a fatality, his mood darkening as the clock counted down to the first bell, at which point he would unleash hell. But now, instead of being in the presence of a dark and unpredictable force, we found ourselves in the company of a serene, Zen-like individual. I found this new Wilder somewhat baffling and wondered whether it was all an act, designed to lull his opponent, former world champion Joseph Parker, into a false sense of security. I asked him midway through the week what had caused this metamorphosis and whether it was, in large part, due to being forced to confront and recover from defeat. He told me that his shift in attitude was a result of becoming older and wiser and a recently acquired penchant for the cleansing properties of ayahuasca, but insisted that he remained as addicted to knocking people out as he always had been. I believed him.

Joshua, on the other hand, was mean and moody and seemed to get more so as the week progressed. Everyone had an opinion on his mental state, with his opponent Otto Wallin, a former sparring partner, suggesting that he carried within his psyche an innate weakness that had been laid bare at the hands of Andy Ruiz, that his days at the top of the sport were well and truly over and that come fight night he would drive him into retirement. Joshua was hard work at times, with one broadcast interview I conducted with him being painful in the extreme, like trying to extract blood from a belligerent, 250lb stone. All he cared about was what happened come Saturday night. He was aware of everything that people were saying, particularly Otto Wallin, and although he insisted it didn't bother him, as the days passed it began to occur to me that the Swede, who had previously given Tyson Fury a very competitive tussle over twelve rounds, could be talking himself into a painful evening.

The consensus was that Deontay Wilder would knock Joseph Parker out, whilst Anthony Joshua would struggle with Otto Wallin, and possibly lose, maybe even get knocked out.

Those forecasts proved very wide of the mark. Deontay Wilder lost on points to Joseph Parker, who stuck superbly to the shrewd gameplan devised by his trainer Andy Lee. Wilder never once looked like detonating the dynamite in his horsehair gloves. The fascination with him had always lain in his ability to knock an opponent out, that was his currency, but as the rounds came and went it became more and more obvious that a knockout, on this night, was becoming less and less likely. He was hesitant, unable to pull the trigger as he'd always been able to do previously. It appeared that the Bronze Bomber had lost his ability to drop bombs, without which his value would greatly diminish.

Joshua, who would have been more than aware of the fate that had befallen his rival by the time he walked to the ring, channelled his irritation of the preceding days into a performance laced with spite. He committed to his punch, hitting Wallin hard from the first bell and punishing his temerity for five rounds, at which point, with an explosive finish looming ever larger, Wallin's trainer Joey Gamache intervened and saved his fighter from the knockout. It was a good decision by Gamache, a former world champion and no stranger himself to a damaging ring battle, and one that he was able to make because he knew what was coming next and was not going to allow the courage of his convictions to be diluted by what anyone else, even his fighter, thought about it. Wallin looked a tortured soul, sat on his stool just a few feet away from me, blinking in disbelief at what had just happened to him. He hadn't believed Joshua capable of inflicting such a merciless and systematic thrashing on him or anyone else; that ability had left him on a balmy summer night in New York, everybody had said so.

In the ring after his defeat was formally announced to the watching world, Deontay Wilder declared: 'I'm a happy fighter. I'll be back. And if not, then it's been a pleasure.'

Listening to him utter those words it occurred to me that the worst possible thing that can happen to a knockout artist had happened to Deontay Wilder: he had become civilized. In the days that followed his defeat, he backtracked, insisting that he would return, that he still wanted to fight Joshua, that it was Joshua who didn't want to fight him, that, delighted at his defeat, AJ would now use it as an excuse to avoid Wilder. He raged against the dying of the light but in amongst the protests, hiding in plain sight, were startling admissions: 'I've got to find my killer instinct back. I'm too at peace, I'm too happy. When I had that dog in me, nobody had a chance . . . I will be a two-time heavyweight world champion.'

The same 'killer instinct', the same 'dog' that Wilder had lost, appeared to have been rediscovered by Joshua, a scenario that very few had predicted. It was a night that for me encapsulated perfectly why I find boxing and fighters who choose to live and die by the knockout, so mesmerizing. The sands are always shifting beneath the fighter's feet, where one swing of a glove can change everything in an instant; they exist in a universe in which jeopardy is their only constant. For individuals like Wilder and Joshua, every day that they enter the ring and answer that bell is a day of reckoning, a day of judgement. Watching what happened to them that week was the perfect way to finish. Where they go from here, nobody knows for sure, but I'll wager that they'll both be rolling the dice again soon and that people will pay to see them do it, as they always have.

The knockout will never lose its lustre. It is, and will remain, sport's most decisive moment: the casting vote, judge and jury, answerable to nobody.

The knockout does not discriminate: acting without passion or prejudice, it neither asks permission nor seeks forgiveness.

A deadly and seductive force, to which nobody is immune.

Bibliography

Augustine, *Confessions*

Frontiers of Neurology, 'How Can a Punch Knock You Out?', October 2020

Homer, *Iliad*

New Zealand Herald, 'Cricket: Former Black Caps captain Brendon McCullum opens up about dismissal in 2015 Cricket World Cup Final', July 2019

Barry McGuigan, *Cyclone: My Story*, 2013

George Plimpton, *Shadow Box: An Amateur in the Ring*, 2010

W.K. Stratton, *Floyd Patterson: The Fighting Life of Boxing's Invisible Champion*, 2012

Mike Tyson and Larry Sloman, *Undisputed Truth*, 2013

Picture credits

Index

INDEX